Land Taxation in Imperial China, 1750-1911

Harvard East Asian Series   73

The East Asian Research Center at Harvard University
administers research projects
designed to further scholarly understanding
of China, Japan, Korea, Vietnam,
and adjacent areas.

Land Taxation in Imperial China, 1750-1911

Yeh-chien Wang

Harvard University Press   Cambridge, Massachusetts   1973

Preparation of this volume has been aided by a grant from the Ford Foundation.

Library of Congress Catalog Card Number 73–80024

SBN 674–50860–2

Printed in the United States of America

To Professor Han-sheng Ch'üan

Acknowledgments

This book is dedicated to Professor Hen-sheng Ch'üan of New Asia College, the Chinese University of Hong Kong. Under his guidance I entered the field of Chinese economic history more than one and a half decades ago and since then have benefited immensely from his continuous instruction and encouragement.

In preparation for this work I received invaluable advice and help from many sources. First and foremost, I owe deepest gratitude to Professors John K. Fairbank and Dwight H. Perkins, who supervised my work from dissertation research to final publication. Their critical comments and constructive suggestions greatly improved the structure and clarity of the book. Professor Lien-sheng Yang has always been a source of inspiration to me; at various stages of my work he has not only corrected many of my mistakes, but provided me with crucial sources for further improvement. I am also very grateful to Professors Ramon H. Myers and Thomas A. Metzger whose remarks were most valuable in shaping the final version of the manuscript for publication.

My deep thanks and appreciation are due also to Professors John R. Watt, S.A.M. Adshead, Winston Hsieh, and Robert Swierenga for their significant suggestions on various aspects of my manuscript, to Professor Grace Bush of the Computer Center at Kent State University for her assistance in analyzing my land tax data, to Miss Joan Ryan of Harvard University Press and Mrs. Olive Holmes of the East Asian Research Center at Harvard University for their editorial help, to the staff of Harvard-Yenching Library for their kind assistance in securing materials for my research, and to my wife Yu-yin and daughter Anna for their active participation in computing, typing, proofreading, and indexing.

Finally, I wish to acknowledge the generous financial support from several academic institutions. Harvard-Yenching Institute and Harvard Graduate School of Arts and Sciences awarded me fellowships for five consecutive years, which enabled me to pursue graduate studies in this country and to accomplish most of the research for the present work. After graduation I received from the East Asian Research Center at Harvard University a summer grant, and later a half-year research fellowship. In addition, Kent State University kindly provided me with a summer grant. Needless to say, I alone am responsible for any errors in this study.

Contents

Tables

Figures

Foreword

A nation's fiscal system is often the key to an understanding of many of the strengths and weaknesses of its government. Nowhere is this more true than in the case of the Manchu government of imperial China. Throughout its rule, the Ch'ing dynasty was increasingly plagued by inadequate funds. Scholars have been generally aware of this continuing fiscal crisis in eighteenth and nineteenth century China, but have been unable to give it a quantitative dimension and thereby come to a fuller understanding of its implications. The data readily available were known to be unreliable and no one possessed the talent or fortitude to come up with better figures.

Yeh-chien Wang has filled this need by carefully reconstructing the Chinese land tax, the principal source of government revenue, from a wide range of primary sources, particularly ones compiled toward the end of the dynasty for the purpose of providing a basis for reforming the system. The result of these efforts is a new estimate of China's land tax substantially larger than the estimates previously in use although still small in relation to the revenues available to a country such as Japan.

However, Mr. Wang does not confine himself to coming up with revised tax figures. He uses his revised figures as a basis for analyzing such fundamental issues as the burden of the land tax on the rural population and differences in that burden between China's various provinces and regions. He also explores, among other issues, the degree to which the tax was able to rise along with the secular increases in prices and income that were occurring throughout much of this period.

This study is being published in two parts. This volume contains the analysis of the relationship between the land tax and China's economy and government administration. The second volume, published separately as a Harvard East Asian Monograph, contains the sources and calculations that went into the derivation of the revised land tax estimates.

Dwight H. Perkins
East Asian Research Center
Harvard University

Land Taxation in Imperial China, 1750-1911

Introduction

The land tax has been the mainstay of government finance and the principal fiscal burden of the peasantry in all agrarian societies. The adequacy of the tax as a source of revenue, the efficiency of its administration, and its burden upon the taxpayers all affect greatly the fortune of government and the welfare of the great majority of people under its rule. Thus the problem of land taxation has always been a primary concern of the ruling elite in an agrarian state and has often occupied the attention of many social scientists and socio-economic historians.

This book is an inquiry into the problem of China's land taxation in the Ch'ing dynasty (1644-1911), especially in the closing decades of the period, in order to better understand imperial China in several respects. First, the land tax system is important as the most essential feature of the Ch'ing fiscal system. As a source of revenue the land tax played a key role in the Ch'ing fiscal administration. Furthermore, there is a commonly accepted thesis that attributes the fall of successive dynasties in Chinese history to oppressive taxation, especially land taxation, of the peasantry.[1] But whether the burden of taxes is a major cause of popular revolution depends on the social and economic conditions of the period in question. This study is intended to test this thesis in the Ch'ing context.

Early in the present century there appeared a number of works on the Ch'ing fiscal system in general and on its land tax in particular.[2] They are inadequate in two important respects. First, the land tax system as described in these works is largely based on laws and regulations contained in such official compilations as *Ta-Ch'ing hui-tien* (Collected statutes of the Ch'ing dynasty) and *Fu-i ch'üan-shu* (The complete book of taxes and labor services). Since the imperial laws and regulations on fiscal matters underwent little modification in response to changes in political and economic conditions, there appeared in the latter part of the dynasty a great difference between the system on paper and the system at work. The generalizations drawn from these official works are therefore at odds with reality. Second, although scholars interested in the financial conditions of the Manchu dynasty have successively pointed out that officially reported figures on tax revenue are much lower than the amounts of actual collection in the late Ch'ing, no one has made a serious effort to reconstruct the tax data on a solid basis. There are estimates but they are mostly speculative in nature.[3] For these reasons the structure of land taxation must be built from the very foundation.

The approach I have adopted is both institutional and quantitative. In the following chapters I shall begin with an anatomy of the Ch'ing economy and the fiscal system in which the land tax system operated. To study land taxation as an institution I will attempt first of all to construct a realistic account of procedures as they were in operation in the late Ch'ing. In other words, how was the land tax actually assessed and collected and how did the prevalent practices differ from imperial laws and regulations? I will also attempt to describe how the land tax was gradually increased over time. Since the increase in land tax revenue took the form of surcharges (the collection of which was with few exceptions not in conformity with imperial statutes), it is essential to analyze the major factors contributing to the growth of land tax surcharges. As far as the quantitative aspect is concerned, this study has three objectives: to assess the fiscal importance of the land tax in the Ch'ing tax structure; to observe changes in the share of land tax contribution from, and shift in relative burden between, areas with different degrees of economic development in the latter part of the dynasty; and to compare the increase of the land tax yields with changes in other major variables (especially prices) affecting the tax burden so as to test the thesis of oppressiveness of taxation. It is hoped that by this two-front approach we shall be able to achieve a far better understanding of the problems.

With regard to source materials such statutory works as *Ta-Ch'ing hui-tien* and *Hu-pu tse-li* are inadequate, for they provide only a framework of land taxation and land tax revenues formally reported, leaving out the actual operation of the system and a substantial part of the revenue it actually produced. Fortunately, there is available a large body of data, both impressionistic and quantitative, especially for the late years of the dynasty. The most precious are the twenty-volume financial reports known as *Ts'ai-cheng shuo-ming-shu* (cited as *TCSMS* hereafter). They were submitted on the eve of the 1911 revolution by all provincial authorities in response to an imperial order to make a thorough survey of the fiscal conditions in each province in preparation for a nationwide financial reorganization. Since the survey was not well planned, these reports vary in quality one from another, and to a great extent appear confusing indeed. Nevertheless, they were undoubtedly the most comprehensive and realistic records of public finance imperial China had ever had.

In contrast with the earlier routine annual reports on revenue and expenditure, those of this survey have three distinct features: First, they were compiled by an *ad hoc* bureau in each province known as Ch'ing-li ts'ai-cheng-chü (Provincial Bureau for Financial Reorganization). Each bureau was under the direction of the financial commissioner. Assisting him were his fellow officers, for example, grain intendant, salt intendant, superintendent of customs, and a number of advisers chosen from the local gentry. Within the bureau there were three sections in charge of compilation, revision, and general administrative work respectively. In addition, the central government directly appointed and sent to each provincial bureau a supervisor and an associate supervisor to watch over this unprecedented undertaking.[4] Hence the survey represented roughly a combined preliminary effort of the central and provincial governments as well as of the local community (represented by the local gentry) to put the country's public economy in order. Moreover, in order to achieve centralized control of the country's financial resources, the imperial government was determined to have it carried out in all provinces; one financial commissioner was immediately dismissed because of his negligence in this newly assigned duty.[5]

Second, the survey was intended to be complete and thorough in coverage. In the latter part of the dynasty, especially after the Taiping Rebellion (1850-64), the annual report of revenue and expenditure required of all provinces became more and more a matter of formality and greatly understated the amount actually collected and spent. It was therefore ordered at the beginning that the survey must cover all kinds of revenue and expenditure including those hitherto not reported to the central government. Also, the Ministry of Finance issued detailed and specific instructions for the provincial bureaus to follow.[6] Even though the survey did not bring to light all concealed facts, it succeeded to a substantial degree in this undertaking. Third, the data in these reports, especially those on the land tax, are much more detailed. There are nine reports which contain information down to the level of the hsien, the lowest administrative unit of China.

Two major deficiencies are apparent in these reports. The degree of reliability varies from one report to another, and surcharges added to and collected together with the tax quota were mostly understated. To a large extent, however, these deficiencies can be made up by materials from other sources.

Besides the financial reports, hundreds of local gazetteers compiled after the 1911 revolution also include some relevant data. Traditionally, almost all local gazetteers contained a record of the land tax. But it was with few exceptions the tax quota of the district, not the amount actually collected, because gazetteer compilation was usually an officially sponsored work and few magistrates would go on record that they exacted more money than the amount specified by law. Soon after the revolution, however, provincial authorities one after another took steps to reduce the complexities of surcharge collection practiced in the previous dynasty and to combine all or most of them together with the quota into a single tax. From then on the magistrates had no need to conceal from the public the tax records of the earlier days, and some of them were thus revealed in gazetteers newly compiled. Finally, there are a number of official reports on taxes submitted and a few privately compiled works published in the Republican period.[7]

1 China's Economy and Fiscal System in the Ch'ing Period

Economic Structure

China has long been an agricultural economy characterized by intensive farming and a high ratio of population to land. From the middle of the seventeenth century to the eve of World War I the world witnessed a series of economic revolutions—commercial, agrarian, industrial, and financial—which transformed one country after another into an industrialized state, while China under Manchu rule experienced no change of this kind at all. Her people continued to follow the same way of life as their forefathers had a millennium before. Although the imperial government made an attempt to build up modern industries as a part of the self-strengthening movement, the effort ended in failure. Moreover, foreign merchants in the treaty ports as well as a number of Chinese entrepreneurs set up modern factories with a view to capturing the market from the handicraft industries. But these new enterprises did not generate enough momentum to transform the economy either. In fact, the traditional sector was able to compete and coexisted side by side with the modern sector.[1] Therefore, China's economy remained agrarian and backward during the Ch'ing period.

Just how backward China's economy was under the Ch'ing can be demonstrated by a single example. When a country experiences modern economic growth, her economic structure is bound to change. The most salient feature of this transformation is the decline of the share of the agricultural sector in both labor force and national product. In Japan, for instance, from 1879 to the eve of World War II (1938), the share of the agricultural sector in the labor force dropped from 83 to 46 percent, while the share of the manufacturing and service sectors combined rose from 17 to 54 percent. At the same time, the share of the agricultural sector in net national product declined from 64 to 20 percent, and the share of the manufacturing and service sectors combined went up from 36 to 80 percent.[2] Although we do not have the figures for Ch'ing China, a recent study made by Ta-chung Liu and Kung-chia Yeh will illustrate the point. According to them, the share of the agricultural sector in the labor force in China still amounted to 79 percent in 1933, while its share in the net domestic product amounted to 65 percent. In the rest of the net domestic product the contribution of the traditional nonagricultural sector accounted for 19.6 percent and that of the government sector for 2.8 percent, thus leaving a share of less than 13 percent produced by the modern sector.[3] These observations point to the fact that China's economy underwent little structural change in the Ch'ing period and remained as late as 1933 at about the same level as that of Japan's economy on the eve of her industrialization in 1879.

Although there was no appreciable change in economic structure in Ch'ing China, her economy did not cease to grow. Instead, it grew extensively. By extensive growth I mean the increase in the output of goods and services in the economy without an accompanying increase in per capita output. In the past few centuries increased production in China has resulted mainly from population growth and expansion of acreage. Capital inputs played only a marginal role, and technological change was the least important.

Thanks to the studies of Ping-ti Ho and Dwight H. Perkins, much has been brought to light on the increase of population and land acreage in the past centuries. As indicated in Table 1.1, China's population grew from between 65 and 80 million in 1400 to 647 million in 1957. That is to say, during the past five and one-half centuries the number of people in China rose between 800 and 1,000 percent. Before the advent of industrialism such a record is impressive. In an agricultural society an enormous increase in population must be accompanied by a similar increase in agricultural output. Then, how could China feed her ever-growing population in the past centuries? This has been reasonably assessed by Dwight Perkins. According to his estimate, while China's population rose tenfold between 1400 and 1957, the acreage under cultivation expanded more than fourfold. The expansion of cultivated acreage alone was not, however, adequate to meet the needs of food consumption. It contributed only about a half of the increased grain output; the rest was attributable to a 100 percent rise in the grain yield of land (see Table 1.1).[4]

In the Ch'ing period the most dynamic change in China's economy was agricultural expansion from the densely populated area to the land-abundant area. I shall say more about this change later. Here it is sufficient to point out two distinct phases of Ch'ing economy. The first phase runs from the mid-seventeenth to the mid-nineteenth century. It was a period of phenomenal growth, for China saw her population triple (from 100-150 million to 410 million) and her cultivated land double (from 600 million mou to 1,210

Table 1.1. China's population and land acreage, 1400–1957

Year (1)	Population (millions) (2)	Cultivated land (million shih mou) (3)	Estimates of grain yields (catties per mou) (4)
1400	65–80	370	139
1600	120–200	670[a]	–
1650	100–150	600[b]	–
1685	–	740	–
1750	200–250	900[c]	–
1770	270	950	203
1850	410	1,210[d]	243
1873	350	1,210	–
1893	385	1,240	–
1913	430	1,360	–
1933	503	1,534[e]	242
1957	647	1,678	276

Sources:
1. Dwight H. Perkins, *Agricultural Development in China, 1368-1968*, pp. 16–17, 216, 240.
2. Ta-chung Liu and Kung-chia Yeh, *The Economy of the Chinese Mainland, 1933-1959*, pp. 129, 178.

Notes:
[a]Perkins' estimate (500 million shih mou) is considered too low. I have replaced it with the figure (converted into shih mou here) calculated from the results of the land survey in 1578–82. See Table 2.1 and the text in Chapter 2.
[b]I have arrived at this figure by assuming that there was an appreciable decrease in cultivated acreage in the first half of the seventeenth century because of internal uprisings and warfare between the Manchu forces and the Ming loyalists.
[c]I have arrived at this figure by assuming that land acreage increased evenly between 1685 and 1770, a period characterized by political stability and economic prosperity.
[d]I added this figure by assuming that land laid waste by the Taiping Rebellion had been by 1873 brought back to cultivation.
[e]Liu and Yeh's estimate is revised to 1,470 million mou by Perkins. However, I do not see sufficient reason for making the revision. For example, the area of cultivated land in Kansu is adjusted upward from 29.2 million mou to 50 million mou. He makes the revision based on John L. Buck's estimate (50 million mou) of the 1930's. Yet, there are other estimates in the 1940's which fall far short of Buck's figure. Among them the following two are the highest: one is 39+ million mou which resulted from a survey by the Committee for the Development of Natural Resources around 1940, and the other is 38 million mou estimated in 1947 by the Department of Reconstruction of the Provincial Government of Kansu. See Kan-su sheng-cheng-fu, comp., *Kan-su-sheng chü-pan t'u-ti ch'en-pao chi-shih* (1942), p. 1; *Chung-kuo ching-chi, 1948* (Canton [?], Hua-nan hsin-wen-she, 1948), p. 145. In view of these two estimates, Liu and Yeh's figure appears more reasonable than Buck's.

million mou) in the course of two centuries. But the second phase extending from the mid-nineteenth century to the eve of world War I was a period of sluggishness in which population increased a mere 5 percent and cultivated acreage gained about 10 percent. In view of the data in Table 1.1, it is obvious that in the first phase population growth was accompanied by both increased acreage and increased yield, but in the second phase it was mainly the extension of cultivated land that supplied additional food for consumption needs. In short, while no modern economic growth occurred during the Ch'ing, China did grow extensively in terms of population and land acreage. At the end of the dynasty, while her economy remained backward living largely on agriculture, it acquired such an enormous size as to dwarf most other nations in the twentieth-century world.

Sources of Public Revenue

Broadly speaking, the revenue sources of the Ch'ing government can be divided into four categories: taxes; contributions; rents and interest; and profits from public enterprises. Rents from public land and interest from government deposits in private businesses were negligible in amount, for they accounted for at most 1 percent of the nation's total public revenue.[5] Profits from public enterprises, which were produced mainly through inflation by excessive issuing of paper notes and copper coins in certain provinces, became to some extent financially important only in the last several years of the dynasty.[6] As in all other countries, taxes were the principal source of public revenue in Ch'ing China. Contributions played a subsidiary role and, in times of emergency, a highly significant one in keeping imperial government finance in balance.

Contribution here refers to the voluntary transfer of resources from private hands into the public treasury. In the Ch'ing period there are two kinds of contribution: one is known as *chüan-na* (the purchase of degrees and offices by contribution), and the other is *pao-hsiao* (lit., "efforts to return the imperial grace"). As is well known, Ch'ing society was formed by two classes, namely, the gentry and the commoners. The gentry may be further differentiated into two layers—the official gentry and the scholar gentry. The official gentry were the ruling class of the society whereas the scholar gentry served as a reservoir of bureaucrats and formed an intermediate group between officialdom and commoners.[7] Any commoner who aspired to attain higher social status could work his way up through civil service examination, or buy his way up through *chüan-na.* While certain academic degrees and honorific titles could be purchased all the time, offices were offered for sale only on specific occasions (military expedition, severe flood, and so on) and only to those who had already acquired gentry status.[8] Hence *chüan-na* was a system that opened up another channel for social mobility and at the same time rendered government a supplemental source of revenue.

In the later part of the eighteenth century and the first half of the nineteenth people contributed roughly three million taels a year to the state through purchasing nominal degrees, titles, and ranks; while the selling of public offices earned on each occasion a sum varying from two million taels up to more than thirty million taels.[9] These proceeds were of particular importance to the central government in the early nineteenth century. According to Lo Yü-tung, the money from *chüan-na* exclusive of the part spent in the provinces accounted for 9 percent of its total revenue (exclusive of the grain tribute) in the Yung-cheng period (1723-35), nearly 17 percent in the Ch'ien-lung period (1736-95), 54 percent in the Chia-ch'ing period (1796-1820), 36 percent in the Tao-kuang period (1821-50), and 23 percent in the Hsien-feng period (1851-61).[10] However, in the last decades of the dynasty when government expenditure grew at an accelerating rate, the receipts from this source of revenue declined. Its role in government financing was therefore greatly reduced.[11]

The other kind of contribution, *pao-hsiao*, was made by big merchants, usually salt merchants in salt-producing areas and hong merchants in Canton. Since they were granted by the imperial government the privilege of monopoly in their respective trades, they voluntarily made or were called upon by officials to make large contributions on special occasions, such as the emperor's tour of the country, natural calamity, war, and so on. The amount of their contributions, according to two scholarly studies, added up to around forty million taels in roughly the Ch'ien-lung and Chia-ch'ing periods.[12] In the long run, however, it is doubtful whether the state treasury did really gain much from merchant contributions. As the merchants might not be able to contribute a large sum of money all at once and the officials having jurisdiction over them were eager to take the credit for fund raising, the *pao-hsiao* money was usually advanced out of public funds and then paid off in installments by them. Consequently, their debts to the government were mounting all the time, and their contributions, as a commissioner of the Lianghuai salt administration put it, existed only in name.[13]

Taxes are the lifeblood of state organization. The Manchu government inherited its whole tax structure from the preceding Ming dynasty (1368-1643) and put it into operation with little change for two centuries. It was only after the Opium War (1840-42) and the outbreak of the Taiping Rebellion (1850-64) that new taxes were added and assumed an increasing role in government financing.[14] In Chapter 4 I shall make a quantitative assessment of the change in the tax structure for the period. For the moment it is enough to describe briefly the major categories of late Ch'ing taxes, which included the traditional taxes as well as the new ones. The traditional

taxes were the land tax, the salt tax, the native customs, and the miscellaneous taxes. The new taxes comprised the maritime customs, likin (a transit tax
on commodities), and various kinds of local levies on commercial transactions
and on commercial establishments.

The land tax was by far the single most important source of public revenue
in the period (see Table 4.8). It generally had two component parts: the
ti-ting tax (lit., "the land tax and the labor services combined") and the grain
tax. The *ti* tax was the land tax proper; whereas *ting* tax was basically a
commutation of labor services required of the adult males, though property
and other criteria were also taken into account in the assessment of the
tax.[15] Because of its excessive regressiveness in the allocation of tax burdens
and of the administrative difficulty in its assessment and collection, the *ting*
tax was abolished and incorporated by apportionment into the land tax
proper in the second quarter of the eighteenth century. In Chihli, for
instance, the *ting* tax was apportioned upon the land tax proper by adding
one fifth to the latter, that is, 0.2 tael more was to be collected for each tael
of the land tax proper. From then on the combined tax took the name of
ti-ting.[16] In addition to the *ti-ting* tax which was paid in money, landowners
in most places had to pay to the government a grain tax. But with increasing
monetization of the economy the latter had been commonly converted into
money payment by the late Ch'ing.

Ranking next to the land tax in fiscal importance was the salt tax. Under
the Ch'ing the whole country had eleven salt producing areas with each
supplying a certain region of consumption. Although the system of collecting
the tax varied from one area to another, the most prevailing one was official
supervision and merchant sales. Under this system the government granted
certain merchants the monopoly of selling salt in assigned regions of
consumption and they paid in return a certain amount of tax in proportion to
the quantity of salt sold. With the introduction of likin following the Taiping
Rebellion merchants transporting salt for distribution had to pay a transit tax
called *yen-li* (salt likin) in addition to the tax they paid at the place of
production.[17] This new levy contributed substantially to the increasing
weight of the salt tax in the public economy.

Before the Opium War native customs stations at places of concentrated
commercial activities or traffic collected taxes on commodities in transit and
a particular station situated in the Canton delta was also in charge of
collecting import and export duties. After the war five ports on the coast
were opened to trade, but native customs officials continued for some time
handling customs duties from foreign trade. It was not until 1858 that a
separate maritime customs administration was established. In the early phase
of the Taiping Rebellion when the rebel forces took over the Yangtze delta,
the imperial government was unable to collect customs duties at Shanghai. At

this juncture the British and other foreign consuls at the port persuaded local Chinese officials in 1854 to permit foreigners to manage the customs on behalf of the Ch'ing government. This makeshift arrangement soon developed into a joint Sino-foreign operation at each treaty port. In order to supervise and coordinate the management of customs duties throughout the country a centralized administration, the Inspectorate General of Customs, was set up in 1858. From then on, owing to the development of trade accompanying the opening of more treaty ports both on the coast and inland, as well as to the efficient administration under the capable inspector general, Sir Robert Hart, the maritime customs soon emerged as a significant source of revenue. On the other hand, after the introduction of likin and the separation of the maritime customs the native customs lost its potential in tapping commercial resources for the state. Hence its contribution to public revenue relative to that of other taxes could not but decline even though its absolute amount still increased somewhat.

Another tax of great importance which was created after the outbreak of the Taiping Rebellion was likin. In 1853 when the rebellion was at its height, Lei I-hsien, a vice-president of the Board of Punishment dispatched to Yangchow for assisting military affairs, tried to raise funds locally for urgent military requisitions by initiating a rather light tax on rice in the nearby market towns. This invention, the origin of likin, proved fruitful. The next year the new tax, consented to by the imperial government, was formally instituted in Yangchow and extended to cover not only rice but also other merchandise. Other provinces soon followed this example in the next few years.[18] Originally the tax was considered a temporary means to meet urgent needs in connection with military operations against the Taiping rebels, and the government intended to abolish it as soon as peace and order was restored. But once it proved to be a rich and dependable source of revenue, it persisted even after the fall of the dynasty.[19]

The merchandise subject to likin levy and its rates varied from province to province. In general, the tax may be classified into three kinds depending on the location of tax collection: likin levied at the place of production; transit likin; and likin levied at the market place. Of these the transit likin was by far the most productive.[20] Surely, many commodities were subject to both taxation of the native customs and likin in the latter part of the nineteenth century. There were, however, three major differences between the two taxes. First, while the native customs was a central government tax, likin was a provincial government tax the administration of which was completely under the direction of the governor or governor-general in individual provinces. Second, whereas the objects of likin were general merchandise, the native customs levied shipping dues in addition to commodity taxes. Finally, likin barriers were much more numerous than native customs houses throughout the country. As a consequence, while likin became a major source of revenue, the native customs submerged into obscurity in the public economy.[21]

The category of miscellaneous tax is composed of a variety of taxes not fitted into the major categories listed above. These included the traditional taxes such as property deeds tax, brokerage tax, pawnshop tax, tax on unloading goods (*lo-ti shui*); and the post-Taiping offshoots like the tobacco and wine tax, tax on slaughtering domestic animals, license fees of various shops, and so on. In the last decades of the dynasty there was not only a proliferation of new taxes of miscellaneous nature but also a sharp increase in the rate of those traditional ones.[22] Hence the combined taxes of this category outran most other taxes and claimed a high place in late Ch'ing finance, primarily in local government finance.

Of the taxes discussed above, all but the land tax and part of the miscellaneous taxes and levies can be classified in general as indirect taxes. Since most taxes created after the Taiping Rebellion were indirect in nature, the public economy was shifting from relying heavily on direct taxes (especially the land tax) towards relying more and more on indirect taxes in the late Ch'ing.

Fiscal Organization

To finance government activities of all kinds the state needs an adequate system of revenue. Equally important is an administrative apparatus that can perform efficiently the task of appropriating resources from the private sector of the economy for meeting public needs. Our knowledge of Ch'ing fiscal administration is at the present still very inadequate, it is a field yet to be explored. What I am attempting to do here is take a bird's-eye view of late Ch'ing fiscal organization and see how governments of different levels coordinated in fiscal matters.

Since fiscal organization is but a part of state bureaucracy, an analysis of essential organizational functions will help us achieve a better understanding of the Ch'ing fiscal mechanism. From the viewpoint of locating administrative responsibility, any office in the state organization is assigned to perform one or more of the following four major functions—executive function, supervisory function, advisory function, and coordinating function. The executive function is designed to carry out a task, general or specific. An executive officeholder may issue orders to his subordinates and direct them to accomplish the assigned work. He may make appointments or dismiss those under his authority, or make formal recommendation on personnel matters. The supervisory function is designed to supervise the performance of certain other offices, that is, to check regularly that tasks assigned to those offices are properly carried out. A supervisory officeholder who finds the performance of those offices under his supervision unsatisfactory may reprimand or impeach those who hold those offices, but he has no authority to remove them. Advisory function here means that an office or officeholder gives advice or makes recommendation on matters usually referred to him by a superior authority. Finally, the coordinating function is to perform a task in coordination with another office or offices.[23] Based on this conceptual framework, an anatomy of late Ch'ing fiscal administration before the reorganization of the Board of Revenue into the Ministry of Finance in 1906 is presented in Figure 1.1. It is without doubt an oversimplified construction, but it serves our present purpose towards understanding major fiscal institutions and their functional relationships at the time.

Before a discussion of the fiscal administration, a few words should be said about the structure of Ch'ing government. Throughout the imperial period the structure of Chinese government had three basic levels: central, provincial, and local. Although there were in the Ch'ing two intermediate territorial units between province and district—circuit and prefecture—the circuit intendents and prefects served merely as supervising agents of the provincial authorities. At the head of the government was the emperor, who appointed all officials within the empire from high ministers at court to magistrates in the district yamen. Ever since the abolition of premiership in the late fourteenth century, the emperor had himself become the chief executive of the country. On the provincial level a governor or governor-general (called governor hereafter) headed the administration. Finally, on the local level a magistrate was in general charge of public affairs.

The most important fiscal institution in the period was the Board of Revenue. It was headed by two presidents and four vice-presidents. Under them were fourteen supervisory departments and a number of specialized agencies, of which the most significant were the State Treasury, the State Granaries, the Mint, and the Office of Contributions (in charge of collecting money from selling academic degrees and offices). As part of the central administration, the Board played two vital roles at all times. First, in relation to the central government it acted as the treasury, the accounting office, and the paymaster general. Second, in relation to the provincial authorities, it supervised their fiscal operations and acted as an auditor of their annual financial reports.[24] In addition, it served the throne as a principal adviser on economic and fiscal affairs. It coordinated with the Tsungli Yamen (the forerunner of China's modern foreign office) on the disposal of maritime customs revenue and with the Board of Works on such matters as coinage and river conservation.

On the whole, however, the power of the board as the central organ of public finance was very limited. While it was a principal adviser to the throne on economic and fiscal matters, the emperor relied for his policy decision

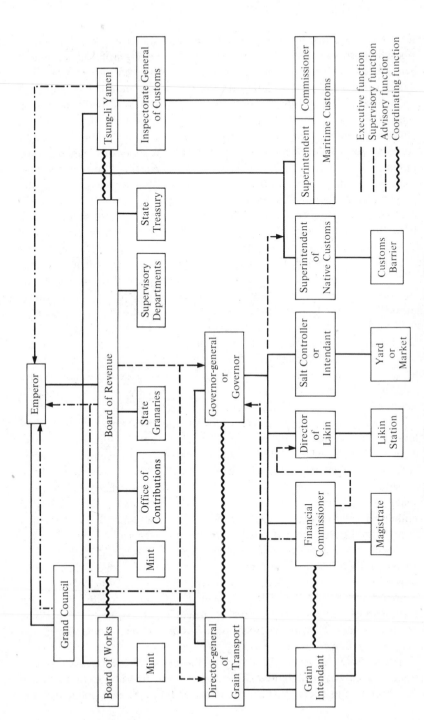

Figure 1.1. Fiscal organization in the late Ch'ing

more upon the Grand Council (the most important policy-making body in the state besides the throne itself) than upon that of the board.[25] Sometimes the emperor might seek the advice of governors. And on matters, financial or otherwise, relating to foreign powers he would usually defer to the opinion of the Tsungli Yamen, which had under its jurisdiction the Inspectorate General of (the Maritime) Customs. Hence the board did not have the exclusive authority of formulating the nation's fiscal policy. Next, while it exercised the supervising role over provincial finance, it could not issue orders to governors. When disagreement occurred between the board and the provincial authorities, the latter could bypass the board and directly memorialize the emperor for a ruling. Moreover, the board itself did not collect taxes; its power of controlling the nation's financial resources depended upon its authority of disposal over the taxes collected in the provinces, save the portion reserved for necessary administrative expenditures. The device to achieve this control consisted of a series of regular communications between the board and the provincial authorities. Each year the provincial authorities had to submit to the board three kinds of financial report: an estimate of next year's expenditure in the province; two half-year reports on the state of provincial treasury; and an annual report of revenue and expenditure known as *tsou-hsiao ts'e*. Although these routine reports went on as usual until the end of the dynasty, the post-Taiping provincial authorities commonly classified a large amount of taxes raised and payments made in the provinces as *wai-hsiao kuan* (lit., "accounts to be reported and cleared outside the capital") and did not report them to the board.[26] As a consequence, the routine reports became simply a matter of formality, and the board's power of disposal over revenues came to be very ineffective.

The fiscal establishment of the provincial administration included a financial commissioner and several other officers, with each taking charge of a specific category of tax. The financial commissioner ranked second only to the governor in the provincial administrative hierarchy and was quite independent of the latter's control before the Taiping Rebellion. However, with the eclipse of the central authority and the rising of regional power in the post-Taiping days the commissioner was often appointed at the recommendation of the governor and thereby became virtually a subordinate of the latter.[27] Like the Board of Revenue in the central government, the commissioner was the treasurer of the province and a top adviser to the governor on provincial finance. But unlike the board, which was basically a supervisory organ, he exercised executive control over magistrates on civil administration and on the collection of the land tax and of the miscellaneous taxes in particular. Moreover, he generally assumed responsibility for supervising the likin administration.[28]

In most provinces there was a grain intendant (two in Kiangsu). His duty was the control of the grain tax in the province for delivery to Peking or to the military units in the provinces. In the matter of the grain tribute (an annual quota of grain to be shipped to the capital) he, together with the governor, was responsible to the director-general of grain transport, whose responsibility was to carry out the task of shipment so as to meet the food consumption need of the metropolitan area.[29] There were, moreover, a director of likin chosen by the governor for administering the newly created tax and a salt controller or salt intendant. Before the Taiping Rebellion the salt tax was a central government tax over which governors often exercised, by imperial order, a supervisory role or even executive control on behalf of the central authority. In the post-Taiping days, however, because of the decline of central power the salt administration virtually became part of provincial establishment.

The native customs and the maritime customs were central fiscal institutions but mostly under the supervision of governors. The native customs was administered by superintendents, some of them commissioned by the emperor, some nominated by the Board of Revenue, and some delegated by governors; but the board assumed jurisdiction over them all.[30] The maritime customs, on the other hand, was put under the joint management of Chinese and foreigners. At every treaty port there was a Chinese superintendent commissioned by the emperor or deputized by the governor and a foreign commissioner chosen by the inspector general (also a foreigner under the jurisdiction of the Tsungli Yamen). Until the very end of the dynasty the function of the commissioner was generally limited to the assessment and accounting of customs duties while the superintendent took charge of the safekeeping and disposal (according to instructions from the central authority) of the revenue. It was only after the 1911 revolution, when China appeared to be unable to meet her foreign obligations on loans and indemnities, that the commissioner took over completely the administration of the maritime customs.[31]

Needless to say, on the local level the magistrate was a tax collector as well as an administrator. He was required to collect the land tax and the miscellaneous taxes in the district under his jurisdiction and to deliver the proceeds, except a specified sum kept for local expenditure, to the financial commissioner and the grain intendant. Moreover, just as governors had to submit an annual report of revenue and expenditure to the central government, the magistrate had to make the same report annually to the provincial authorities (specifically, the financial commissioner). It should be also mentioned that, although there were tax officers from other services (likin, native customs, and so on) scattered in various districts, especially at centers of commercial activity, they were but local agents of the provincial or central fiscal establishment, not in any sense a part of the local administration.

While it is generally true that the collection of the land tax and the miscellaneous taxes was the responsibility of local magistrates, there were a number of exceptions. First, in some provinces prefects and officials on the same administrative level (independent department and independent subprefecture) collected part of the land tax within the area under their jurisdiction. In certain areas of Manchuria and Sinkiang there was no administrative subdivision below the prefectural level, and the prefects therefore assumed all the responsibilities of a magistrate as a matter of course. Second, in the city where their yamen was located prefects usually collected some sort of local sales tax such as *shang-shui* (lit., "the commercial tax") or *lo-ti shui.* [32] Third, after the Taiping Rebellion provincial governments established one after another special agencies for collecting certain new levies in the category of the miscellaneous taxes, especially those financially highly productive ones. The tobacco and wine tax in Chihli, the tax on the export of rice in Hunan, and the gambling tax in Kwangtung are the clearest examples. [33]

Intergovernmental Fiscal Relations

Having thus far presented an overall picture of Ch'ing fiscal organization, we can examine briefly intergovernmental fiscal relations, that is, how government agencies on different levels coordinated their efforts in appropriating private resources for meeting public needs. This is a problem every state organization faces. The devices to solve this problem in various countries are generally a combination of the following four types: separation of tax sources, tax sharing, supplementation, and grants-in-aid. Foremost among these is a separation of tax sources. Under this system the major tax sources are divided among different levels of government with each having exclusive jurisdiction over a specific tax or set of taxes. For instance, in the United States customs duties are solely a federal tax, property tax almost completely a local tax, and general sales tax and motor vehicle license fees are generally state taxes. Tax sharing is a device through which the collection of a tax or certain taxes is concentrated in one level of government and the revenue collected is shared by other levels of government according to whatever arrangement is made by the parties concerned. In this respect, two examples may be cited. In the United States the estate tax is shared by the federal government and all but three states. In Canada the corporation income tax is shared by the federal government and the provinces. Supplementation means that a higher level of government collects, in addition to its own tax rate, a supplementary rate for the lower units of government which need it. This device is very common in Scandinavian countries. Finally, grants-in-aid, employed frequently by the federal government of the United States, is a method by which a higher level of government gives aid to lower levels of government either for implementing certain programs or simply for relieving their financial strains.[34] In coordinating intergovernmental fiscal relations Ch'ing China also adopted a variety of devices, yet in a rather different manner.

In traditional China all land within the empire theoretically belonged to the emperor. It followed logically that all taxes were to be at the emperor's disposal. Hence the provincial and local governments did not have separate tax sources. What the early Manchu rulers designed was roughly a combination of tax sharing and grants-in-aid. In the first place, taxes collected by the local government were divided into two parts: one part known as *ts'un-liu* (withheld taxes) kept in the local yamen for stipulated local expenses, and the other called *ch'i-yün* (taxes to be delivered) for delivery to the provincial authorities.[35] In general, the same was true on the provincial level: a part kept in the provinces for approved expenses, and the rest left to the disposal of the central government.[36] In the second place, the central government could order that part of revenue at its disposal to be shipped either to the capital or to other needy provinces, or to both with each receiving a portion of it. The revenue to be delivered to the capital was called *chieh-hsiang* or *ching-hsiang* (central government fund); the revenue to be sent to other provinces was called *hsieh-hsiang* (fund for subsidies)[37] The latter item was similar to the grants-in-aid. The only difference between them is that grants-in-aid are directly granted by a higher governmental authority to a lower level of government whereas the *hsieh-hsiang* is a kind of transfer payment from one province to another.

In view of great differences in financial resources between provinces the central government established in the early eighteenth century a system of delivery and subsidies. Under this system the provinces were classified into three categories depending on their degree of affluence and financial needs: the self-sufficient, the deficit, and the surplus. Included in the self-sufficient category were those provinces (Fukien, Kwangtung, and Kwangsi) whose tax revenue exclusive of the salt tax and native customs was just sufficient to support the military and administrative establishments of the province. Hence these provinces were not required to deliver their tax revenue either to the capital or to other provinces. The deficit group was made up of those provinces (Shensi, Kansu, Szechwan, Yunnan, and Kweichow) whose tax revenue fell far short of the expenditure needs of the province. Not only were they not required to deliver taxes outside but were also entitled to receive subsidies from other provinces. The surplus category contained those more affluent provinces (Shansi, Honan, Chihli, Shantung, Kiangsi, Hupei, Hunan, and Chekiang) whose tax receipts exceeded their expenditure. These provinces were therefore called upon to hand over their surplus revenue to the capital or to needy provinces.[38]

Nonetheless, the system of delivery and subsidies, however adaptable to reality it may have been, was found inadequate from the start; other devices had to be employed. As I shall discuss at some length in Chapter 3, the amount of tax that was allowed to be withheld for local expenditure was insufficient to meet the actual needs of the local government. Moreover, the amount as fixed in the early part of the dynasty remained hardly changed in spite of population increase and price inflation. Inevitably, local officials had to find ways to finance local government activities and to maintain their administrative staff. And since they were the ones who actually collected taxes, it was natural for them to look upon the collection of tax surcharges as the best possible solution to the fiscal problem of local administration. As a result, supplementation became the prevailing method of local finance.

Furthermore, an insufficient and static "budget" was not merely a local problem, but a virtually universal phenomenon on all levels of government. While local governments found their way out by means of surcharges, administrative offices on higher levels saw it as more convenient to solve their problem by way of *kuei-fei* (customary fee) and *t'an-chüan* (assigned contribution).[39] It was an established custom that lower-level governments conducting official business with a high-level yamen had to pay various kinds of fee such as *fan-shih yin* (food money) or *chieh-fei* (delivery fee) for the latter's upkeep. To meet many kinds of expenses not, or only partly, covered by the "budget" the provincial authorities frequently resorted to requiring local officials to make regular or special financial contributions. Since the "contribution" was forced upon the local government and its amount was determined by the provincial authorities, it was called an assigned contribution. Customary fees and assigned contributions were but a device through which lower-level governments paid or helped pay the expenses of higher-level yamen. It was in short a grant-in-aid in reverse.

In the last few decades of the dynasty the government came to rely more and more heavily on the latter two devices. Because of successive catastrophic defeats the central government expenditures such as the service of foreign loans, indemnities, and national defense were increasing at an alarming rate. Unable to meet these obligations with regular revenue flowing into the capital the Manchu government ordered the provincial authorities to make financial contributions to tide over the crisis by assigning each with a "fair" share.[40] After the Boxer disaster there arose in various provinces a modernization movement, for example, railroad building, modern schools, modern police force. All those required a tremendous amount of money. Then, how did the provincial administration raise funds for paying "contributions" assigned by the court at Peking and for starting these new adventures in the provinces? Among other things, adding land tax surcharges and raising the salt price were the methods most commonly resorted to.[41] In other words, it was supplementation and grants-in-aid in reverse that in the late Ch'ing played the most important role in coordinating intergovernmental fiscal relations.

2 The Administration of the Land Tax

Land Registration

The administration of the land tax is made up of three essential parts—land registration, tax assessment, and tax collection. Undoubtedly, the existence of complete and up-to-date land records is most essential for an efficient and just administration of the land tax. Since land tax assessment is based on such information as the size, classification, rent, yields, and value of land property, incomplete and inaccurate records would result in the loss of revenue on the part of government and the inequitable distribution of fiscal burden among the taxpayers. An unfair assessment will in its turn encourage tax delinquency as well as raise tax-collecting costs. Beyond the fiscal field, land records are essential for the settlement of property disputes between individuals. In modern times these records also serve in many states as a basis for planning agricultural development and for land tenure reform. Needless to say, the quality of the records depends upon the system of land registration.

In most countries there have been two types of land registration: one being the cadastral survey made at intervals, regular or irregular, the other being the day-to-day recording of changes in ownership or physical conditions. A cadastral survey aims at property identification and property valuation. The cadastre, which is the product of the survey and the official record of land property covered by the survey, normally consists of a set of maps on which each plot of land within a specified area appears and corresponding registers which contain the information needed to identify each plot. Depending on the country the information in the cadastre may be rudimentary or very detailed, but it generally includes the location, size, shape, value, and ownership of each plot of land surveyed. Because a satisfactory cadastral survey entails a large investment of money and technical skill, many countries made it only at infrequent intervals. Even in countries where periodic survey (mostly ranging from one to four decades) is required by law, the requirement is not always observed in practice.[1]

. Apart from a cadastral survey made at intervals, there is an apparent need for another type of land registration in order to keep land records up-to-date, expecially at times of rapid change. Between the intervals many changes may occur. For instance, many plots may change hands because of sale or inheritance. A severe flood may wash away a large tract of land or render it unproductive. The construction of a water control work, on the other hand, may transform a hitherto barren area into a highly productive field. Should these changes be left unrecorded, the cadastre may become out of date long before the next survey is undertaken.

In Ch'ing China the land records and land registration devices of the preceding Ming dynasty were inherited without major change by the Manchu rulers, so it is of vital importance for an understanding of Ch'ing land statistics to see what heritage they received from the defunct Ming house. Throughout Chinese history probably the most ambitious land survey was undertaken by the founder of the Ming dynasty, Emperor Hung-wu (reign: 1368-98). Under his direction the government carried out two major land surveys and succeeded in the compilation for most provinces of a cadastre known as Yü-lin t'u-ts'e (lit., "the fish-scale maps and books"). This work described the size, boundary, grade, and owner of each plot of land surveyed. At the same time he also ordered the registration of the entire population within the empire and the compilation of another important work called Huang-ts'e (lit., "yellow registers"), which contained information not only on the number of persons in each household and their age, sex, and occupation, but also on the land owned, the land tax, and labor services borne by each household.[2] In the last quarter of the sixteenth century the government again made a nationwide cadastral survey and subsequently compiled an additional workbook on taxes, *Fu-i ch'üan-shu* (The complete book on taxes and labor services).[3] The latter embodied the data on the acreage of registered land, the number of *ting* (lit., "male adult"), the land tax, labor services, miscellaneous taxes, the amount of taxes to be delivered to the higher authorities, and the amount to be withheld for local expenses in each district. With infrequent modification from time to time these three books constituted the basis of land tax administration in the Ming and Ch'ing periods.

But the most striking thing of the Ming heritage with regard to land registration was that the records of the late sixteenth-century survey had from the start of the Manchu dynasty become a virtually unalterable institution—an unequivocal and enduring standard that was observed to a surprisingly high degree by all officials in the empire. Accordingly, the records of the late sixteenth-century land survey are of great significance. Although the Ming government made three large-scale cadastral surveys, it never compiled follow-up land statistics. While scholars like Fujii Hiroshi and Dwight Perkins have made strenuous efforts to evaluate the available land data of early Ming and to reconstruct the results of the first two surveys, no one has as yet undertaken a similar study on the third survey.[4] But Shimizu Taiji has certainly rendered a great service in this respect by pointing out with indisputable evidence that the 1578 official land data were by no means the results of the Ming government's last land survey, which started in 1578 and lasted until 1582.[5] After an investigation I found that most of the survey results are preserved in local gazetteers and that these results are the best approximation of the actual cultivated acreage at the time.

In Table 2.1 the land data under column 3 are gathered from Shimizu's work and a number of provincial gazetteers compiled in the Ch'ing and Republican periods. The figures for Honan, Shantung, Shansi, Shensi, Hukwang (Hupei and Hunan), Szechwan, and Kwangsi were the acreage reported immediately after the survey in 1578-82,[6] those for Kwangtung and Chekiang were dated 1600 and 1610 respectively, those for Kiangsi and Yunnan were dated the Wan-li period (1573-1620) and late Ming respectively, and those for Kiangnan (Kiangsu and Anhwei), Chihli, Fukien, and Kweichow were the "original quotas (of land acreage)" (yüan-o) at the beginning of the Ch'ing period. In fact, all can be identified as the post-survey acreage in the late Ming.

After the Manchus gained control of China in 1644, the first emperor issued an order that the tax quotas of the Wan-li period, specifically the quotas in the Fu-i ch'üan-shu compiled in the period, should be the basis for the assessment of the land tax and labor services. Accordingly, what the original quota then referred to was the official acreage of the Wan-li period.[7] Since the Fu-i ch'üan-shu of the Wan-li edition was compiled after the 1578-82 survey, the original quota of land acreage apparently meant the post-survey acreage.

Second, because the survey was carried out in the early years of the Wan-li period, which lasted for almost half a century, and the Fu-i ch'üan-shu was compiled late in the period, one wonders whether there are marked differences between the acreage data immediately after the survey and the acreage data in the Fu-i ch'üan-shu.[8] It appears to me however that the differences, if any, would be very small because the government did not possess an efficient apparatus for keeping land registration up-to-date short of a nationwide survey. It is hard to find land data in a time sequence for the late Ming, but those shown below illustrate clearly that there was little change in official acreage after 1582 survey.[9]

Year	Mou
Wu-chin District (Kiangsu)	
1582	1,723,433 (survey result)
1583	1,723,356
1588	1,723,333
1603	1,723,333
1604	1,723,357
1645 (of the Ch'ing Period)	1,723,357 (original quota)
Ju-Kao District (Kiangsu)	
1583	3,039,215 (survey result)
1613	3,008,349
Beginning of the Ch'ing	3,018,787 (original quota)
Ch'ao-chou Prefecture (Kwangtung)	
1582	3,666,304 (survey result)
1592	3,600,269

Finally, the Yunnan acreage (6.8 million mou), which is arrived at by adding together the acreage data of all prefectures and independent subprefectures in the province, is much larger than the pre-survey acreage (1.8 million mou). One can hardly imagine that the reported acreage could be nearly quadrupled without a major land survey. If there were a province-wide survey in this province, it must have been undertaken in the relatively peaceful Wan-li period.[10] In short, all figures on land acreage under column 3 (Table 2.1) are the results of a nationwide land survey accomplished in the last quarter of the sixteenth century.

Not only are most of the 1578-82 survey results available, but they are probably very close to the country's actual acreage at the end of the sixteenth century. There are two good reasons for believing the validity of the survey data. First, scholars may doubt whether the 1368 and 1398 surveys were on a national scale; there is no doubt, as shown in Shimizu's article and numerous early Ch'ing local gazetteers, that the 1578-82 survey covered virtually the entire empire. The marked difference between the pre-survey data and the post-survey data indicates that the last survey was by no means a business-as--usual undertaking.[11] Second, comparing the figures in column 2 and those in column 3 we find a surprisingly high degree of parallel development between population and land in the two centuries between 1400 and 1600. Taking 1400 as the base year, the acreage of Chihli, Shantung, Honan, Shensi in the north, and of Anhwei, Hukwang (Hupei and Hunan), Szechwan in the south had generally doubled or even more than tripled by 1600 (see column 4 in

Table 2.1. Registered land in the Ming and Ch'ing periods (1,000 mou)[a]

Province (1)	c. 1400 (2)	c. 1600 (3)	(3) as percentage of (2) (4)	1661 (5)	1753 (6)	(6) as percentage of (3) (7)	1908 (8)	(8) as percentage of (6) (9)
Chihli	26,971	67,439	250	45,977	65,719	97	68,589	104
Shantung	54,293	112,734	208	74,134	99,306	88	98,283	99
Honan	27,705	94,949	343	38,340	78,832	83	71,685	91
Shansi	39,081	45,724	117	40,787	54,548	119	50,000	92
Fengtien	-	-	-	61	2,524	-	39,162	1,552
Kirin	-	-	-	-	-	-	31,200	-
Heilungkiang	26,066[b]	-	-	-	-	-	15,000	-
Shensi	-	50,358[b]	193	37,329[b]	29,244	101[b]	30,593	105
Kansu	-	-	-	-	21,649	-	18,781	87
Sinkiang	-	-	-	-	-	-	10,555	-
Kiangsu	56,026	71,984	128	95,345[c]	70,430	98	75,117	107
Chekiang	47,234	47,865	101	45,222	46,153	96	46,778	101
Fukien	13,517	13,654	101	10,346	13,614	100	13,452	99
Kwangtung	23,734	33,417	141	25,084	33,411	100	35,227	105
Anhwei	24,991	43,731	175	-	38,033	87	34,064	90
Kiangsi	40,235	47,786	119	44,430	98,565	102	47,343	97
Hupei	13,548	83,852[d]	350[d]	79,335[d]	58,738	111[d]	59,220	101
Hunan	10,428	-	-	-	34,317	-	34,874	102
Kwangsi	10,785	10,317[e]	96	5,394	8,940	87	8,652	97
Szechwan	10,787	40,935[f]	379	1,188	45,915	112	47,062	102
Yunnan	-	6,844	-	5,212	8,990	131	9,319	104
Kweichow	-	1,985	-	1,074	2,569	129	2,679	104
Total	425,401	773,574[g]	182	549,258	761,597	98	847,635	111

Sources:

1. For figures in column 2, see Dwight H. Perkins, *Agricultural Development in China*, p. 225.

2. For figures in column 5, see *WHTK*, pp. 4860–4861.

3. For figures in columns 6 and 8, see Tables 4.1 and 4.4.

4. For figures in column 3, see Shimizu Taijii "Chō kyosei no tochi jōryō ni tsuite," *Tōyō Gakuhō*, 29.2 (May 1942), 167–198; *Yun-nan t'ung-chih* (1835), 59.1–31; *Kuang-tung t'ung-chih* (Taipei, Chung-hua shu-chū 1959), 161.2942–2946; *TCSMS* (Chihli), 1.1–2; *Chiang-hsi t'ung-chih* (1880), 83.3b–4; *Che-chiang t'ung-chih* (Shanghai, The Commercial Press, 1934), 67.1296–1303; *An-hui t'ung-chih kao* (1934), "Ts'ai-cheng k'ao," 5.3–9; *Kuei-chou t'ung-chih* (1692 preface), 11.1–2; *Shan-hsi t'ung-chih* (1892), 65.31; *Fu-chien t'ung-chih* (1737 preface), 12.3–7; *Chiang-nan t'ung-chih* (1684 preface), 17.7–10.

Notes:

aSome figures considered apparently unreasonable have been replaced with other official figures of approximate date by Fujii Hiroshi, Dwight H. Perkins, and myself.

bIncluding registered land in Kansu.

cIncluding registered land in Anhwei.

dIncluding registered land in Hunan.

eSum of the 1393 official figure and the acreage discovered in 1782 survey.

fSum of the 1578 official acreage and the additional acreage discovered in the 1582 survey.

gThe results of land survey in the late sixteenth century.

Table 2.1). Note that these provinces either suffered from mass depopulation prior to the establishment of the Ming dynasty and witnessed a massive rehabilitation afterwards (Chihli, Honan, Shantung, Anhwei), or had attracted mass immigration in these two centuries because of the existence of abundant but undeveloped natural resources (Hukwang, Szechwan, and southern Shensi).[12] Hence the late sixteenth century land data are highly compatible with those of 1400 reconstructed by Dwight Perkins.

When we proceed to examine the land data of the Ch'ing period in Table 2.1 and to compare them with the 1600 data, we find three distinct features. First, there was a substantial decrease in registered acreage in the first half of the seventeenth century. Second, the registered acreages of various provinces between 1600 and 1753 are remarkably close and the national totals between these two dates are only two percent apart. Third, save in Manchuria and Sinkiang—two outlying areas brought under the Chinese administrative system in the late Ch'ing—there was practically no change in official acreage between 1753 and 1908. The 1661 land data were arrived at by deducting the acreage laid waste in the few decades prior to the dynastic changeover from the post-survey acreage of the Wan-li period of the preceding Ming dynasty (that is, the "original quota" in Ch'ing official nomenclature).[13] The imperial government laid down no strict rules for determining the devastated acreage in the provinces. Some provincial and local officials may have made a careful survey of the land under their jurisdiction, but many probably could only undertake a very rudimentary check or simply relied on self-reporting by landowners.[14] There is no way to ascertain the accuracy of these data, but considering the intensity of warfare and the pervasiveness of natural calamities in the second quarter of the seventeenth century a decrease of 200 million mou in cultivated acreage is probably not a gross exaggeration.

The land data of 1753 and 1908 are, however, undoubtedly subject to a substantially downward bias; for if they are considered to be indicators of China's actual acreage, it would mean that the area of cultivated land in China proper had by 1600 virtually reached the saturation point in spite of a roughly 50 percent increase in population between 1600 and 1750 and another 100 percent increase between 1750 and 1913 (see Table 1.1). Short of a technological revolution (industrial or agricultural) this would be impossible. To what extent China's cultivated land was underregistered can be roughly measured. As indicated in Table 1.1, her cultivated acreage increased by 300 million mou between 1650 and 1750 and by 460 million mou more between 1750 and 1913, but the registered acreage shown in Table 2.1 increased by about 200 million mou in roughly the first period and by less than a hundred million mou in the second period. The comparison between these two sets of data suggests that at least a third of the newly cultivated land in the first century of the Ch'ing dynasty and about four fifths in the next one and a half centuries went unregistered.

The extent of land underregistration, then, demonstrated the ineffectiveness of the Ch'ing system of land registration. The most serious weakness of the registration system was undoubtedly the absence of a cadastral survey on a national scale. While the Ming government undertook three major land surveys, the Manchu regime did nothing in this regard. Instead, it relied basically on the late Ming records with infrequent and minor revisions done by officials on the provincial and local levels. There were three main reasons why no nationwide land survey was ever made in the Ch'ing. First, the cadastral and land-tax records left over by the defunct Ming dynasty were considered by the early Manchu rulers to be adequate in providing financial resources for government needs. As a matter of fact, before the Taiping Rebellion the government lived well within its means depending mainly on the land tax. Since there was no need for more taxes, there was no compelling desire for a major land survey. Second, in the early years of the dynasty there were many instances of officials conducting local land survey and resorting to various kinds of abuses (such as demanding onerous fees from the landowners), and popular opposition to this undertaking was aroused. Hence emperors and high officials at the court deemed it not only financially unnecessary but also politically undesirable to embark on a cadastral survey.[15] Finally, after the Taiping Rebellion the government was beset with increasing financial difficulties and therefore did not have the wherewithal to undertake a nationwide land survey even though scholars like Feng Kuei-fen (1809-1874) strongly advocated it.[16]

Short of a cadastral survey on a national scale the Manchu regime sought to update the land records by establishing a number of regulations. The important ones can be stated briefly. Local officials were required to report to the provincial authorities at the end of each year the land acreage newly brought under cultivation within the district under their jurisdiction. Areas along the coast and river subject to frequent changes had to be surveyed every five years by local officials under the direction of provincial authorities. In cases such as unclear boundaries and inaccurate size or grade of certain plots in official land records, the appearance of newly reclaimed land, or the devastation of farms by flood, local officials were required to make a survey in the off-season. People who bought or reclaimed land were required to report the acquisition to the government. The *Fu-i ch'üan-shu* was to be revised every ten years.[17] However, for one reason or another soon to be described, none of these rules was faithfully observed with the result that under-registration became increasingly conspicuous, especially in the newly developed areas.

While the Ch'ing government devised certain rules for updating the country's land data, it unwittingly set up, or allowed to exist, obstacles that rendered virtually unworkable its land registration system. The perpetuation of the original quota, the institution of *k'ao-ch'eng* (evaluation of accomplishment), the lack of financial resources for a land survey, and the practice of mou conversion all had the effect of keeping registered acreage from increasing. Soon after the Manchus assumed control of China in 1644, the post-survey land acreage and land tax of the Wan-li period in the provinces were adopted as the original quota of the new regime, and the current acreage and land tax quotas in each province and district were determined by deducting from the original quota the acreage then devastated and taxes then uncollectable. In the first century of Manchu rule the reported acreage showed a steady increase and by the mid-eighteenth century had approximately reached the 1600 level, that is, the original quota of acreage.[18]

It is understandable that the reported acreage should steadily increase in the first century of the dynasty because the imperial government not only expected the rehabilitation of devastated land accompanying the restoration of peace and order, but actively pursued a policy of extending cultivated acreage by granting land free to the people who brought it back to productivity and by rewarding officials who succeeded and punishing those who failed in promoting land cultivation.[19] But why had there not been an appreciable increase in registered land over the 1753 level in the latter part of the dynasty (except in Manchuria and Sinkiang)? An easy answer would be the deterioration of administrative efficiency together with the dynastic decline. It seems to me, however, that a matter of utmost importance in this regard is the perpetuation of the original quota established at the beginning of the dynasty.

In traditional China light taxation (*ch'ing-yao pao-fu*) was always upheld as a golden canon. An official who succeeded in reducing the tax quota of a locality was always praised by the local community. To win the respect and support of local people, especially of local gentry, officials from governors down to magistrates had a strong inclination not to increase registered land (in effect, not to increase the land tax) within their jurisdiction. In the early part of the dynasty they could not refrain from reporting increase in land acreage because there existed a substantial gap in many provinces and districts between the original quota and the current quota and because they were instructed by the emperors to narrow and fill the gap. But as soon as the original quota was reached, the pressure from above for updating land data vanished while the pressure from below for maintaining the status quo grew stronger. As a consequence, throughout the country officials managed to conform approximately to the quota in reporting the amount of land and land tax in the area under their jurisdiction.

The fact that the local community wanted to keep the registered land and the land tax quota of the district from increasing needs no explanation. Yet, why the imperial government lost its interest in updating land data after the attainment of the original quota deserves further discussion. One of the reasons for the total inaction of the Manchu government with respect to a nationwide survey of land was the adequacy of the late Ming post-survey land and land tax data in providing for public expenditures. The same can be said of its indifference to the increase through other devices of registered acreage beyond the 1600 level. In fact, there appeared to officials of both high and low rank a clear indication from successive imperial instructions that registered acreage did not need to be increased. In 1658 the imperial government ordered that officials need not conduct land surveys in areas where the current registered acreage matched the Wan-li acreage (as appeared then in the *Fu-i ch'üan-shu*) of the preceding dynasty.[20] In 1713 came the highly-praised decree of *yung-pu chia-fu* (never raise taxes). This decree provided that the amount of the *ting* tax in 1711 be considered the permanent quota and that the increased number of male adults afterwards would no longer be liable to the tax.[21] But officials throughout the empire interpreted the phrase *yung-pu chia-fu* literally and applied it to the land tax, especially after the merger of the *ting* tax into the land tax in the second quarter of the eighteenth century. Naturally, no increase in the land tax implied no increase in registered acreage.

In the middle of the eighteenth century the government moved further along this direction by decreeing that odd pieces of newly reclaimed land in the provinces were permanently exempted from taxation (that is, exempted from registration).[22] Although the maximum size of odd pieces in each province was clearly defined in imperial regulations, local officials applied them quite liberally.[23] For example, in 1841 when the land property of a local rebel in Kweichow was confiscated, governor Ho Ch'ang-ling (1785-1848) found out that the property which totaled 48 mou in official registers was after an ad hoc survey as large as 828 mou. Upon inquiry the local magistrate replied that those plots of land beyond the registered 48 mou were all odd pieces legally exempted from registration. It is interesting that neither the governor nor the emperor had any objection to the magistrate's reply.[24]

Later, another regulation on land reclamation provided that no punishment should be imposed on people who did not immediately report newly reclaimed land to the government or on the local officials who failed to detect it, and that tax assessment began from the year when the land was reported, not when it was reclaimed.[25] This no-punishment regulation would undoubtedly encourage evasion of land registration on the part of proprietors and relaxation of land registration on the part of local officials.

The evidence just noted illustrates that while the imperial government at Peking showed no interest in pushing the registered acreage beyond the 1600 level, provincial and local officials saw in those instructions unmistakable enunciation of imperial benevolence towards the people. They felt that it was their moral responsibility not to surpass that level when reached. Conformity then took precedence over actuality. Reporting land acreage and land tax became a mere formality. Hence, what had been termed the original quota of land acreage at the beginning of the dynasty was by the middle of the eighteenth century transformed into a practically permanent quota. Although minor changes occurred in official land acreage from one year to another, they were by nature fictional.

Apart from moral and political grounds there were practical considerations on the part of local officials that made them either unable or unwilling to update the land data. Local governments under the Ch'ing were understaffed. Unless local residents voluntarily reported their reclaimed land to the government, magistrates could not possibly keep land records up to date without a land survey. But many people simply chose not to register their land in order to evade tax payment. And there were legal loopholes such as the "odd-pieces" and "no-punishment" regulations that encouraged evasion of land registration. Most magistrates would have found land survey—the most effective way of updating land records—financially impossible even if they had wanted to do it for the sake of administrative efficiency or fiscal equity. The part of taxes earmarked for local expenses was far from adequate to meet the basic administrative expenditure. Most local governments managed to make ends meet by collecting surcharges and customary fees. Few could set aside a sizable amount of money for undertaking a cadastral survey. Therefore, the most local officials could do was rely on the existing land records in the office, however outdated these were, as the only information for the purpose of taxation.

Finally, under the system of k'ao-ch'eng the record of tax collection was one of the basic criteria by which officials at higher levels evaluated the administrative performance of local officials. The latter were rewarded or punished according to the evaluation. For example, if a magistrate failed to collect 50 percent or more of the land tax quota in the district under his jurisdiction, he was subject to dismissal.[26] On the other hand, the lower the tax quota in a district, the easier it was to collect the tax in full, whereas the higher the quota, the more difficult was the task of tax collection. Hence the higher the tax quota, the greater the risk of being punished, whereas the lower the quota, the greater was the chance of being rewarded. Such being the case, local officials would certainly not be interested in updating the land data for the simple reason that more registered land meant more tax quota to be collected. Even when they did make a land survey and uncover large tracts of land hitherto unregistered, for moral and practical reasons they would almost without exception purposely keep the reported increment at a minimum or totally conceal it by the device of mou conversion—converting several actual mou into fiscal mou—as Ping-ti Ho has dwelt at length.[27]

Assessment of the Land Tax

Tax assessment occupies a central position in the administration of the land tax and, in fact, of all other taxes. While land registration can be properly considered a prerequisite of land tax assessment, the collection of the tax is the implementation of whatever assessment made. The task of assessment is comprised of two phases: the selection of a base and the determination of a rate structure. The base is the object which is taxed; the rate is what is applied to that base so that the amount of taxes to be collected can be calculated. Whether a tax is equitable in the allocation of fiscal burden, adequate in revenue yields, economical in administration, and desirable in its effects on economic growth depends to a large extent upon the decision made by the government on the base and rate. To see what effects the decision might produce on all segments of a society and on the economy as a whole, one needs only to compare the medieval tithe (which is based on the gross-income concept and taxed at a flat rate) with the modern progressive income tax (which is based on the net-income concept and taxes at an elaborate rate structure). The former is easier to administer but generally less adequate in yields from the standpoint of the government and far less equitable from the standpoint of taxpayers than the former.

As far as land tax assessment is concerned, there have been three major types of tax base among various countries: land area, land value, and land yield or income. Under the land area system the land tax is assessed on the basis of land area, for example, so many dollars per acre. The amount of tax to be paid by property owners is the product of the area of their landholding and the tax rate decided by appropriate officials or tax agencies. The rate may be a uniform or a classified one. If it is uniform, all land is levied at a flat rate in spite of differences in the quality of the soil, the topography of the field, the accessibility to irrigation and market, and so on. If it is classified, land is divided into a number of categories depending on productivity and use; in general, high tax rates are applied to the land in higher categories. Under the land value system the land tax is assessed either on the annual rental value or on capital value. Under the land yield system the tax is assessed on land yield or land income (including yield from other cooperative inputs: labor and capital), gross or net. Under the latter two systems as well, tax policymakers may adopt either a flat tax rate or a multitude of rates.[28]

Before describing the land tax assessment system of the Ch'ing period let me first put down two formulas as follows:

Land tax quota = land area × tax rate
Amount of land tax = land tax quota × rate of collection

Just like the preceding Ming government, the Manchu regime had adopted at the beginning the first formula as its system of land tax assessment and by and large statutorily maintained the formula until its last days; but owing to fiscal necessity it had to allow the development of the second formula as the practical system of assessment. In other words, the first was the statutory system; the second was the system actually in operation.

The statutory system of assessment was based on land area with a classified-rate structure. Throughout the country all types of land under cultivation were classified by their fertility or topographical condition into several categories such as *t'ien* (paddy land), *ti* (dry land), *shan* (terrace land), *tang* (marsh land). Each category was further divided into a number of grades. While the classification of cultivated land into three main grades and of each main grade further into three sub-grades was considered a standard pattern, the number of categories and grades varied from one province to another and from one district to another.[29] In general, paddy land or land of the upper grade was assessed at a higher tax rate than the land in other categories or of lower grades. Among all provinces Kiangsu had the most complicated rate structure, for there existed more than two hundred grades there.[30] On the other hand, in a less developed area like Fengtien the rate structure was rather simple; a number of districts there even had a flat rate.[31] The tax thus assessed was in either silver or grain or both. In Kansu it also included straw.

Nevertheless, as Ping-ti Ho has rightly pointed out, there was another method of assessment at work in many parts of the country. That is, instead of assessing land of diverse productivity at different rates, some officials in charge of land tax assessment fixed a standard rate for land of diverse productivity by converting several mou or more of lower-grade land into one mou of upper-grade land, or into one fiscal mou.[32] This was a scheme to do away with multiplicity of tax rates and to keep the registered land and land tax quota of a district in conformity with the established quota of acreage and taxes. As mentioned before, the practice of mou conversion was one of the major factors accounting for the downward bias of Ch'ing land statistics.

Within an administrative area, whether a district, a prefecture, or a province, the total amount of taxes thus arrived at (that is, the assessed rate times land area, actual or fiscal) constituted the tax quota of the area. By regulation the quota should be revised every ten years in connection with the revision of *Fu-i ch'üan-shu*. However, after the middle of the eighteenth century revision of tax quota was apparently minimal, except for those provinces which suffered heavily from ravages of war during the Taiping Rebellion, or from the Moslem Rebellion in the third quarter of the nineteenth century (see Tables 4.1 and 4.4).[33] The reasons for the nonincrease of tax quota in the latter part of the Ch'ing period are just the same as those contributing to the practically unchanged registered acreage. Suffice it to say that land tax quotas in most districts throughout the country had virtually become a fixed quantum after 1750. As far as the assessment of the quota is concerned, all the magistrate cared to do, when the *Fu-i ch'üan-shu* was being revised, was to adjust the tax rates of the land in the district so that the current quota could be approximately maintained. Since the registered acreage changed little, neither did the rates.

A fixed land tax quota meant a fixed revenue from land taxation. Since the land tax occupied a predominant position in the Ch'ing tax structure, a fixed land tax revenue would presume a more or less fixed "budget" for the government. One could hardly imagine that such a system of land tax assessment could work for years, much less for centuries. When the tax quota, even fully collected, could not meet the financial needs of the government, officials had to levy surcharges to finance public activities if the quota could not be increased. When surcharges were levied, the most convenient way was to have the quota as tax base, for example, 10 percent surcharge as *hao-hsien* (lit., "the meltage fee") for each tael of the *ti-ting* quota. In this case the rate of collection was 1.1 taels per tael of the quota. As financial needs increased, officials in charge of land tax administration simply added more surcharges and thereby raised the rate of collection without any change in the tax quota. This was the system that was at work in the Ch'ing period and particularly in the latter part of that period.

The factors causing the increase of land tax surcharges will be discussed in Chapter 3. The question now is who decided the rate of collection and on what criteria the rate was determined. Some, if not most, scholars with special interest in nineteenth-century China have stressed official corruption in tax collection as if local magistrates had a free hand in determining the rate of collection.[34] It should be immediately pointed out that no magistrate under the Ch'ing could carry out his official responsibilities without collecting surcharges beyond what was allowed by rigid imperial regulations. Therefore, if the rate of collection was set at a reasonable limit, not only governors but even the emperor would not object to the extra-legal collection on legal ground.[35] The general attitude of the higher authorities towards this matter was that the rate should be so determined as to be satisfactory to both the government and the people (*kuan min liang-pien*) or, more specifically, that magistrates should consult at first with the local community on the imposition of a land tax surcharge so that any decision made would be willingly accepted by the general public.[36]

In a pre-modern society and in a country as extensive and diversified as

China there were certainly many instances in which local magistrates decided the rate of collection at their own discretion. However, it appears that there were at work in the Ch'ing period two prevalent patterns with regard to the determination of the rate. The first was that whenever the magistrate considered it necessary to raise the rate of collection he made the decision in consultation with local gentry and in some districts with local elders, as well. Moreover, a prudent magistrate may have submitted the rate thus determined to the provincial authorities for approval. The second type was that the decision of either increasing or decreasing the rate was made by the provincial government and subject to imperial approval. The first type had been in existence from the early Ch'ing, if not earlier; but the second became a rather common pattern only in the latter part of the nineteenth century.

That local gentry had to be consulted on matters of taxation was apparent because, by virtue of their influence in the society, their advice and cooperation was necessary for the fulfillment of the magistrate's official duties, and by virtue of their connection with officialdom, they could appeal to the higher authorities to overrule the magistrate's decision to which they objected or even to impeach him.[37] In Cheng hsien of Chekiang, for example, before governor-general Tso Tsung-t'ang (1812-85) fixed the rate of collection in 1863-64, there was a land tax commission called *liang-hsi*. Twice each year (once on the fifth day of the second month and once on the fifth day of the eighth month) the magistrate called into session the local gentry both in the city and in the countryside to decide the rate of collection. Because of such an institution, it was said in the district gazetteer, local taxpayers were free from fraudulent exaction for more than a hundred years.[38] Similar institutions also existed in Nan-ch'uan hsien of Szechwan.[39] Whether this system of a regularly convened ad hoc commission was widely used is unknown, but some sort of consultation or deliberation with local gentry can be found in numerous places, for example, in Tan-t'u hsien of Kiangsu (1815), in various districts of Kuang-hsin Prefecture of Kiangsi (1868), in Tzu-yang hsien of Shensi (1884), in Lo-p'ing chou of Yunnan (1886), in Chen-yüan hsien of Kansu (1906).[40] In all these cases local gentry played an important role in the determination of the rate of collection.

Local gentry often enjoyed a preferential rate of collection, discriminatory against the peasants. Considering the social structure at the time, this discrimination, if not carried to the extreme, would usually be tolerated by the peasants. It does not mean, however, that the magistrate could regard their interests lightly. An unreasonable and arbitrary increase of the rate by the magistrate frequently resulted in refusal to pay taxes or even rioting on the part of the peasants.[41] And these undesirable consequences would in turn probably cost him his entire official career. For example, a riot occurred in Huang hsien of Shantung in 1828 as a consequence of a 200-cash increase in the rate of collection by the magistrate. When the report of this incident reached the court, he was immediately dismissed.[42] Needless to say, a magistrate with his career in mind would do everything possible to avoid angering the peasants, who formed the great majority of the local population.

The second pattern of determining the rate of collection can be traced back to the second quarter of the eighteenth century when the imperial government legalized a surcharge called *hao-hsien* and authorized governors to fix the rate of collection in their respective provinces.[43] The rates then fixed by the provincial authorities and approved by the emperor were subsequently codified as part of imperial regulations on land taxation.[44] However, as will be shown in Chapters 3 and 4, these rates were inadequate to meet the financial needs of local governments from the start and became even more so as population and prices increased over time. As a consequence, in spite of imperial regulations magistrates throughout the country set their own rates of collection by necessity (often in consultation with local gentry). By the eve of the Taiping Rebellion these rates had become widely variant among districts and provinces because of differences in local conditions an in personal character of the magistrates. They were generally burdensome largely because of severe deflation at the time (see Chapter 6). It was in the midst of the rebellion that the second major effort for the removal of the decision-making power on the rate of collection from the local to provincial level started, a process that was not finished until the end of the dynasty.

During and after their bitter struggle against the Taipings the emerging Chinese scholar-generals felt that the best policy to win popular support to their cause was to reduce the tax burden of the people, and that in order to reduce the tax burden it was necessary to lower the rate of collection or land tax quota. While some succeeded in both directions, all managed to take over the power of determining the rate of collection from the local government. The man who initiated this process was Lo Ping-chang (1792-1867). In 1855, as governor of Hunan, he instructed all magistrates in the province to consult with the gentry and people on reducing the current rate of collection and to report to him the rate agreed upon. The reported rates considered to be reasonable were approved and those exorbitant ones were rejected. Finally, all magistrates were ordered to collect the land tax according to the approved rate. After a few years of successful experimentation he reported this operation to the emperor in 1858 and received the latter's approval.[45]

Lo Ping-chang's successful reform in Hunan was soon copied with some modification by other provincial leaders in south China—by Hu Lin-i (1812-61) in Hupei, Tseng Kuo-fan (1811-72) and Shen Pao-chen (1820-79) in Kiangsu, Chiao Sung-nien (1815-75) in Anhwei, Tso Tsung-t'ang in Chekiang, Li Hung-chang (1823-1901) and Ting Jih-ch'ang (1823-82) in Kiangsu, and Chiang I-li (1846-87) in Kwangtung.[46] In the last quarter of the dynasty two more provinces in the north (Shansi and Shantung) followed suit.[47] In all these provinces the power to raise or lower the rate of collection was thus transferred from the local government to the provincial government. There certainly were magistrates who collected land tax over and above the approved rate, but on the whole the provincial ruling prevailed.[48]

It should be added, however, that final authority still rested with the imperial government. While the latter always approved the decision made by governors to reduce the rate, it did not automatically grant permission to do otherwise. For instance, a proposal made by the acting governor-general of Liang-kiang in 1906 to raise the rate by 200 cash in Kiangsu was at first turned down; it was not until after two years' repeated arguing by the provincial authorities that approval was finally granted.[49] Moreover, although the imperial government approved the rate of collections as submitted by the governors in the post-Taiping years, no effort had been made to incorporate these authorized rates into imperial regulations on public finance. Accordingly, provincial and local officials still had to conform to the outdated regulations while making their annual report of revenue and expenditure. In other words, as far as tax revenue is concerned, what they reported to the capital was still the quota, not the actual amount of collection (the tax quota times the rate of collection). Ironically, this requirement for conformity left the central government with no effective institutional control over the taxes collected over and above the quota.

The second question is by what criteria the rate of collection was determined? Suppose that R is the rate of collection, Q a unit of tax quota (tael or shih), S a surcharge per unit of tax quota, and n the number of surcharges, then the rate of collection can be expressed by an equation:

$$R = Q + S_1 + S_2 + \ldots + S_n$$

Since Q is constant, the rate of collection (R) depends on variables S_1, S_2, $\ldots S_n$. In other words, if we know how these variables are determined, we know how R is determined. On the determination of surcharges there was no single conventional rule in the Ch'ing period. Instead, on different occasions or under different circumstances officials involved in the decision making might well decide the rate of surcharges on different principles. On the whole, however, four considerations are discernible. They are fiscal equity between individual taxpayers or between different districts, the financial needs of the local government, the social status of taxpayers, and the cost of tax collection.

In Ch'ing China a tax was commonly considered fair if it was a proportional tax, that is, in proportion to taxpayers' income or wealth. In principle, a taxpayer who owned ten mou of land was assessed with a tax quota ten times as much as that assessed on a taxpayer who owned only one mou (provided the productivity of land owned by both was the same). In the same manner, most surcharges were levied at a certain percentage of or by a certain amount of money per each unit of tax quota the taxpayer owed to the government. For instance, the surcharge for the Boxer Indemnity was assessed at 200 cash per tael of the *ti-ting* quota in Kiangsu, 400 cash per tael in Fukien, and 0.3 tael per tael in Kwangtung.[50] In short, a taxpayer had to pay an amount of surcharge in proportion to the tax quota he bore as a property owner.

While proportional taxation was a dominant philosophy in the Ch'ing, there were cases in which surcharge exemption was given to the poor districts or the taxpayers with a minimal amount of tax quota. Szechwan is a case in point. Among the 146 districts of the province, thirty were exempted from a surcharge called *chin-t'ieh* (subscription to military provision) and twenty-three from another surcharge known as *chüan-shu* (contribution to military and indemnity funds) because of general poverty in these districts. Moreover, people with a tax quota less than 0.08 tael were free from the latter levy.[51] Another interesting case is the imposition of the surcharge for the Boxer Indemnity in Ching-men chih-li chou (independent department) of Hupei. Exemption was granted to those people who had a tax quota less than 0.01 tael (*ti-ting*) and/or 0.01 shih (grain). The surcharge rate was progressive from 70 to 300 cash per piece of the tax receipt for those who had a quota from 0.01 tael to one tael (*ti-ting*) or from 0.01 shih to one shih (grain). A proportional rate at 300 cash per piece of the receipt was applied to all those who had a minimum quota of one tael or one shih.[52]

However, for one reason or another the principle of fiscal equity had to give way to other considerations. Among these reasons, the most urgent was how to meet the required expenditure of the local administration (a consideration which in fact overshadowed the principle of fiscal equity, accounting for the differences in the rate of collection among different provinces and districts. See Chapter 5). A realistic solution was to measure the revenue by expenditure. Since the land tax was the most important revenue of local governments and the grant-in-aid in whatever form was, if any, minimal, officials would naturally look upon the collection of land tax surcharge as the most effective means to make both ends meet in local finance. Under these circumstances, a heavy burden was likely to fall on poor districts (districts which had a small amount of tax quota) because only a high rate of surcharge could compensate for the meagerness of the quota and thereby meet the necessary expenditure of their administration. On the other hand, rich districts (districts which had a large amount of tax quota) could adequately support their administration with a moderate rate of surcharge in spite of the fact that the administrative expenditure of rich districts was usually much greater than that of their poor neighbors. The grain tax of Anhwei in the late years of the dynasty is illustrative. In those districts that had a large amount of grain quota the rates of collection were around 4,000 cash per shih (exclusive of the surcharge for the Boxer indemnity), but in those districts that had only a small quota the rates ranged from 5,000 to 6,400 cash per shih.[53]

Another good example of measuring revenue by expenditure is seen in the way Governor Ting Jih-ch'ang (1823-82) regulated the rates of collection in northern Kiangsu after the Taiping Rebellion. He divided the districts in the area into three categories: the big-quota districts, each with a quota of more than 20,000 taels (*ti-ting*) or shih (grain); the medium-quota districts, each with a quota between 10,000 and 20,000 taels (or shih); and the small-quota districts each with a quota of around 3,000 taels (or shih). The rates of collection he authorized were generally in reverse correlation with the amount of quota each district had; the big-quota districts yielded, as he put it, plenty of surplus, and therefore the rates of collection should be somewhat reduced.[54] The same consideration was put into effect by Governor Hu Lin-i in Hupei in 1857 and by Governor-general Tso Tsung-t'ang in Chekiang in 1864.[55]

In determining the rate of collection for the land tax, local officials were often compelled to take into account the taxpayers' social status and set different rates for different groups of people. In rural China of the Ch'ing the population was generally composed of two groups: gentry and peasants. It has been pointed out that the gentry were influential in the society and closely connected with official hierarchy. To perform their official duties successfully magistrates had to seek the advice and cooperation of the gentry. In return, the latter were given privileges in one form or another. One of these privileges was a preferential tax rate. Accordingly, in many districts local officials classified the taxpayers into two groups. The privileged group was generally known as gentry households or big households; the unprivileged group was known as commoner households or small households. In certain localities there were subdivisions within each group. As a rule, the higher the taxpayer's social status, the lower the rate of collection for each unit of tax quota he owed to the government.

On the eve of the Taiping Rebellion this kind of inequity existed to a considerable degree in a number of southern provinces. For example, the top gentry households in the Soochow area paid the grain tax in money at rates about 120-130 percent of the quota but the commoner households paid at rates as high as 300-400 percent. In northern Kiangsu some gentry paid nothing, some paid 2,000-3,000 cash for each shih of the grain quota; but the commoner households had to pay 6,000-7,000 cash, or even as high as 15,000-16,000 cash per shih.[56] A similar situation prevailed in Chekiang and Hupei.[57] During and immediately after the rebellion the highest authorities in these provinces made a vigorous effort to do away with the multiple rates among taxpayers of different social status. The reform was a success but irregularities later reappeared in a number of districts (see Table 2.2). Besides the three provinces mentioned, multiple rates also existed in other areas. However sporadic, the evidence presented in Table 2.2 demonstrates two social characteristics of late Ch'ing land tax structure: (1) the gentry class's enjoyment of a preferential tax rate was a widespread phenomenon; and (2) the gap between the rates applied to the gentry and those applied to commoners varied widely among different districts and provinces.

Many magistrates also set different rates of collection for different sections of their districts because the backward condition of transportation made the cost of tax collection differ considerably between the city and the country-side. In this respect the most common practice was a division of tax collection stations into two sorts: one was known as *ch'eng-kuei* (lit., "city chest"), that is, money chests for receiving taxes were put in the district yamen; the other was known as *hsiang-kuei* (lit., "country chest") or *hsiang-cheng* (collection in the countryside), that is, additional tax collection stations were set up in the countryside to facilitate tax payment by the peasants. But to set up the *hsiang-kuei* the magistrate had to bear the costs of stationing clerks and runners in the countryside and of shipping the tax funds collected there to his yamen. For this reason, people in the village would generally not oppose a higher rate of collection for taxes collected in the countryside than in the city (for an illustration, see Table 2.3).[58] Since only gentry and merchant landowners lived and could afford to live in the city, this measure again put a heavier burden on the peasants than on the city dwellers and had the effect of encouraging absenteeism.

Collection of the Land Tax

Collection of the land tax and delivery of a specified portion of the tax to the provincial authorities were among the paramount responsibilities of local magistrates. Success or failure in this aspect of the land tax administration was of particular concern to them because at stake were not only the financial stability of local administration but their whole official career. To achieve the best possible record in their performance as tax collectors, magistrates in the Ch'ing period learned to adapt themselves to diverse local conditions through various arrangements. Generally speaking, there were at work four major systems of collection and delivery throughout the country, namely:

Direct collection and direct delivery or official collection and official delivery (magistrates assumed direct control over the collection and delivery of the land tax).
Indirect collection and indirect delivery (magistrates received an agreed-

Table 2.2. Differential rates of collection for the *ti-ting* quota in the 1900's

| Province and District (1) | Rate of collection (number of cash per tael of quota unless otherwise indicated) | |
	Gentry household (2)	Commoner household (3)
Kiangsu		
Yüan-ho hsien	Discount	Full
Chekiang		
Shui-an hsien	1,700–1,800	2,800
Anhwei	Lower	Higher
Hupei		
Some districts	Payment in silver (usually lower)	Payment in cash (usually higher)
Fukien[a]		
Cheng-ho hsien	1,400–2,000	2,600
Lung-yen chou	1.5 taels	1.93 taels
An-ch'i hsien	1,910	2,500
Yung-ch'un chou	1.3 taels	1.8 taels
Lung-ch'i hsien	1.44 taels	1.73 taels
Shang-hang hsien	1.24 taels	1.49 taels
Honan		
Ku-shih hsien	1,950–2,800	3,300
Kwangsi		
Li-p'u hsien		0.1 tael more than the rate paid by the big households
Fu-ch'uan hsien		0.24 tael more than the rate paid by the big households
Pin chou		0.52 tael more than the rate paid by the big households
Yung-fu hsien		0.75 tael more than the rate paid by the big households
Hsiang-an hsien		1.0+ tael more than the rate paid by the big households
Kweichow		
Ch'ang-chai subdistrict	0.5–1.5	1.5–2.0 taels
Fengtien		
K'ai-yüan hsien	1,220 (*tung-ch'ien*)/mou	1,990 (*tung-ch'ien*)/mou
T'ieh-ling hsien[b]	0.08 tael/mou	0.14 taels/mou

Sources:
1. *CKCTNYS*, p. 345.
2. *TCSMS* (Chekiang), R–L, 11; *TCSMS* (Anhwei), R–L, 8, 3–4; *TCSMS* (Hupei), p. 2; *TCSMS* (Fukien), R–L, 5–8; *TCSMS* (Honan), R–L, 40; *TCSMS* (Kwangsi), *Ko-lun shang–kuo-shui pu*, 92; *TCSMS* (Kweichow), R–L, 85–86.
3. *K'ai-yüan-hsien chih* (1917), 5.62b.
4. *T'ieh-ling-hsien chih* (1931 preface), 6.1b.

Notes:
[a]Surcharges for the Boxer indemnity and railway building not included.
[b]Converted from rates in terms of silver dollars at the ratio of one dollar to 0.72 tael.

Table 2.3. Differences in the rate of collection between *ch'eng-kuei* and *hsiang-kuei* in Fukien

| District | Rate of collection for the *ti-ting* quota, cash/tael[a] | |
	Ch'eng-kuei	Hsiang-kuei
Ku-t'ien hsien	2,100	1,700
Yung-fu hsien	2,380	2,250–2,400
Nan-p'ing hsien	2,300	2,460
Shun-ch'ang hsien	1,800	2,460
Ch'ang-t'ing hsien	1.465 taels per tael	1.515 taels per tael
Yung-an hsien	2,560	2,580
Kuei-hua hsien	1,900	2,000

Source: TCSMS (Fukien), R–L, 5–8.

Note: [a]Surcharges for the Boxer indemnity and railway building are not included.

upon sum of money from tax farmers and left the business of collection and delivery entirely to the tax farmers).

Direct collection but indirect delivery.

Indirect collection but direct delivery.[59]

Under the last two systems magistrates directed one phase of the collection-delivery operation but let out the other phase to tax farmers. Within each major system, moreover, there was a variety of arrangements in tune with local conditions and with the administrative ability of magistrates. On the whole, delivery was much less a problem than collection, for the latter involved thousands of taxpayers with diverse social and economic status who were scattered over a large area in the countryside. Once collection was successfully accomplished, delivery was a rather simple matter.

By regulation the magistrate had to direct his staff at the office of revenue, where tax records were kept, to perform the following tasks: preparing and sending to each taxpayer a tax notice specifying the amount of taxes to be paid within a limited period of collection; setting up in the district yamen money chests for depositing tax money; and recording the amount of taxes received from each taxpayer.[60] On the other hand, taxpayers had to deposit in person their tax payments in the chests; only those who had a tax quota of less than one tael of silver and who lived far away from the district yamen could arrange with someone to pay on their behalf.[61] While this system existed in all provinces, few, if any, districts could adhere completely to it. For transportation between countryside and city took days and entailed a fair expense. Many peasants simply could not afford the expense which might amount to several times their tax payment itself.[62]

To remedy the situation local officials often offered taxpayers one or both of the following alternatives while still assuming direct control over tax collection. One was frequently dispatching clerks and runners to or stationing them in the countryside to collect taxes from individual taxpayers in the tax collection period.[63] This method of collection had two serious defects, however. Clerks and runners might exact from individual taxpayers, especially the ignorant or timid, more payment in the name of fees and expenses than what was authorized by the magistrate. They might also embezzle a portion of the money collected from taxpayers and report it as uncollected.[64]

Another alternative was to set up during the tax collection period money chests in the countryside and to levy a limited amount of surcharge for this operation. It was convenient for taxpayers and less costly than the first method. For these reasons there appeared to be a trend in the late Ch'ing, as indicated in the financial report of Hupei, of shifting from the first alternative towards the establishment of more tax-receiving chests for accommodating taxpayers.[65] Moreover, while the extent of the first alternative is unknown, the *TCSMS* does reveal the prevalence of country chests in Fukien, Kwangsi, and Kweichow.[66] In view of this evidence, however inconclusive it is, the second arrangement had probably become the most common practice in the closing decades of the Ch'ing as an alternative to the centralized collection at the district yamen.

Indirect collection means tax farming. In Ch'ing times there were two kinds of tax farming. One was generally called *pao-shou* or *pao-cheng* (a contract for collection). It was made by magistrates and tax farmers. By mutual agreement or by official order the magistrate authorized the tax farmer to collect taxes at a certain rate and received taxes from the tax farmer instead of from individual taxpayers. The other kind, known as *pao-lan* (a contract for payment), was made by taxpayers and tax farmers. Not only had the magistrate no part in such a deal but he also often had no knowledge of it. However, it was similar to the first kind, in that between local officials and taxpayers there was a group of tax farmers acting on behalf of one party or the other. Most active as tax farmers were two groups: clerks and runners in the district yamen and the local gentry. In some localities, merchants, usually money shopkeepers, and common people also took part in it.[67]

In most districts where *pao-cheng* or *pao-shou* was practiced, it was largely a monopoly of clerks and runners. The reasons clerks and runners occupied a leading position in this business can be found mainly in the defects of the Ch'ing administrative system. By regulation a magistrate was not permitted to hold office in his native province and his tenure was normally three years at most.[68] Therefore he was not familiar with conditions in the area where he held office, and his short tenure often discouraged him from making changes in yamen personnel, however necessary these appeared to him, except in a few key positions like the secretaries of law and finance. On the other hand, clerks and runners were natives; many of them had remained on their job for years or decades. They were the ones who kept land tax records. Hence their cooperation was necessary to a magistrate for carrying out his official duties.[69] As a rule, he assigned them various tasks in connection with tax collection and delivery and gave them a reasonable share of the surcharges in lieu of salaries or wages. But an inexperienced and less competent magistrate might well choose an easy way by leaving the matter entirely in the hands of his yamen underlings and content himself with a lump sum of money turned over to him by them. Moreover, in certain poor districts where the costs of tax collection and the rate of tax delinquency were high, even an experienced and capable official might find it economical and expedient to render a contract to clerks and runners for collecting all or part of the land tax in the district.[70]

Undoubtedly, this group of clerks and runners entered into a contract (*pao-shou*) with the magistrate for material gain. Let us see where their profits came from. Under contract they were usually authorized to levy a surcharge for collection expenses in addition to the rate of collection proper (that is, the rate of collection exclusive of the surcharge for collection expenses). Thus, a part of their profits was obviously derived from the surcharge. It should be pointed out that whether under the system of indirect collection or under the system of direct collection the surcharge for collection expenses was a universal levy throughout the country. What matters is whether this surcharge was generally higher under the indirect than under the direct system. If the data for Fukien are typical, the answer is negative. In Table 2.4 there are nineteen districts where the surcharge for collection expenses is known. The simple arithmetic average of the surcharge for all nineteen districts is 0.1 tael for each tael of the *ti-ting* quota. Of these districts seven were on the direct collection system. The rates of the surcharge for this group of districts range from 0.03 tael to 0.41 tael and average at

Table 2.4. Differences in the surcharge for collection expenses in Fukien, 1908 (direct collection versus indirect collection)

System of Tax Collection	Number of Districts	Surcharge for collection expenses (tael per tael of the *ti-ting* quota)	
		Range	Average
Direct Collection	7	0.03-0.41	0.12 (0.08)[a]
Indirect Collection	12	0.04-0.23	0.08
Total	19	0.03-0.41	0.10

Source: TCSMS (Fukien), R–L, 9–10.

Note: [a]One district with an exceptionally high rate of surcharge (0.41) is excluded.

0.12 taels for each tael of quota. The figures for the remaining twelve districts which were on the indirect collection system are 0.04-0.23 tael and 0.08 tael respectively. Even if we exclude from the first group one district having an exceptionally high rate of surcharge for collection expenses (0.41), the average rate of the surcharge for this group of districts still amounts to as much as that for the second group of districts. In other words, under normal circumstances taxpayers did not pay more through indirect collection than through direct collection. Therefore, whatever amount of profit clerks and runners earned by contract, they earned it at the expense of the magistrate with whom they concluded a contract (and hence at the expense of the government), not of taxpayers, provided that they collected the surcharge as authorized.

There were certainly cases in which clerks and runners with the contract for tax collection intended to and did exact more from taxpayers than what was authorized by the magistrate. Nonetheless, two practical considerations would deter them from doing so and therefore precluded excessive collection as a dependable means of making profit. First, even with a modern and efficient administrative apparatus the success of tax collection depends to a great extent upon the cooperation of taxpayers. Needless to say, their compliance is even more important to tax farmers in a premodern society. Extortion could arouse popular resentment. Tax delinquency and the costs of tax collection would be high. The tax farmers might well end up with a net loss instead of a sizable gain.

Second, clerks and runners who collected taxes without authorization ran the risk of losing not only profits but also their jobs. One of the sure ways for a magistrate to gain fame and popularity in local community was to dismiss and punish dishonest clerks and runners. For this reason most of them dared not grossly abuse the power delegated to them; some would even go bankrupt rather than violate the contract. For example, a group of clerks in the district yamen of Tz'u-ch'i hsein in Chekiang turned in their resignation in 1826 because the magistrate rejected their request for an increase in the rate of collection for meeting office expenses.[71] Obviously, if they could increase the rate in one way or another without authorization, they would not choose to quit. Another revealing case is found in Hsin-ch'ang hsien (Chekiang) during the T'ung-chih period (1862-74). By contract the clerks of the revenue office in the district yamen were authorized to collect the land tax in cash at a specific rate of collection and were required to pay to the local government taxes in silver. Since the value of silver in relation to cash had risen rapidly at the time, they were financially ruined for making good the tax deficit caused by monetary fluctuations.[72] Again, if they could have raised the rate of collection by any means, they would not have had to incur such a heavy loss.

Clerks and runners did not by any means always act prudently, however.

On occasion they would not hesitate to exploit for unjustified gain taxpayers who were almost without exception the poor and hapless. People were supposed to pay their taxes within a specified period of collection each year, but there were always some who could not. At the same time the yamen tax farmers had to fulfill the contract without delay—to pay taxes in full before the deadline. Accordingly, it was common practice for them "to advance money for tax payment" (generally called *tien-liang*). Since those taxpayers could not possibly obtain credit from other sources, the clerks and runners were in a strong position to dictate the term of loan in their favor. Local officials had to accept such practices in order not to jeopardize the administration of tax collection.[73] As a consequence, clerks and runners were able to earn an exorbitant amount of interest for the loans in addition to the normal profit through tax farming.

Besides the contract for tax collection by mutual agreement, there was in operation in some localities another type of contract which was dictated by the magistrate. That is, for the purpose of tax collection the local population was organized by officials into a number of units like *li, chia, t'u*, with each comprising a number of households. The head of such units, either elected by the people or selected by the government, had the duty of collecting taxes from all households within his unit. If any household failed to pay, he would have to make good the deficit.[74] However, unless the unit was formed by a tightly knit clan, such a system could not have persisted long because the head might easily be ruined by the tax delinquency of other members of his unit. This type of contract was therefore far less common than the first type—contract by mutual agreement.

While clerks and runners played a leading role in the business of *pao-shou* or *pao-cheng*, in the business of *pao-lan* it was local gentry who occupied an unchallengeable position. *Pao-lan* is a contract for the payment of taxes, that is to say, by a mutual agreement the gentry promised to pay taxes on behalf of commoner-proprietors or less privileged gentry-proprietors. In southern Kiangsu certain prominent gentry even set up a special type of business concern called *tsu-chan* (the landlord bursary). It managed the land properties of its owner and those entrusted to it by other landowners, thereby collecting rents from tenants and paying taxes for all lands under its management.[75]

Two major factors gave rise to the business of *pao-lan*. In many districts the gentry enjoyed a preferential rate of collection for taxes they paid. They stood to gain by *pao-lan* because they could take advantage of the difference in the rate of collection between the gentry-household and the commoner-household, and between the city chest and the country chest (some gentry lived in the city). On the other hand, commoner-proprietors often sought this arrangement in order to save time and traveling expenses in bringing their taxes to the city yamen and to avoid possible embarrassment or obstruction by the yamen runners (note that most peasants were illiterate). Again, as in the case of *pao-shou*, tax farmers in the *pao-lan* business gained by and large at the expense of the government, not of the taxpayers who paid the tax farmers generally no more than what they had to pay under direct collection.

It is hard to say with certainty how these systems were geographically distributed; many local officials actually put to work different systems in different seasons of the year or in different sections of the district under their jurisdiction as they saw fit.[76] Although the evidence is inconclusive, a few observations can be made here. First, in two provinces where information on the systems of collection is adequate, direct collection was much more prevalent than indirect collection. Direct collection prevailed in seventy-nine out of 106 districts in Honan, and in fifty-two out of seventy-two districts of collection in Kweichow.[77] Second, in Hupei there was a movement from indirect collection to direct collection and from sending clerks and runners to collect taxes in the countryside to establishing more country chests.[78] Finally, the *pao-lan* activities appeared to be widespread in the lower Yangtze valley probably because the gentry wielded stronger power there than in the rest of the country.[79]

Needless to say, for any tax collection system to work with efficiency it must be accompanied by certain provisions for the enforcement of tax payment. In the late Ch'ing, it appears to me, although both the assessment and collection of the land tax worked against poor proprietors, these two phases of the tax administration were by and large conducted in order. What were most onerous to the taxpayers were measures taken against those who failed to pay their taxes in time. In general, local governments would use one or more of the following three kinds of pressure or punishment to enforce tax payment after the expiration of the period of collection: sending "land tax hasteners" (*ts'ui-ch'ai*) to the countryside, summoning the delinquent taxpayers and inflicting corporal punishment upon them, and imposing a fine. To the taxpayer these penalties meant psychological harassment, physical suffering, and economic degradation.

To provide for the travel expenses of the yamen runners assigned as tax hasteners some local administrations collected a special surcharge called *ch'ai-fei* (expenses for tax hasteners) from all taxpayers; some set aside money out of surcharges for administrative expenses. But in most cases it was the delinquent taxpayer who had to bear the costs of food, lodging, and travel for the tax hasteners.[80] It is conceivable that these costs, even charged according to the officially fixed rate (by day or by distance), could often amount to several times the taxes they owed to the government. Where local officials did not fix the rate of charge, the yamen runners would almost certainly exact more, for example, food, wine, medical expenses, and so on. Moreover, as in the case of *pao-cheng*, they might personally give a loan for tax payment to the hapless taxpayers and demand that it be paid back at an exhorbitant rate of interest.[81]

If the taxpayer failed to pay off his taxes even under the pressure of a tax hastener, he was summoned to the district yamen at the deadline hearing and flogged.[82] Severe physical punishment was considered an effective measure for enforcing tax payment, and the fear of such punishment gave the tax hastener added leverage for extortion and intimidation.

A rather common substitute for the two methods of enforcement in the late Ch'ing was the imposition on the delinquent taxpayer of a fine by way of raising the rate of collection after deadline. The extent of increase in the rate differed from one province to another and, in some provinces, from one district to another. For instance, in the Soochow area of Kiangsu the rate of collection for the grain quota was to be increased, so ruled the provincial government, by 500 cash per shih after the end of the year.[83] In Kiangsi the rate was to be raised by 300 cash per shih after deadline and by 500 cash one month later.[84] In Kweichow local administration set its own rule with regard to the deadline and the rate increase. Many districts there limited the period of collection to 10-30 days and the rate advanced after the deadline cumulatively by every month or every 10-15 days.[85] These samples indicate therefore shorter tax collection periods and heavier fines for delayed payment in the poor provinces than in the relatively affluent provinces.

In conclusion, it is safe to say that the weakest link in the land tax administration of Ch'ing times was its system of land registration. Throughout the entire period the imperial government never made a nationwide cadastral survey. Instead, it mainly relied upon the data of the late sixteenth-century survey inherited from the preceding Ming dynasty. While the government did lay down a number of rules for updating the land records (for example, annual reporting of land reclamation by local officials, quinquennial survey of the land along lakes and rivers, decennial revision of Fu-i chüan-shu, reporting of land acquisition by the owner), these rules were nevertheless rendered almost completely unworkable by the canonical decree of yung-pu chia-fu, by legal loopholes like that of "odd-pieces" and of "no-punishment," and by the reluctance and inability on the part of local officials to undertake land survey owing to the k'ao-ch'eng regulations and the lack of financial resources respectively. As a consequence, when the registered acreage reached by the mid-eighteenth century the level of 1600, it ceased to increase (except for the outlying areas of Manchuria and Sinkiang) in spite of the fact that the country's cultivated acreage had expanded by more than 400 million mou in the remaining one and one-half centuries of the dynasty. Underregistration was therefore the greatest weakness of the Ch'ing land tax administration.

As far as the taxpayers were concerned, what proved to be most onerous were measures taken after the deadline for the enforcement of tax payment. It was the follow-up of the tax-collection process which left the unscrupulous clerks and runners much room to exploit and victimize the poor. To those who could not afford to pay off their taxes in time, these penalties together with the tax hasteners' harassment and extortion were not only oppressive but indeed dreadful.

3 Increase in Land Tax Surcharge

Local Finance and Land Tax Surcharges

A peculiar characteristic of Ch'ing government finance was the existence of a dualistic structure. There was a rigid system designed in the early part of the dynasty to govern all conceivable fiscal activities. Under this system officials in charge of public finance were required to perform their duties in strict conformity with imperial regulations established in such works as *Ta-Ch'ing hui-tien, Hu-pu tse-li* (Regulations of the Board of Revenue), and *Fu-i ch'üan-shu.* Any violation of, or deviation from, the established order would, with few exceptions, result in rebuttal or even disciplinary action from the superior authorities.[1] Being based on imperial statutes this system may well be called the statutory or formal system.

On the other hand, because of the inadequacies and inflexibility of the statutory system in meeting the ever growing requirements of Ch'ing fiscal administration there gradually developed of necessity an irregularly controlled system—a multitude of practices some of which owed their existence to imperial sanction or to the approval of provincial authorities, some to precedents or customs. Yet virtually all were generally tolerated by bureaucratic hierarchies and the people at large. This latter system may be called the nonstatutory or informal system. The presence of the informal system in the Ch'ing fiscal structure made the management of public economy fragmentary and even chaotic, but it was the system, informal yet flexible, that kept public administration in operation.

This kind of fiscal dualism is conspicuously manifest in the financing of local government.[2] By regulation the local government was required to collect each year a specified amount (quota) of the land tax and miscellaneous taxes plus rent from public land, and, as mentioned in Chapter 1, to divide the revenue into two parts: *ch'i-yün* for delivery to the provincial

49

government and *ts'un-liu* for stipulated local expenditure. In fact, local administrators spent far more money than the amount of *ts'un-liu* because many expenses necessary for maintaining local administration were not provided for or not adequately covered. They also delivered to the superior authorities a great deal more than the amount of *ch'i-yün* because they had to send to the latter many assigned contributions, fees, and gifts which were not in any statutory works on public finance. Obviously, they could not meet these additional outlays without collecting additional revenues. Since tax quotas were practically fixed at all times, these additional revenues took the form of surcharges, fees, and various levies. Thus the structure of Ch'ing local finance can be shown as in Table 3.1.

Such fiscal structure brought into being the practice of keeping two sets of accounts in local fiscal administration—one for recording statutory revenues and outlays simply for the sake of conformity with the *tsou-hsiao* regulations; the other for recording funds that were raised and disbursed over and above statutory ones and that were handled in accordance with superiors' executive orders, or with established precedents, or with the magistrate's own discretion. As statutory funds were fixed, what concerned local officials most were funds in the nonstatutory category, for example, the amount of surcharges and fees to be collected, the amount of assigned contributions to be sent upward, the amount to be left as their personal income (deficit was by no means unusual). It is only against this background can we understand such terms as *fei-ch'üeh* or *mei-ch'üeh* (lucrative post), *chung-ch'üeh* (medium post), *chi-ch'üeh* (lean post) then current in official circles.[3]

For most local governments a predominant part of their nonstatutory revenue came from surcharges imposed on the land tax. Hence the increase of revenue on the local level in the Ch'ing was largely produced through increase in land tax surcharge. Before we trace the factors that accounted for the

Table 3.1. Fiscal structure of local government in the late Ch'ing

Classification	Revenue	Outlay
Statutory	Land tax quota	Taxes to be delivered (*ch'i-yün*)
	Miscellaneous taxes quota	Statutory expenses (*ts'un-liu*)
	Rent from public land	
Nonstatutory	Surcharges	Administrative expenses
	Fees	Assigned contributions, gifts, etc.
	New local levies	Donations

accumulation of surcharges from time to time, however, it is advisable to know first what these surcharges were. Partly because their complexity and irregularities almost defy systematic description and analysis, and partly because they were not recorded in the officially compiled works on finance and taxation until the last days of the dynasty, no one has ever made a special study of this area. The *TCSMS* exposes for the first time a massive amount of surcharge data, especially those in connection with administrative expenses, throughout the country. However incomplete these reports may be, they nonetheless provide us a factual basis for examining the subject. The nature of the surcharges and some terms often seen in these reports can be classified roughly into four groups as follows: [4]

Group 1. Surcharges for administrative expenses
    Those for general administrative expenses:
        Hao-hsien (lit., "meltage fee")—collected mainly for providing *yang-lien yin* (lit., "money to nourish integrity") to the officials. This surcharge was the only one of its kind which was incorporated into imperial statutes.
        P'ing-yü (extra silver).
        Kung-fei (public expenses).
        Yü-liang (extra grain).
    Those for tax collection and delivery:
        Cheng-fei or *cheng-shou fei* (collection expenses).
        Chieh-fei (delivery expenses).
        Ts'ui-liang fei (expenses incurred for enforcing tax payment).
    Those for clerks and runners:
        Fan-shih yin (food money).
        Ch'uan-p'iao fei or *p'iao-fei* (tax receipt fee).
        Fang-fei or *kuei-fei* (money for office clerks).
        Chih-pi fan-shih (money for stationery and food).
    Those in lieu of labor service:
        Ch'ai-yao (labor service).
        Fu-ma (labor and horse).

Group 2. Surcharges for local welfare
    Chi-ku chüan (contribution to local public granary for famine relief).
    Ho-kung chüan (contribution for the maintenance of river embankment).
    T'ang-kung chüan (contribution for the maintenance of embankment along the seashore).

Group 3. Surcharge for the Boxer indemnity
    Liang-chüan or *sui-liang chüan* (lit., "contribution collected together with the land tax"), or *ting-ts'ao chia-chüan* (lit., "contribution collected together with the *ti-ting* tax and the grain tribute").

Group 4. Surcharges for modernization needs
  Those for modern schools and police forces:
    Mou-chüan (lit., "contribution assigned by mou").
    Hsüeh-chüan or *hsüeh-t'ang chüan* (contribution for the establishment of schools).
    Hsün-ching chüan (contribution for the establishment of police forces).
  Those for railroad building:
    T'ieh-lu chüan (contribution for railroad building).
    Tsu-ku (lit., "subscription out of rent").
  Those for army training:
    T'uan-fei or *T'uan-lien fei* (money for army training).
  Those for preparation for self-government:
    Tzu-chih chüan (contribution for self-government).

It should be pointed out that the above is a generalization. By no means all these surcharges existed in all provinces. In the absence of any general regulation, and in a country as extensive and diverse as China, the combination of the surcharges was bound to vary, and the consequent burden to be uneven among different parts of the country and among different districts of the provinces.

Institutional Weaknesses

Land tax surcharges existed outside the formal framework of Ch'ing statutes governing public finance. They carried numerous names and covered a wide range of public expenses. Moreover, as the fiscal demand of government increased over time, they inevitably grew in number as well as in amount and thus drove up the rate of collection. Between 1753 and 1908 the nationwide average rate of collection increased from 1.2 to 2.4 taels for each tael of the *ti-ting* quota and from 1.9 to 4.3 taels for each shih of the grain quota.[5] How then did these surcharges pile up in the course of the dynasty? To be sure, institutional, economic, and political factors all played a considerable role in the process. But the factor of vital importance was undoubtedly institutional rigidity of the Ch'ing fiscal system.

The first and foremost of the institutional weaknesses lies the fact that the statutory system of land taxation lacked income- and price-elasticity because of the selection of land area as tax base. As pointed out in the last chapter, for the purpose of tax assessment there are three possible bases of land taxation, namely, land area, land value, and land yield or income. Under the first system the land tax is assessed on the basis of land area, the rate may be unitary or differentiated into multiple grades. Under the second system the tax is assessed according to land value (rental or capital value). And the third system takes land yields (gross or net) as the basis of assessment. As far as the tax administration is concerned, the uniform rate of the first system is the simplest among the systems just mentioned. Even the multiple rate has two advantages over the remaining two other systems. First, it is easier to classify land into a number of categories than to assess land value or land yields. Second, reassessment of land value and land yields must be made more frequently than that of land categories. However, in terms of economic equity and revenue productivity, the system based on land area is far less desirable than the other two.

Under the system based on land value or land yield, the land tax will automatically increase at the time of rising land value and productivity, and the tax will automatically decrease at the time of falling land value and productivity, provided reassessment is kept up-to-date. In other words, these two systems have a built-in mechanism to adjust tax receipts with changes in the state of the economy and in the income of taxpayers. Under the system based on land area, however, taxes will not increase in times of inflation and general rise in land productivity unless the government raises the tax rate. Nor can the burden of taxpayers be reduced in time of deflation and hardship unless the government reduces the tax rate or remits the taxes.[6]

China's land tax system under the Ch'ing was, by regulation, one of the classified-rate area type (that is, land tax quota = land area × tax rate). Under this system the land tax will grow only through: raising the tax rate or increasing land acreage or a combination of both. Nevertheless, for reasons discussed in connection with land registration and land tax assessment in the preceding chapter, both tax rate and registered acreage were practically fixed in all but a few provinces from the mid-eighteenth century until the end of the dynasty in 1911. Hence the land tax quota of the country remained virtually unchanged (see Tables 4.1 and 4.4). But in this period China's cultivated acreage did expand substantially and her land yield also registered a moderate gain (see Table 1.1) largely owing to a tremendous increase in population and the development of the middle and upper Yangtze valley and Manchuria. As cultivated acreage and land yields increased, so did the agricultural income of the country. Yet the statutory system with fixed tax quota was totally unresponsive to increase in the income of the agricultural sector. Therefore, we may conclude that under the statutory system, except in times of natural calamity, the income elasticity of the tax revenue was near zero.[7]

Not only was the land tax quota completely inflexible with respect to agricultural income, but it was also conspicuously unresponsive to changes in the price level. As we shall see in Table 4.1 and 4.4, the Ch'ing land tax quota included a greater part in money and a smaller part in kind. In times of inflation the tax revenue actually depreciated in spite of the fact that the same amount of money was collected as before; in times of deflation the reverse was true. But during most of the Ch'ing period the movement of prices was generally upward.[8] It follows that the statutory revenue from land was in fact shrinking because of the decrease in the purchasing power of money. Under these circumstances, unless government spending could be reduced, or adequate revenue could be secured from other sources, the imposition of land tax surcharges in one way or another became inevitable.

Added to the revenue inflexibility of the land tax system was the rigidity of the Ch'ing fiscal administrative system. The types of expenditure for local administration were specified by regulation, and each type of expenditure was provided with a specific amount of money.[9] Under the rigid and virtually unchanged regulations, the items of expenditure and the amount of money formally earmarked for each item remained the same for centuries.[10] This is what James T.K. Wu called "the static budget."[11] This system had two very serious defects: First, from the start the provision made for the maintenance of local administration fell far short of actual expenditure needs. Second, the system was unresponsive to changes in social and economic conditions; therefore, in Wu's phraseology again, "reality was sacrificed for regularity."[12]

The funds formally provided to local governments were limited to those for statutory expenses such as salaries, wages, post station expenses, expenses for sacrifice, and rations to the poor. In the late Ch'ing, however, there was little resemblance between what existed on paper and what was actually spent by the local government. The actual expenditure, as illustrated in Table 3.1, consisted of three categories: administrative expenses, assigned contributions and gifts, and donations.

Notable among the administrative expenses were salaries of secretaries, allowances of clerks and runners, meals in the yamen, costs of collecting and delivering taxes, in addition to personal and family expenses of the magistrate and his subordinate officials. Within the yamen the most important staff members were secretaries. They were not, however, members of the regular bureaucracy and were not on the official payroll. Instead, they worked for the magistrates on contract and received pay from the latter. The number of secretaries varied from one district to another, but in general even in a small district two secretaries were indispensible, one in charge of lawsuits and another in charge of taxation.[13] In the late Ch'ing the annual salary of a secretary ranged from about 100 taels to as high as 2,000 taels, depending on the responsibility of the post and the revenue productivity of the district.[14] Since magistrates themselves received only a nominal salary of 45-80 taels and a supplementary salary (yang-lien yin) ranging from 400 to 2,259 taels,[15] it is apparent that in many cases their salary could not cover even the cost of employing secretaries.

Among the personnel of local governments the most numerous groups were clerks and runners. The annual wage of clerks, usually 10-12 taels, was totally cut from the early K'ang-hsi period (1662-1722); that of runners, generally 6 taels, was too meager to meet their living expenses.[16] Consequently, these two groups had to maintain themselves almost completely by surcharges on taxation and customary service fees on other business, for example, fees on lawsuits. Besides, it was a custom that the local magistrate provide meals to all of his staff working in the yamen. This expense also was not among the statutory ones.

The maintenance of local order and the collection of taxes were the two paramount responsibilities of the magistrate. By regulation, however, nothing was provided for the costs of investigating and examining civil as well as criminal cases nor for the costs involved in tax collection and delivery. Again, it was surcharges and customary service fees that enabled him to perform these all-important functions.

The fact that formal funds provided for administrative expenses fell far short of actual needs was not limited to local government. Rather, it was a phenomenon common to government units at all levels. Lacking the institutional power to collect land taxes themselves, officials above the local level devised a number of schemes to tap the resources of the local government so as to maintain their administrative activities and their personal living. Thus a magistrate had to find means to make up the substantial shortage of funds not only for his own administrative and personal expenses but also for that of his superiors. The most obvious of these informal channels, through which part of the resources at the command of the local government were transferred to the government at higher levels, was assigned contribution. It weighed heavily on a magistrate, for he was required to make contributions, regular as well as special, to every provincial administrative office above him (including that of governor or governor-general, financial commissioner, judicial commissioner, educational commissioner, grain intendant, and prefect).

These contributions often numbered a few score and amounted to several thousand taels a year. For example, in the last years of the Ch'ing the amount of the annual regular contributions (60 in number) that the magistrates of Shensi were required to make ranged from 4,000-5,000 taels down to something more than a hundred taels, depending on the financial condition of the post.[17] In Fu-ning hsien of Kiangsu the contributions, regular and special ones as well, numbered sixty and amounted to about three thousand taels.[18] In Ch'uan-sha t'ing of the same province they were fifty-one in number and more than nine thousand taels in amount.[19]

Besides the assigned contributions, two more informal groups of transfer payments proved to be a considerable burden on magistrates. Customary fees (*kuei-fei*) of various kinds constituted one group, gifts on different occasions the other. The most important among the first group was *chieh-fei*, which was usually composed of a number of minor items. When delivering the tax quota to the financial commissioner or grain intendant, magistrates were required to pay an extra amount over and above the quota so as to provide funds for administrative expenses of the higher offices.[20] The *chieh-fei* was 5 percent of the tax quota delivered in southern Kiangsu, 3.3-3.4 percent in Hunan, and 3.5 percent in Kwangsi.[21] Moreover, whenever official business took place between a local government and the administration above it, it was customary that the former pay the latter such fees as *t'ou-wen fei* (fee for presenting documents), *kua-hao fei* (register fee), *ts'e-fei* (records fee), and *ch'e-p'i fei* (fee for delivered-tax certificate).[22] Additionally, the magistrate of a *shou-hsien* (the district containing the office of the governor or the prefect) was obliged to supply the office furniture and maintain the office building of his superiors. These expenses alone could cost the local government hundreds or even thousands of taels a year.[23]

To finance the personal expenses of the officials above the local level and their secretaries, there was a custom of presenting gifts, usually in money. These included seasonal gifts, birthday gifts, and errand gifts. The last, known as *ch'ai-ching*, were presented to superiors or their representatives when they made a tour through the district or a regular inspection of the local administration. In T'ai-k'ang hsien of Honan, for example, these outlays amounted to more than 3,500 taels a year in the last decade of the dynasty.[24]

The expenditure in the third category was the least important. It often included donations for public welfare such as education, poor relief, welfare land, and temple building.[25] Of course, if there was an urgent need to store grain in preparation for famine, or to build a big water-control project and the magistrate could not make an adequate donation, imposition of a specific surcharge often became necessary.

To what extent were the funds for statutory expenses insufficient to meet the actual expenditure needs of local government? Two precious, though incomplete, accounts found in local gazetteers may serve as a good example. Tables 3.2 and 3.3 illustrate immediately the enormous gap between the amount the local administration was allowed to spend in accordance with the regulations and the amount it actually spent. Against a total annual expenditure of more than 18,000 taels, the administration of Hsiang-t'an hsien in Hunan was provided by regulation with an amount of less than 3,000 taels. In another district, Ch'uan-sha t'ing in Kiangsu, the local administration was allowed to withhold out of taxes an amount less than 1,800 taels a year for statutory expenses, but its actual expenses also totalled more than 18,000 taels. In other words, the funds formally made available for local administration accounted for less than one-sixth of the actual outlay in one case and less than one-tenth in another. The proportion that had to be supplied by various sorts of surcharges and fees thus amounted to more than 80 or 90 percent.

Table 3.2. Statutory and actual expenses of the administration of Hsiang-t'an hsien, c. late 1880's (in taels)

Statutory expenses		Actual expenses	
Sacrifice	130	Administrative expenses	6,000
Postal stations	1,380	Collection expenses	1,000
Yang-lien-yin for		Chieh-fei to superior	
assistant officers	180	yamen	4,000
Wages of runners	1,190	Assigned contributions	7,000
		Personal expenses	?
Total Less than	3,000	More than	18,000

Source: Hsiang-t'an-hsien chih (1889), 6.15–16.

Table 3.3. Statutory and actual expenses of the administration of Ch'uan-sha t'ing, c. 1908 (in taels)

Statutory expenses		Actual expenses	
Salaries of the subprefect		Administrative expenses:	3,000
and his lieutenant		Salaries of secretaries	
(regular and supple-		Meals	
mentary salaries)	1,172	Prisoners' rations, etc.	
Wages of runners	456	Expenses of tax collection	
		and delivery	2,800
Rations to the poor	66	Assigned contributions	9,077
Sacrifice	52	Chieh-fei to superior yamen	1,546
		Gifts to superiors	1,000
		Donations	467
		Personal expenses	?
Total Less than	1,800	More than	18,000

Sources:
1. Ch'uan-sha-hsien chih (1937), 8.47b–54.
2. Ch'uan-sha-t'ing chih (1879), 4.29b–33, 14.25–32.

Population Growth and Price Inflation

While institutional rigidity made the collection of surcharges inevitable, economic changes in the period made a higher surcharge necessary. Among other things, population growth and changes in the value of money were two most relevant factors contributing to the increase of the surcharge, or in other words, to the rise in the rate of collection. When the economy witnessed a substantial increase in both population and prices, the government was bound to increase its expenditure if it intended to maintain or expand its activities.

China experienced a substantial growth of population during the Ch'ing period. Between the middle of the seventeenth century and the start of World War I her population tripled (see Table 1.1). As the population multiplied, the administrative expenditure had to be increased continuously. With respect to the administrative expenditure, the increase in the number of the extra clerks employed in various yamen is highly illustrative. In the government there were three groups of clerks—the regular clerks, the extra clerks, and the nominal clerks. The number of the first group in various yamen was fixed in the early years of the Ch'ing and increased only slightly throughout the dynasty. The last group had nothing to do with official business because they neither performed administrative work of any kind, nor did they receive any pay from the government.[26] Thus, when more manpower was needed to handle the growing load of work, the government employed more extra clerks.

In the early part of the eighteenth century the number of the extra clerks had already far exceeded that of the regular clerks. In 1729 a court official suggested that the number of the regular clerks in the various yamen from the provincial down to the district be doubled and that all the rest (the extra and nominal clerks) be dismissed. This suggestion was strongly opposed by T'ien Wen-ching, then director-general of the conservation of the Yellow River and the Grand Canal, who held that doubling the number of the regular clerks was simply not enough to carry out the administrative work. To support his argument he put forward the case of his administration. He said that the regular clerks in his yamen numbered only twenty, but there were actually more than 200 clerks working under him. Even with this greatly expanded staff he still found it difficult to transact official business without delay. Accordingly, he concluded that it was absolutely impossible to carry on the administration if the above suggestion were adopted.[27]

On the local level a revealing case is the tenfold increase of tax clerks in Huai-ning hsien of Honan. In a governor's message dated 1911, it was said, the district was divided for the purpose of tax collection into nine li (rural zone). The number of clerks in charge of tax collection in each li which started at three in earlier years had by then gone up to thirty.[28] Although the extent of increase in the number of extra clerks in local yamen certainly varied from one district to another, an upward trend was present almost everywhere throughout the country. For instance, while by regulation the number of regular clerks in the magistrate yamen ranged, with a few exceptions, from ten to fourteen in the late Ch'ing, the clerks actually employed (including the regular and extra clerks) numbered about sixty (1873-75) in Shang-hai hsien of Kiangsu and around seventy in Kuan hsien of Szechwan.[29] In Kwangtung, moreover, it was observed in the late nineteenth century by a contemporary scholar, the magistrate in a busy district had to employ more than a hundred extra clerks; even in a district with light official duties he still needed several tens of them in order to carry on the administrative work.[30] With the employment of additional staff from time to time, the costs of administrative personnel must have risen correspondingly.

Another good indication of the increase of administrative expenditure is the accumulation of assigned contributions. The assigned contribution was an informal device by which local governments were made to bear the costs of administration at higher levels. When administrative expenses were rising, assigned contributions would undoubtedly rise with them. Take the case of Shensi, for example. Between 1739 and 1908 sixty-four items of regular "contribution" were successively assigned by the provincial authorities. Almost all these were imposed on the local governments for the defraying of one kind of administrative expense or another incurred at higher-level yamen. Of the sixty-four items, the first twelve occurred in the Ch'ien-lung period (1736-95), seven more were added in the Chia-ch'ing period (1796-1820), fifteen more in the Tao-kuang period (1821-50), three more in the Hsien-feng period (1851-61), two more in the T'ung-chih period (1862-74), and twenty-five more in the Kuang-hsü period (1875-1908).[31] By the end of the dynasty assigned contributions thus became a heavy drain on the revenue of local governments.

Population growth resulted in an increase not only of administrative expenditure but of other expenditures as well. For instance, the expenditure for poor relief in Kuan hsien of Szechwan doubled in the later part of the nineteenth century.[32] Such being the case, government revenue had to increase in one way or another. Since formal revenue was inflexible, informal revenue was destined to play an increasingly important role in financing government activities.

An equally if not more powerful factor that forced local officials to raise the rate of collection was the movement of the value of money in the market. There were two elements involved which affected the upward adjustment of the rate of collection: one was the silver-cash ratio, and the other was the price level. A rise in the value of silver relative to copper cash or a rise in the price level would have the effect of pushing up the rate of collection. A rise in the price level means the decline in the value of money. Accordingly, it is understandable that land tax officials would most likely collect more to compensate themselves at least partly for the loss of purchasing power of money if they depended heavily upon the tax revenue for financing their administration. But to understand how the changes in silver-cash ratio brought about an adjustment in the rate of collection we shall need first a brief account of the mechanism of the Ch'ing monetary system as well as of the monetary aspect of Ch'ing fiscal administration.

The Ch'ing monetary system was fairly close to what economists called "parallel bimetallism."[33] Two kinds of metal—silver and copper cash—served as money and they were independent of each other without a fixed relationship in their relative value. Although the government set an ideal ratio at one tael of silver to 1,000 cash,[34] the ruling was scarcely followed in the market because of the government's lack of control over the quantity of money. In the first place, the government did not issue silver coins except in its last two decades; the metal was circulating in whatever form it might take: bullion, ingot, Mexican dollar, and so on. From the analytical point of view, therefore, the silver sector was hardly different from a metallic system with free and unlimited coinage. In the second place, in spite of the monopoly of the government to coin copper cash, it could not effectively control the supply of cash because it was unable to check counterfeiting and illegal melting. Consequently, the market ratio fluctuated beyond the control of the government. When the market supply of silver increased (other things being equal), its value in terms of cash fell. Conversely, when the market supply of copper increased, the value of silver in terms of cash rose.

As is well known, Ch'ing land tax quota was collected in silver or grain or both. From the middle of the eighteenth century, however, two distinct trends appeared in tax payment—commutation of the grain tax into money payment, and payment of the tax in cash instead of silver. The prevalence of cash over silver was largely due to enormous expansion of copper production in Yunnan in the last two-thirds of the eighteenth century.[35] Before the outbreak of the Taiping Rebellion (1850-64) a governor in the south observed that 80-90 percent of the people in the country paid their land tax in cash.[36] On the other hand, local officials were obliged by regulation to send to the governments at higher levels the part of the tax known as *ch'i-yün* in silver. Under these conditions, they had to raise the rate of collection (when taxes were collected in cash) at the time of rising value of silver in terms of cash. For instance, in the mid-eighteenth century when silver-cash ratio was around 750 cash to a tael, magistrates who collected the *ti-ting* quota at a rate of something less than 1,000 cash to a tael could manage to meet their fiscal obligations to the superior yamen and to maintain local administration. But a century later when the ratio rose to more than 2,000 cash to a tael, no magistrate, however capable and incorruptible he was, could carry on his duties without increasing the rate of collection to something more than 2,000 cash to a tael of the quota (see Table 3.4).

It is worth examining the behavior of money and prices in the Ch'ing to see how they affected the rate of collection. I have gathered in Table 3.4 three series of data, indicating the movement of general prices, the silver-cash ratio, and the rate of collection for the *ti-ting* tax for the period of 1750-1910 in the most prosperous area of the country, the Yangtze delta. Three conclusions may be drawn from observing the three variables. First, the rate of collection closely followed the movement of the silver-cash ratio. When the value of silver in relation to cash was rising in the century between 1750 and 1850 and in the 1900s, it pushed up the rate of collection steadily. When the value of silver in relation to cash was declining in most of the half century between 1850 and 1900 it brought down the latter. Second, there was a positive correlation between rising prices and rising rate of collection, as

Table 3.4. Changes in the value of money and in the rate of collection in the
Yangtze delta, 1750–1910

Approximate date (1)	Index number of prices in silver (1750 = 100) (2)	Silver-cash ratio Number of cash per tael (3)		Rate of collection Number of cash per tael of the *ti-ting* tax (4)	
1750	100	750	(Soochow, 1759)	880	(Chia-ting, 1759)
1800	150	1,080	(Hsiao-shan)	1,360	(Hsiao-shan)
1850	75	2,080^{-b}	(Shanghai)	2,600	(Ningpo, 1852)
1864	250+	1,540^{-b}	(Ningpo, 1862)	2,200	(Chia-ting, 1866)
1875	120	1,750^{+b}	(Ningpo)	–	
1895	180	–		–	
1900	220^a	1,300^{+b}	(Ningpo)	2,000	(Chia-ting)
1910	300	1,800^{-b}	(Ningpo)	2,470	(Chia-ting)

Sources:
The index numbers of prices are derived from my article "The Secular Trend of Prices
during the Ch'ing Period." For the rest, see Ch'en Chao-nan, *Yung-cheng Ch'ien-lung
nien-chien ti yin-ch'ien pi-chia pien-tung* (Taipei, 1966), p. 17; Sasaki Masaya; *Yin-hsien
t'ung-chih* (1935), "*Shih-huo chih*," pp. 43b–44; *North China Herald*, Sept. 4, Oct. 19,
Nov. 16, 23, Dec. 21, 28, 1850.

Notes:
[a]A rough estimate.
[b]Converted from the ratio expressed in the number of cash per silver dollar (1 silver
dollar = 0.72 tael assumed).
[c]Converted from the ratio expressed in the number of copper coins per silver dollar
(1 copper coin = 10 cash assumed).

demonstrated in the latter part of the eighteenth century and in the first
decade of the present century. During most part of the Taiping Rebellion
(1850-64) when the Yangtze delta was the scene of frequent battles between
the imperial armies and the Taiping insurgents, however, the government
could not collect taxes there. Hence the soaring prices had no effect on
taxation whatsoever. Third, when prices were falling, the rate of collection
would continue to increase if, as in the early nineteenth century, the
silver-cash ratio was persistently on the rise. But certainly a combination of
falling prices and declining silver-cash ratio would make it easier to bring
down, at least moderately, the rate of collection.

The Boxer Catastrophe and the Movement
for Modernization

In the last decade of the dynasty political factors emerged as a major force
contributing to the increase in the rate of collection. Following the Sino-
Japanese War of 1894-95 three political movements appeared in China—anti-

foreignism, reform, and revolution. The antiforeignism culminated in the
Boxer uprising in 1900; the reform movement, cut short in 1898, revived in
the last decade of the dynasty which ended with the revolution of 1911. The
first two movements gave rise to new land tax surcharges in various provinces.

The antiforeign movement grew out of China's successive military defeats
and the subsequent foreign encroachments on Chinese territory and sover-
eignty. After the conclusion of the Treaty of Shimonoseki (1895) the foreign
powers began a scramble for concessions and proceeded to map out their
respective spheres of influence. A widespread fear of the "breakup of China"
was in the air. It was during this unprecedented crisis that the Boxer
movement switched its aim from being antidynastic and antiforeign to
prodynastic and antiforeign. Meanwhile, following the failure of the Hundred
Day Reform of 1898 the ultraconservatives held power in the Ch'ing court
and in a number of provinces. Under their patronage the movement burst out
in 1900 into violent and indiscriminating attacks upon foreigners. But the
result was again a disastrous and humiliating defeat by the allied forces of the
eleven powers; and the Chinese people were forced to shoulder an exorbitant
indemnity of 450 million taels![37]

The Boxer indemnity was to be paid in gold with interest over forty years.
Even if the extra burden due to appreciation in the value of gold in relation
to silver is excluded, the total (including interest) amounted to nearly one
billion taels. Consequently, the Ch'ing government had to raise for the
indemnity an additional revenue of from about 19 to 35 million taels, or an
average of 25 million taels a year, which was about 10 percent of the total tax
revenue of the country (see Table 4.3). To meet this enormous payment the
imperial government decided in 1901 that the bulk was to be allotted among
the provinces (the three provinces of Manchuria being exempted) and a small
part was to be raised by reduction of its own expenditure and by the
appropriation of the remaining customs revenue after servicing the foreign
debt incurred prior to 1900.[38] The allotment (totalling 18.8 million taels)
varied from one province to another, depending on the financial capacity of
each province. Kiangsu, the richest of all, was required to contribute 2.5
million taels a year and Kweichow, the poorest, 0.2 million taels a year (see
Table 3.5).

It was left to the provincial authorities how to raise the money needed for
this purpose in each province. All of them resorted to an increase in taxes.
Common among those subject to increased levy were the land tax, the salt
tax, the likin (especially that on opium), the tax on property deeds, and the
tax on business establishments.[39] As is shown in Table 3.5, of the nineteen
provinces required to share the indemnity burden, twelve used an imposition
of land tax surcharge for this specific purpose; only in Chihli, Hunan, and the
backward provinces of the southwest and northwest were the land proprietors

Table 3.5. The allotment of the Boxer indemnity and the imposition of land tax surcharge

Province (1)	Allotment (taels) (2)	Land Tax Surcharge	
		Ti-ting (amount per tael) (3)	Grain (amount per shih) (4)
Kiangsu	2,500,000		
Soochow		200 cash	–
Kiangning		100 cash	–
Szechwan	2,200,000	6.66 taels (av.)[a]	–
Kwangtung	2,000,000	0.30 tael	0.30 tael
Chekiang	1,400,000	300 cash	–
Kiangsi	1,400,000	200 cash	300 cash
Hupei	1,200,000	700⁻ cash (av.)[b]	650⁺ cash (av.)[b] (until 1904)
Anhwei	1,000,000	300 cash	300 cash
Shantung	900,000	amount varying[c]	–
Honan	900,000	300 cash	–
Shansi	900,000	0.15 tael (until 1906)	–
Fukien	800,000	400 cash	400 cash
Chihli	800,000	–	–
Hunan	700,000	–	–
Shensi	600,000	0.37 tael (av.)[b]	–
Sinkiang	400,000	–	–
Kansu	300,000	–	–
Kwangsi	300,000	–	–
Yunnan	300,000	–	–
Kweichow	200,000	–	–
Total	18,800,000		

Sources:
1. See my work, *An Estimate* . . . , chap. 1.
2. *CKCTNYS*, pp. 315, 319.
3. *Pao-ying-hsien chih* (1934), pp. 108–109.
4. Wei Sung-t'ang, comp., *Hu-pei ts'ai-cheng chi-lüeh*, pp. 2, 7b, and the table between pp. 24 and 25.
5. *TCSMS* (Honan), R–L, 43.
6. *TCSMS* (Shantung), R–L, 2.

Notes:
[a]Average rate of surcharge for *chüan-chin*, of which the surcharge for the Boxer indemnity was merely a part.
[b]Average rate obtained by dividing the total surcharge for the Boxer indemnity by total tax quota.
[c]Before 1900 the highest rate of collection among the districts was 2,400 cash (i.e., 4,800 Ching-ch'ien) per tael of the tax quota. To raise funds for the indemnity the provincial authorities ordered in 1901 that the rate be increased to 2,400 cash in all districts.

exempted from this surcharge. Its amount varied from 100 cash in Kiangning area of Kiangsu to nearly 700 cash in Hupei (generally even higher in Szechwan) per tael of the *ti-ting* quota. In some provinces, moreover, the surcharge was imposed on the grain tax as well as on the *ti-ting* tax.

While the steady advancement of foreign powers and Western civilization into China produced a violent reaction in the Boxer uprising of 1900, it nevertheless also brought about some constructive results. Although few Chinese in the late Ch'ing doubted the superiority of their own cultural value over that of the Occident, more and more officials and intellectuals increasingly recognized the need of modernizing their country to meet the challenge from the West. In the last half century of the dynasty the movement in this direction may be roughly divided into two stages: a stage of industrialism from the 1860s until the Sino-Japanese War of 1894-95, and a stage of institutional reform from the end of the war through the 1911 revolution. In the first stage the emphasis was laid on the establishment of industrial enterprises such as arsenals, shipyards, and coal mining so as to strengthen China's military power.[40] After the great humiliation in the war with Japan in 1894-95 China then entered into the second stage in which the emphasis was shifted to the reorganization of educational, military, and governmental institutions. This movement, which was first led by K'ang Yu-wei, failed completely in 1898 mainly because of the conservative *coup* in the court. Immediately after the Boxer disaster it was revived by the government in an effort to save the dynasty. Yet, it did not proceed far before the collapse of the Manchu regime in 1911.

It is beyond the scope of this study to describe various reforms put into effect in the last decade of the dynasty.[41] What is relevant here is how they affected the land tax. Of all innovations in the decade of reform, only the establishment of Western-style schools and police forces made some progress. But it also brought into being a new tax surcharge in a number of provinces. In the matter of education, the central government took a giant step by abolishing the time-honored examination system through private study of classics. Instead, it proclaimed a three-level national school system with a mixed Sino-western curriculum—primary school on the local level, high school on the provincial level, and the Imperial University at Peking.[42] In the matter of maintaining law and order, it instructed the provincial authorities to establish a taotai of police affairs in the provincial city, and to appoint a police chief in each district of their respective provinces.[43] To finance these new undertakings, provincial as well as local governments were compelled to tap various sources, among which the land tax again became an attractive one. Accordingly, there were *mou-chüan* or *hsiang-chüan* in Chihli and Manchuria, *hsüeh-t'ang chüan* and *hsün-ching chüan* in Kiangsu and Hupei. Of all provinces eight are known to have had this kind of surcharge levied on land by the end of the Ch'ing. The relative amount of the surcharge varied greatly from one province to another. For example, it was less than 10 percent of the quota in Kiangsu but about 300 percent in Fengtien (see Table 3.6).

In addition, a surcharge known as *t'uan-fei* was collected to provide funds for army training in Yunnan and some districts of Szechwan. Furthermore, after the proclamation in 1908 by the imperial government of a nine-year program to prepare for constitutional government, another kind of surcharge bearing the name of *tzu-chih chüan* or *hsin-cheng chüan* appeared sporadically in a number of districts in various provinces. Nevertheless, the *t'uan-fei* was limited to two provinces only, and the *tzu-chih chüan* or *hsin-cheng chüan* was too late to develop into a fairly common surcharge; therefore, their impact on the land tax was marginal.

Along with the reform movement in the last decade of the Ch'ing there was a popular movement for railway building—a political development signifying both a rising tide of nationalism against foreign encroachment and an intensified spirit of provincialism against the weakening regime at Peking. At the opening of the present century a part of the Chinese population—gentry, merchants, and students—was finally awakened by a series of tragic events: the Sino-Japanese War, the scramble for concessions, and the Boxer catastrophe. They saw their country in imminent danger of being cut up by foreign

Table 3.6. Surcharges for modernization needs, 1900's (amount per tael of the *ti-ting* quota, unless otherwise specified)

Province (1)	Education and police (2)	Railroad building (3)
Chihli	0.5–2.0 taels	–
Shantung	200 cash (1909–11)	–
Shansi	–	0.15 tael (1906 on)
Fengtien	3.0 taels (av.)	–
Kirin	1.4 taels+	–
Heilungkiang	1.2 taels (av.)	–
Kiangsu (Soochow)	50–100 cash, and 50–100 cash per shih of grain	–
Fukien	–	200 cash, and 200 cash per shih of grain
Kiangsi	0.1 tael⁻ (av.)	–
Hupei	700 cash (1904 on) and 650 cash per shih of grain (1904 on)	–
Szechwan	–	3.0 taels (av.)
Yunnan	–	200 cash

Source: See my work, *An Estimate of the Land Tax* . . . ; *TCSMS* (Kiangsu-Soochow), *Shui-Hsiang* (taxes), 34.

powers and their government at Peking totally incompetent to lead the
nation. They realized the need to take the initiative to modernize their
country and to ward off further encroachment by foreigners. Since they
looked upon the railway as the secret of the military and economic power of
the Westerners and as a tool for their political and economic penetration into
China's territory, railway building naturally became a focal point of national-
istic sentiment.[44] In this movement the Cantonese took the lead by
constructing with their own resources the southern section of the Canton-
Hankow Railway. Gentry and merchants in Kiangsu and Chekiang followed
suit and built a railway connecting Soochow, Hangchow, and Ningpo.
Meanwhile, railway companies sprang up one after another in other provinces.[45]

But railway building needs an enormous amount of capital investment. The
promoters in other provinces soon realized that the capital that could be
raised by private subscription fell far short of their aims. It was under such
circumstances that an ad hoc land tax surcharge was imposed in three
provinces: Fukien, Szechwan, and Yunnan (see Table 3.6). In another
province, Shansi, the surcharge was originally imposed for the Boxer indemnity, but it was later appropriated by imperial approval for railway and mining
purposes. Even with a combination of private subscription and land tax
surcharge, the result was a great disappointment. In these four provinces only
nineteen miles in Fukien and fourteen miles scattered in Szechwan and Shansi
had been constructed by the end of the dynasty.[46]

4 The Fiscal Importance of the Land Tax

Having dealt with the institutional aspects of Ch'ing land taxation, I shall now make an attempt to assess the amount of the land tax and its place in the Ch'ing tax structure.[1] The land tax has been the principal source of public revenue in all agrarian societies. However, the fiscal importance of the land tax relative to that of other taxes tends to decline over time. This happened in Tokugawa Japan. In the early years of the regime *bakufu* finance depended almost entirely upon the land tax of its domain, but in the mid-nineteenth century about one-half of its income came from nonagricultural taxes.[2] A similar trend also occurred in British India. Near the end of the eighteenth century land revenue amounted to around 70 percent of the total revenue of her central and state governments combined. By the first decade of the present century the proportion had declined to one third.[3] The experience of Ch'ing China followed the same pattern.[4]

The Tax Structure as of 1753

To evaluate the fiscal importance of any tax, it is necessary to assess the revenue produced at the same time by all other taxes. Before we start such evaluation, however, two crucial problems should be solved: one is the definition of tax revenue; the other is the selection of tax data. Tax revenue is here defined as the sum total of the basic tax (tax quota) and surcharges of various kinds combined.[5] The basic tax was the fixed amount that officials in charge were required to collect according to rates set by imperial regulations. Mostly not visible in official tax returns, the surcharges included the statutory ones such as *hao-hsien* and the nonstatutory ones for expenses of public administration, social welfare, and various special projects and payments—expenses that had no counterparts in imperial statutes.[6] Nonstatutory surcharges should nonetheless be considered part of tax revenue; for they were necessary not only for keeping all levels of administration at work but also for stabilizing the state and society, explicitly or implicitly consented to by superior authorities and generally tolerated by the public. But outright corruption or excessive exaction of taxes that were against established rules, either official or customary, should be excluded. Also, the tax revenue to be assessed here means the total taxes collected and shared by all levels of government—central, provincial, and local.

It is a well-known fact that, except for the revenues of the maritime customs (which were under Sino-foreign joint management), reports of most taxes during the Ch'ing reflect merely the tax quotas fixed by the central government, not the tax revenues actually collected from the people. Hence official tax returns should be used with great caution and, whenever possible, estimates of the unreported portion of revenue have to be made. To assess the structural change in taxation I have selected the years 1753 and 1908 for observation. Two reasons stand out for such a choice. First, there are available more reliable and complete data on tax revenues for these two years. Second, these years represent two contrasting points in the dynastic cycle, one the height of the Manchu dynasty and the other near its collapse.

Official tax returns of the mid-eighteenth century are generally more reliable than those of the rest of the dynasty because the central government's efforts to bring nonquota revenue under public control were relatively successful. During the second quarter of the century the Manchu government under the vigorous leadership of the Yung-cheng Emperor (reign: 1723-35) carried out significant reform on all major taxes. To reduce the complexity and irregularity of land tax surcharges, he gave his formal approval to the collection of one kind of customary surcharge (hao-hsien) and ordered the elimination of all others. The proceeds from hao-hsien were largely used for providing a meaningful salary known as yang-lien yin (lit., "money for nourishing integrity") to officials from governors-general down to magistrates. In the field of the salt and customs administration he required all tax officials to make public the customary fees they had been collecting together with the basic tax and had the hitherto concealed revenue divided into two parts[7]—one for defraying administrative and personnel costs and for providing funds for other public needs in the provinces and the rest sent to the central government as ying-yü (surplus) or simply incorporated into the quota. As a result, the prevailing practice of under-reporting tax revenue was substantially eliminated. Numerous tax officials reported surplus (ying-yü) in addition to the quota.[8] Throughout the early part of his reign the Ch'ien-lung Emperor (reign: 1736-95) was able to maintain and even improve the efficiency of the fiscal administration inherited from his father. Hence we have good reason to regard the official tax returns at the time as relatively reliable.

From the late eighteenth century onwards, however, the imperial government had failed to change or modify its fiscal regulations in response to changing socio-economic conditions such as population growth and price fluctuation. Local and provincial officials who took charge of tax collection had to increase taxes in one way or another so as to keep their administration functioning. They also had to conform to the outdated regulations which left no room for an increase in either expenditure or revenue. As a result, the difference between reported taxes and collected taxes widened. While the reporting of annual revenue and expenditure went on as usual until the very end of the dynasty, the quality of official tax returns deteriorated. Accompanying this development was the weakening of control of the central government over the nation's financial resources. It was against this kind of fiscal anomaly that the Manchu government in its last days resolved to undertake a nationwide financial survey. And it was the results of this survey that made an approximate assessment of late Ch'ing tax structure possible.

Of all published official tax returns in the eighteenth century only those of 1753 cover all major taxes from all provinces, salt administrations, and native customs stations throughout the empire. These data are surely far from perfect, but given the relative orderliness of fiscal administration at the time, they may be taken as a basis for estimation. As defined above, tax revenue is the sum total of tax quota, statutory surcharges, and nonstatutory surcharges. However, official tax returns include merely revenues in the first two categories; hence it is necessary to investigate the amount or magnitude of the nonstatutory surcharges so that a reasonable estimate of tax revenue can be made. With regard to the land tax revenue in 1753 I have concluded that the nonstatutory surcharges amounted to as much as the statutory ones, which generally ranged from 10 to 15 percent of the quota depending on the province in question. It follows that surcharges of both categories combined came to roughly a quarter of the tax quota. The figures in Table 4.1 are estimated with few exceptions on this assumption.

Scattered evidence also reveals in the case of the salt tax and native customs a magnitude of surcharge rather close to that of the land tax. In Kansu, for example, merchants were required to pay 0.2155 tael as the basic tax and 0.049 tael as surcharge for public expenses and other operating costs for each shih of salt they shipped out of the area of production.[9] In another province, Hupei, where no salt was produced, merchants distributing this particular commodity there had to pay to various yamen certain customary fees in addition to an annual tax quota of about 653,000 taels. According to a memorial submitted in 1729 by Fu Min (1673-1756), acting governor-general of Hukwang, these fees totaled 160,000 taels a year.[10] In both cases the amount of surcharge was approximately a quarter of the tax quota.

With regard to the native customs, the imperial government authorized in

Table 4.1. An Estimate of China's land tax revenue, 1753 (in 1,000 taels unless otherwise specified)

Province (1)	Area of registered land^a (in 1,000 mou) (2)	Ti-ting			Grain			Grand total (9) = (5) + (8)
		Quota^a (3)	Hao-hsien Approx. percentage of quota (4)	Total estimated^b (5)	Quota^a (in 1,000 shih) (6)	Estimated value of quota^c (7)	Total estimated^d (8)	
Chihli	65,719	2,411	12	2,990	101	152	190	3,180
Shantung	99,306	3,397	14	4,348	508	762	953	5,301
Honan	78,832	3,506	13	4,417	249	374	468	4,885
Shansi	54,548^e	3,029	13	3,817	169	254	318	4,135
Fengtien	2,524	38	10	46	76	76	95	141
Shensi	29,244	1,544	15	2,007	325	325	406	2,413
Kansu	21,649^f	299^f	15	389	508^f	508	635	1,024
Kiangsu	70,430	3,407	7	3,884	2,211	3,759	4,699	8,583
Chekiang	46,153	2,830	7	3,226	1,130	1,921	2,401	5,627
Fukien	13,614	1,222	12	1,515	193	328	410	1,925
Kwangtung	33,411	1,259	17	1,687	441	750	938	2,625
Anhwei	38,033	1,798	10	2,158	945	1,323	1,654	3,812
Kiangsi	48,565	1,895	10	2,274	900	1,260	1,575	3,849
Hupei	58,738	1,161	11	1,416	380	532	665	2,081
Hunan	34,317	1,262	10	1,514	278	389	486	2,000
Kwangsi	8,940	391	10	469	130	156	195	664
Szechwan	45,915	659	15	857	14	17	21	878
Yunnan	8,990^g	211^g	20	375^h	237^g	284	355	730
Kweichow	2,569	100	14	128	155	186	233	361
Total	761,497	30,419		37,517	8,950	13,356	16,697	54,214

Source: See Table 27 in my work, *An Estimate of the Land Tax* . . . .

Notes:

[a] Including *min-t'ien* (private land) and *t'un-t'ien* (land held on military tenure). The *t'un-t'ien* data are however those of 1766.

[b] Including quota and surcharges which are estimated to be two times as much as the *hao-hsien*.

[c] For estimated grain prices, see Table 26 in my work, *An Estimate* . . . .

[d] Including quota and surcharges which are estimated to be 25 percent of the quota.

[e] The official figure of 1766 (*min-t'ien* and *t'un-t'ien*).

[f] The official figure of 1745.

[g] The official figure of 1736.

[h] Including *kung-chien*, a special surcharge in Yunnan authorized in the early Ch'ing.

general a 10 percent surcharge (20 percent at certain customs stations) for defraying administrative expenses. An investigation ordered by the emperor in 1763 shows, however, that about two-thirds of the customs stations in the country, which yielded more than three-quarters of total customs revenue, still collected fees of various kinds without authorization. And after a close examination the emperor himself considered some of the unauthorized surcharges necessary for the maintenance of administrative efficiency.[11] This indicates again that actual collection exceeded to some extent what was permitted by imperial regulations. All these facts appear to suggest that the 1753 official figures on salt and native customs revenue should also be increased by about a quarter so as to cover the unreported portion.

Among all taxes in the Ch'ing the most under-reported was the group under the heading "miscellaneous taxes." Since their miscellaneous nature rendered centralized control extremely difficult and since they were considered financially insignificant, they were left untouched when the government undertook a wide range of tax reform in the second quarter of the eighteenth century. To what extent the miscellaneous taxes were under-reported may be roughly indicated by the following two cases. One is the tea tax in the northwestern provinces. According to the 1753 official report, the tea tax in Shensi and Kansu was 6,266 taels; but a memorial submitted in 1725 by the governor of Kansu discloses that his office alone received an annual income of 32,000 taels from customary fees on tea and horse trade.[12] Another is the property deeds tax in Kwangtung. The annual quota of this tax in the province appears to have been fixed at about 10,000 taels in 1729, but in the next five years local officials collected on the average of 40,000 taels a year over and above the quota.[13] Although the degree of under-reporting undoubtedly differed greatly from one province to another and even from one district to another, the 1753 official figure on the miscellaneous taxes should, in view of the above-mentioned evidence, be revised upward at least five times or to an amount no less than the native customs revenue. Given all these modifications and adjustments, an estimate of China's tax revenue in the mid-eighteenth century is summed up in Table 4.2, which shows a total amount of collection of approximately 74 million taels.

The estimate, it should again be pointed out, is merely a tentative one based on a small number of samples. I hope further revision will be made as soon as more evidence comes to light. Nonetheless, the margin of error in the present estimate, it seems to me, is not likely to be unusually wide. The reasons are twofold. In the first place, there are unmistakable testimonies that the mid-eighteenth century was indeed fiscally the most orderly period in the Ch'ing. Speaking on the irregularities of land taxation in the early nineteenth century, Yao Wen-t'ien (1758-1827), formerly vice-president of the Board of Revenue and a scholar with a special interest in taxation, said with nostalgia

Table 4.2. An estimate of China's tax revenue, 1753 (in 1,000 taels)

Taxes (1)	Quota (2)	Surcharge estimated (3)	Total (4) = (2) + (3)
Land Tax			
Ti-ting	30,419[a]	7,098	37,517
Grain	13,356[b]	3,341	16,697
Salt Tax	7,014	1,754	8,768
Native Customs	4,324	1,081	5,405
Miscel. Taxes	1,053	4,352	5,405
Total	56,166	17,626	73,792

Sources: For tax quotas, see *HT* (1764), 10. 2b-6, 16. 1-2, 17.5; *HTTL* (1764), 45. 1-67. For surcharge estimates, see the text.

Notes:
[a]An adjusted figure; see Table 4.1.
[b]Converted from adjusted amount in kind; see Table 4.1.

in 1822 that "there was no excessive collection (*fou-shou*) before the thirtieth year of the Ch'ien-lung period (1736-95)."[14] On the other hand, the compilers of a documentary work on tax reductions in Kiangsu noted several decades later than "since the Chia-ch'ing period (1796-1820) tax collection has gradually become more and more excessive.[15] To be sure, given an extensive empire physically and economically as diversified as China and given the decentralized nature of tax collection in the country, it is not hard to find instances of tax abuse on the part of bureaucracy; one should not, however, construe a sporadic instance as a common phenomenon. On the whole, extra collection beyond the limits of official regulations was an established practice in the mid-eighteenth century as it was necessary for keeping public administration at work, but it was generally within bounds of customary rules.

In the second place, the costs of a tax administration that consumes a fifth or a quarter of the total taxes it collected are certainly too high in a modern industrial state, but they are not so in a traditional society.[16] While it is difficult to make appropriate comparison of administrative efficiency in different pre-modern societies until more research is done, the costs of tax collection were universally high. For example, Louis XIV's tax collection system reportedly consumed nearly 20 percent of receipts, and collectors in eighteenth-century Egypt kept as theirs 25 percent of the taxes they collected.[17] Hence the tax administration of Ch'ing China is quite compatible with those in other agrarian countries.

The Tax Structure as of 1908

In the last decade of the dynasty the Ch'ing government twice made public the state of revenue: one being the 1903 report of the Board of Revenue and the other being the 1911 budget. Besides, foreign experts also made some estimates. As shown in Table 4.3, there are wide differences between these data. The figures presented in the 1903 report are too low because a large portion of tax revenue collected in the provinces was classified as *wai-hsiao kuan*, and thus not reported to the central government. The 1911 budget which was drawn immediately after a nationwide financial survey is undoubtedly of better value as a measure of the country's tax receipts than the 1903 report. However, we should note that the budget was worked out in haste by the newly reorganized Ministry of Finance; the ministry did not have time to verify and digest the reported data from the survey (some reports probably did not even reach the capital before the completion of the budget). While the ministry was better informed on those taxes that were under the control of special agencies, central or provincial, it unavoidably underestimated by a great deal those taxes that were collected and relied upon as the only source of financing by local governments.

The Morse estimate is simply a product of speculation. For example, his estimate of the land tax was based on a single piece of evidence—George Jamieson's report to the (British) Foreign Office on taxes paid by a British company for the land it bought in seven districts of Honan. I have made in a separate volume a critical appraisal of the Jamieson report and demonstrated that the average rate of the land tax paid by the company, when applied to the whole province of Honan, would distort the state of land taxation in this province.[18] An uncritical application of a single rate to the whole country, as is the case for Morse's estimate, would in all probability result in even greater distortion. On the other hand, the Williams estimate is a patchwork, piecing together the 1911 budget and the Morse estimate. Although he made a few modifications, they are by and large guesswork without solid evidence. Accordingly, neither the official data nor private estimates can serve as a satisfactory yardstick for the evaluation of the late Ch'ing tax structure.

Not satisfied with those data discussed above, I have undertaken to reassess independently all major sources of revenue; the results are presented in the last line of Table 4.3. On the land tax I have made in a separate volume a detailed assessment (out of which a simplified province-to-province version is produced in Table 4.4) and have come to the conclusion that the tax collected in 1908 amounted to around 102 million taels, or at least twice as much as the budget (1911) figure.[19] On the maritime customs the data published by the Inspectorate General of Customs are the most reliable and therefore can be accepted without modification. In the year 1908 this tax yielded 32.9 million taels, or nearly one-third of the land tax produced in the

Table 4.3. Reported and estimated tax revenues in China, 1902–1911 (in 1,000 taels)

Report or estimate	Land tax	Salt tax	Likin[c]	Maritime customs	Native customs	Miscellaneous taxes	Total
1903 report[a] (1902)	35,360	13,000	18,200	31,500 (1905)	3,900	3,500	105,460
1911 budget[b] (1911)	49,670	47,622	44,177	42,139[d]	–	26,164	209,772
Morse estimate (1904–05)	127,763	81,000	42,537	35,111	3,699[e] (1906)	10,839	300,949
Williams estimate (1910–11)	69,000	57,000	43,000	36,000	6,100	38,000	249,100
My estimate (1908)	102,400	45,000	40,000	32,900	6,700	65,000	292,000

Sources:

1. *Shina keizai zensho*, comp. Tōa Dōbunkai (Tokyo, 1908), I, 470–539.
2. Chia Shih-i, pp. 25–26.
3. H.B. Morse, pp. 85–110.
4. E.T. Williams, "Taxation in China," *Quarterly Journal of Economics*, 26.3 (May 1912), 482–510.
5. For my estimate see the text to follow.

Notes:

[a] A small part of the data which were missing from the report were estimated by the compilers of *Shina keizai zensho*. Tax receipts expressed in cash are converted into those in silver at the rate of 1,000 cash to a tael.

[b] There are two versions of the 1911 budget—the original and the revised. The figures presented here are those of the revised budget. Nevertheless, the differences between the two versions are almost negligible.

[c] Including the excise on native opium.

[d] Including the native customs.

[e] Native customs revenue collected by the maritive customs administration.

Table 4.4. An approximation of China's land tax collected in 1908 (in 1,000 taels unless otherwise specified)

Province (1)	Area of registered land (in 1,000 mou) (2)	Ti-ting		Grain		Total (4) + (6) = (7)
		Quota (3)	Amount collected[a] (4)	Quota, (in 1,000 shih) (5)	Amount collected[a] (6)	
Chihli	68,589	2,445	6,185	97	531	6,716
Shantung	98,283	3,339	6,244	437	2,357	8,601
Honan	71,685	2,839	6,093[c]	231	1,508[c]	7,601
Shansi	50,000	2,988	4,478	117	351	4,829
Fengtien	39,162	543	2,718[d]	131	1,359[d]	4,077
Kirin	31,200	486	1,400	–	–	1,400
Heilungkiang	15,000	253[b]	800	–	–	800
Shensi	30,593	1,623	3,247	198	712	3,959
Kansu	18,781	225	585	330	1,062[e]	1,647
Sinkiang	10,555	–	–	302	1,036[e]	1,036
Kiangsu	75,117	3,038	5,882	1,674	8,566	14,448
Chekiang	46,778	2,767	5,479	900	3,465	8,944
Fukien	13,452	1,228	2,608	96	415	3,023
Kwangtung	35,227	1,223	2,786	380	1,842	4,628
Anhwei	34,064	1,588	3,187	387	1,666	4,853
Kiangsi	47,343	1,930	4,439	829	2,405	6,844
Hupei	59,220	1,170	3,401	306	1,396	4,797
Hunan	34,874	1,246	2,371	297	823	3,194
Kwangsi	8,652	379	775	144	432	1,207
Szechwan	47,062	669	7,906	–	–	7,906
Yunnan	9,319	293	631	204	673	1,304
Kweichow	2,679	96	198	163	405	603
Total	847,635	30,368	71,413	7,223	31,004	102,417

Sources: See Table 2 in my work, *An Estimate of the Land Tax* . . . .

Notes:
[a]Surcharge for collection expenses included.
[b]The quota of Heilungkiang is not known. The figure is converted from the reported amount of collection in 1908 (1,140,434,019 local cash) according to the ratio of one tael to 4,500 local cash (chung-ch'ien).
[c]It is assumed that surcharge for labor services was imposed on the *ti-ting* and grain tax in proportion to the amount of collection from each tax, i.e., 80 percent on the *ti-ting* tax, and 20 percent on the grain tax.
[d]It is assumed that one-third of the revenue was collected from the grain tax for the reason that the grain quota valued about one-third of the total quota.
[e]The amount collected from straw quota included.

same year.[20] For a thorough assessment of other taxes, much research is still needed. At the present moment only a very rough estimate can be made.

Between the appearance of the 1903 report and the 1911 budget the government brought to light two more figures on salt revenue—a sum of about 30 million taels reported in 1907 by the Ministry of Finance, and a sum of 45 million taels disclosed in 1910 by the newly created General Salt

Administration (Tu-pan yen-cheng ch'u), which was designed for wresting the control of this source of revenue from the provincial authorities.[21] There is strong evidence to support the figure of the Salt Administration and to reject the ministry's. Immediately following the fall of the dynasty an investigation undertaken by a Japanese expert at the request of the Six-Nation Banking Syndicate revealed that China's salt revenue had lately been about 47.5 million taels a year.[22] Moreover, some ad hoc investigations of salt revenue in several salt distributing areas in the last decade of the dynasty disclosed, as shown in Table 4.5, that the budget figures are very close to, though slightly higher than, the amounts collected from those areas. It is understandable that those who worked out the budget should anticipate a slight increase in the salt revenue over the latest amount of collection because of price inflation and population growth. For all these reasons I consider the figure released by the General Salt Administration the best approximation.[23]

Lo Yü-tung's pioneer study is a remarkable contribution towards an understanding of the administration of likin and its significance. Nevertheless, his data on the revenue from this source are based on official reports without taking into account various surcharges customarily withheld by likin collectors. Hence it is necessary to estimate the amount of surcharges concealed from the reports. These unreported surcharges were mainly of two kinds: one was a surplus created out of monetary manipulation, that is, instead of collecting the tax in silver, most likin stations required cash payment at an exchange rate artificially fixed in their favor, but they reported the collection in silver according to the prevailing market exchange rate between these two kinds of money. The other consisted of a number of fees and fines which were normally not reported. To what extent Lo's data should be revised is a

Table 4.5. The salt revenue in some areas, 1900s (in 1,000 taels)

Area	1911 budget	Amount of collection (year)
Lianghuai	14,015	12,000–13,000 (after 1903)
Liangkwang	6,055	5,800 (1911)
Szechwan	6,722	6,888 (Av.) (1903–1910)
Yunnan	1,338	1,250 (1909)

Sources:
1. *T'an-yen ts'ung-pao*, no. 1 (April 1913), "T'iao-ch'a," pp. 1–4; no. 6 (September 1913), "T'iao-ch'a," pp. 1–2.
2. *HWHTK*, p. 7934.
3. Ting En, *Kai-ke Chung-kuo yen-wu pao-kao-shu* (1922), II, 107b.
4. S.A.M. Adshead, *The Modernization of the Chinese Salt Administration, 1900–1920* (Cambridge, Harvard University Press, 1970), p. 22.

question to which the answers thus far are speculative in nature.[24] Again, a new assessment is needed.

After the Sino-Japanese War of 1894-95 the revenues of certain likin stations were pledged for the payment of a foreign loan, and the control of these revenues was passed over to the Inspectorate General of Customs (called I.G.C. hereafter). Following the transfer of administration G.F. Montgomery, deputy commissioner of eastern Chekiang collectorate, reported in 1898: "As to the actual amount of 'squeeze' made it is of course difficult to say, but I do not believe it amounts to anything like 50 percent of the reported collection."[25] A decade later the financial reports of Fukien and Shensi revealed nearly the same range in the unreported portion. In the last decade of the dynasty the reported annual revenue of likin in Fukien was around 800,000-900,000 taels; the unreported amount was estimated by the provincial authorities to be no less than 300,000 taels a year.[26] At the same time, the financial report from Shensi listed all kinds of hitherto unreported surcharges in various stations. Examining the data I found that the unreported collection varied generally from 20 to 50 percent of the reported collection.[27] In view of these facts it seems reasonable to increase the official returns of likin by 40 percent. According to Lo's calculation, the revenue from this tax was in the range of 20.4-21.1 million taels in 1908.[28] It follows that the actual collection of likin might very well be approaching the level of 30 million taels in the same year.

Besides likin, there was a special tax, an excise on native opium, which yielded to the government a substantial amount of revenue in the last decade of the dynasty. The collection of this tax was first vested in the likin bureau (in this case the proceeds were accounted for separately) or in a special agency created by the provincial authorities, but was taken over in 1906 by the central government with the understanding that part of the proceeds be returned to the provincial governments. In 1909 Ko Feng-shih, superintendent of the excise on native opium, reported that more than 20 million taels had been collected in the past two years.[29] In other words, 10 million taels a year should be added to the likin revenue if we put the excise on native opium in the latter category.

After the introduction of likin, the native customs apparently lost its position as a potential source of revenue. The relative insignificance of this tax in the late years of the dynasty is therefore not to be wondered at. In official returns the tax revenue from this source was less than three million taels a year in the last two decades of the nineteenth century but rose to 3.9 million taels in 1902.[30] It should be noted, however, that in 1902 the native customs stations within the radius of 50 li of the treaty ports came under the control of the I.G.C. as a consequence of the Boxer uprising. We should also bear in mind that the I.G.C. was then run much more efficiently than other governmental institutions in China. After the partial transfer of the native customs, the anarchical fee system came to an end in one place after another; all collections were gradually brought into account.[31] Thus, the increase of revenue undoubtedly resulted from the change in administration.

Now, let us make an estimate of the native customs in 1908. In Table 4.6 the figures without parentheses are official returns, and those in parentheses are my projections. First, from the known data in columns 3 and 4, we may figure that those native customs outside the 50-li radius of the treaty ports yielded 1.6 million taels in 1902. Second, supposing that the increase of revenue between 1899 and 1902 was entirely brought about by those customs under the I.G.C., the revenue in 1899 produced by this group of customs stations (that is, those later put under the I.G.C.) and the revenue yielded by all the rest of the native customs would be 1.3 million and 1.6 million taels respectively. Third, in 1908 the group of customs under the I.G.C. brought in 3 million taels, or more than twice the amount before their takeover. If the rest of the customs were also put under the administration of the I.G.C. or underwent the same kind of reform as did the transferred group, the revenue from those customs would likewise more than double within the same period. Then, adding together the projected and reported amounts, we arrive at a total revenue of 6.7 million taels for the year 1908.

Again, the miscellaneous taxes which include a variety of items, old and new, are the most difficult to assess and therefore most underestimated. Fortunately, the financial reports of 1908 shed some light on this perplexing problem. Among the reports those from Kwangtung, Kwangsi, and Kweichow give much more (though by no means complete) information on the miscellaneous taxes than the rest. Since these three provinces represented two

Table 4.6. The native customs revenue, 1899–1908 (in 1,000 taels)

Year (1)	Under the administration of the native customs (2)	Under the administration of the I.G.C. (3)	Total (4)
1899	(1,600)	(1,300)	2,900
1902	(1,600)	2,300	3,900
1908	(3,700)	3,000	(6,700)

Sources:
1. J. Edkins, *The Revenue and Taxation of the Chinese Empire* (Shanghai, 1903), p. 126.
2. Inspectorate General of Customs, *Native Customs Trade Returns*, no. 3 (1902–06), Shanghai, 1907, p. 1.
3. *RT* (1908), part 1 (A), p. 5.
4. *Shina keizai zensho*, I, 539.

extremes in economic conditions—Kwangtung was highly commercialized whereas Kweichow and, to a lesser extent, Kwangsi were economically very backward, their data in the aggregate may form a basis for estimating the national total of this category of taxes. As shown in Table 4.7, the three provinces, which had an aggregate land tax revenue of about 6.5 million taels (see Table 4.4) produced an aggregate revenue from miscellaneous taxes amounting to more than 8.4 million taels. It should be pointed out, however, that Kwangtung was the only province where the gambling tax played an important role in public finance. In order to avoid upward bias in our estimate, we should exclude Kwangtung's gambling tax (4.3 million taels) from the aggregate and count it separately. The aggregate of miscellaneous taxes thus adjusted still amounted to more than four million taels, or about 60 percent of the aggregate land tax. If we apply this rate to the whole country, we arrive at a total sum of 65 million taels (the gambling tax in Kwangtung included) as of the nation's revenue from this last category of taxes. In sum, my estimate indicates that the country's tax revenue was around 292 million taels near the end of dynasty (see Table 4.3).

Relative Decline in Importance of the Land Tax

The overall assessment or reassessment we have just undertaken has laid a foundation based upon which the changes in tax structure over the last one

Table 4.7. Major items of the miscellaneous taxes in Kwantung, Kwangsi, and Kweichow, c. 1908 (in 1,000 taels)

Item	Kwangtung	Kwangsi	Kweichow
Property deeds tax	761	209	10
Pawnshop tax	362	45	74[b]
Commercial tax	632	116	–
Household tax	376	–	–
License fees[a]	375	–	–
Tax on slaughtered animals	218	–	–
Prostitutes tax	296	–	–
Gambling tax	4,355	152	–
Other levies	330	–	122
Total	7,705	522	206

Sources:
1. *TCSMS* (Kwangtung), R–4.22-66, R–7.4-80.
2. *TCSMS* (Kwangsi), *Ko-lun shang–kuo-shui pu*, chap. 15, pp. 57–58; *Ko-lun shang–sheng-shui pu*, chap. 10.
3. *TCSMS* (Kweichow), R–1.2-6, R–2.1-55.

Notes:
[a]Including license fees of opium shops, liquor stores, and ferry boats.
[b]Brokerage tax and commercial tax included.

and a half centuries of the Ch'ing period can be readily observed. As indicated in Table 4.8, of all the taxes the land tax held an undisputedly dominant position throughout the period, but the percentage of its contribution declined. In 1753 its contribution made up 73.5 percent of the total tax revenue; all other taxes combined accounted for merely a little more than a quarter. In 1908, however, the share of the land tax in the total fell to about 35 percent though its absolute amount had increased to more than 100 million taels. To put it in another way, at the height of the Manchu dynasty approximately three out of four tax dollars came from the land tax, but on the eve of its downfall only about one in three was yielded by the tax. The decline in importance of the tax in the public economy came about because, notwithstanding its unchallenged position, it was increasing at a much slower rate than most other taxes in the late Ch'ing. Taking the amount of taxes in 1753 as 100, for example, we find that the land tax had by 1908 hardly doubled while other taxes combined had jumped up almost ten times. As a result, the index of total tax revenue was able to move up twice as fast as that of the land tax; in 1908 the former stood at 396.

Moreover, there had been also a noticeable change in the structure of the land tax during the same period. As shown in the same table, the share of tax quota in the total land tax declined relatively from 80.7 percent in 1753 to 53.1 percent in 1908 while the share of surcharges increased from less than

Table 4.8. Changes in the tax structure of China in the Ch'ing period

| Tax | Percentage of total tax revenue[a] | | | | Index number in 1908 (1753 = 100) |
	1753		1908		
Land Tax		73.5		35.1	189
Quota	(80.7)		(53.1)		124
Surcharges	(19.3)		(46.9)		460
Other taxes		26.5		64.9	968
Salt Tax	11.9		15.4		513
Native Customs	7.3		2.3		124
Maritime Customs	–		11.3		–
Likin	–		13.6		–
Miscel. Taxes	7.3		22.3		1,203
Total		100.0		100.0	396

Sources: Tables 4.1, 4.2, 4.3, 4.4.

Notes:
[a]Figures in parentheses indicate the percentage share of tax quota or surcharges in the total land tax. Grain quotas are converted into their monetary equivalents according to the estimated prices in column 7 of Table 1 and column 3 of Table 26 in my work, *An Estimate of the Land Tax . . .*

one-fifth to about 47 percent. That the increase in the land tax revenue mainly took the form of surcharges has been discussed in detail in Chapter 3.

Then why did the growth of the land tax fall far behind that of most other taxes in the late Ch'ing? To answer this question four principal reasons may be suggested, which I have also discussed before. It is sufficient here to state each of them briefly. The first was the availability of other taxes. The creation after the mid-nineteenth century of the maritime customs, likin, and a variety of miscellaneous taxes, both local and provincial, all proved to be highly productive; thus there was less pressure for the increase of the land tax than would otherwise be the case.

Second, there was a great difference in revenue elasticity between the land tax and most other taxes. Unlike the land tax, most other taxes were commodity taxes and therefore highly responsive to changes in income and prices. That is to say, when the income of a society (aggregate or per capita) rises (provided no appreciable change occurs in the distribution of income), its consumption will naturally increase. Consequently, commodity taxes will likewise increase. Moreover, even if the real income of a society remains the same as before, the absolute amount of revenue from commodity taxation would still multiply in a time of rising prices. Furthermore, if there is a trend towards commercialization so that more and more self-consumed goods find their way into the market, commodity taxes would certainly grow. All the above happened to be characteristic of the Ch'ing economy. As indicated in Table 1.1, between 1750 and 1913 China's population increased from 200-250 million to 430 million, her land acreage expanded from 900 million mou to 1,360 million mou, and her land yields showed at least a modest improvement. Therefore, the aggregate consumption in the country must have had a substantial increase during this one and a half centuries. Moreover, as shown in Table 3.4, the price index was up to 300 in 1910 (1750 as base year), and China's economy was increasingly monetized in the eighteenth and nineteenth centuries.[32] All these changes contributed substantially to the increase of commodity taxes. However, based on land area instead of land value or land yields, the Ch'ing land tax system was hardly responsive to rising prices or rising yields. Consequently, the percentage contribution of the land tax diminished as a matter of course.

Third, even without income- and price-elasticity the land tax could still be increased if the government could keep land registration up-to-date or raise the tax rates. Nevertheless, except in Manchuria the country's registered land hardly increased in the latter part of the dynasty. This resulted, as has been discussed in Chapter 2, partly from the absence of nationwide cadastral survey, partly from official conformity to a practically unchanged quota in reporting registered land, and partly from the inability and unwillingness to undertake a land survey of any kind on the part of most local officials. In other words, the Manchu government never made a land survey on a national scale and showed no interest in updating the country's land data beyond the level reached in 1600. On the other hand, local officials saw conformity to the established quota (1600) as the most practical way to manage the land tax administration. First, given a very rigid "budget" and a small number of yamen staff, they simply considered a land survey beyond their reach even if they had intended to make one. Second, since any increase in registered land meant an additional tax quota to be collected and an additional tax burden on the local community, officials who endeavored to attain best *k'ao-ch'eng* records and to win the respect and support of the local population would naturally not take the initiative to make such a survey even if they had the wherewithal to do so. Third, although certain officials sometimes did make some sort of survey, their purpose was in general to equalize or lighten the tax burden of the local population. Hence they would report little increment, if any, beyond the land already under registration.

Fourth, the forces of tradition and the voice of the local community also proved to be very strong in curbing the increase in the land tax. In traditional China light taxation on the peasantry was always upheld as a golden canon. While many officials advocated reduction of the land tax, few had the courage to propose an increase. In the early Ch'ing the principle of light taxation was crystalized in the K'ang-hsi Emperor's exalted decree of *yung-pu chia-fu* issued in 1713. The decree had the effect of fixing the land tax quota in the country once and for all and established a sacred tradition that no successors could ever violate. Later on, all increases in the land tax took the form of surcharges with the implication that they were merely a makeshift levy to be removed as soon as conditions permitted.

In time of financial difficulties both the central government and the provincial authorities usually looked for sources other than a land tax surcharge to make up deficits, for example, selling academic degrees and offices, raising salt prices, or imposing new taxes. With few other sources of revenue to exploit, the local government depended most heavily upon land tax surcharge for financing its activities. However, the freedom of local officials in this field was far from broad. A prudent magistrate always consulted with local gentry before taking any action on this matter because he needed their assistance and cooperation in carrying out his official responsibilities. As a matter of fact, it was a customary rule, rather than an exception, that the assessment of surcharge rates were the joint decision of local officials and gentry. Moreover, in the post-Taiping period the rates were decided in many provinces by the provincial authorities usually in consultation with the gentry rather than by local magistrates. Finally, the peasants who constituted the majority of local population could not be ignored either. There were many instances in which in direct response to the arbitrary increase of their tax burden they resorted to riot, the worst thing that could happen to a career official. Consequently, although there was an ever increasing demand for the increase of land tax surcharges, it was nonetheless constantly constrained by traditional, administrative, and social forces.

5 Geographical Differentials in Land Taxation

*Regional Economic Development and Changes
in Land Tax Yield*

In the discussion on the economic structure of Ch'ing China, I have pointed out that while no modern economic growth took place, there was a tremendous increase in population and a substantial expansion of cultivated acreage without simultaneous rise in per-capita income. Essentially, the kind of growth that occurred in the Ch'ing as well as in earlier periods of Chinese history took the form of extension of the agricultural frontier.

The process of development can be simply stated as follows: First, population growth moved people to settle in the hitherto unexploited land. Next, interregional migration not only brought more land under cultivation but also led to an intensive effort, wherever possible, to construct water control works and to experiment with various kinds of seeds. This process was further promoted by interregional trade. Finally, with the extension of cultivated and irrigated acreage, the country was able to increase grain output to meet the food demand of a growing population.[1] It was this extensive growth that determined China's peculiar nature in the present century, enormous in size yet backward in technology, abundant in manpower but short of land and especially capital. This chapter is intended primarily to inquire into the changes in geographical distribution of land tax yield and of the land tax burden in the context of the expansion of China's agricultural frontier under the Ch'ing. Hence it is necessary to see in a broad perspective over what areas the frontier was being extended.

From the point of view of extensive growth, China under the Ch'ing may be divided into three areas: the developed area in the east, the developing area in the mid-west, Taiwan, and Manchuria, and the undeveloped area in the far west and Mongolia. The outstanding features of the developed area in this context were: well-developed agricultural resources, a high ratio of population to land, and the growth of handicraft industries (later joined by a tiny sector of modern industry). The developing area was characterized by a relatively low population-land ratio and general development of primary resources. And the undeveloped area was distinguished by an extremely low population-land ratio and the predominance of pastoral life in the economy.

To mark off the three areas, a line can be drawn from Shanhaikwan (the gate between China Proper and Manchuria) westward through Peking to Ho-ch'ü on the border of Shansi and Shensi and then southward through T'ung-kuan, Hankow, Ch'ü-chiang to the southern tip of Lei-chou Peninsula on the edge of the Gulf of Tongking, and another line from Lu-pin in Manchuria southwestward along the Mongolian border to Chia-yü-kuan (the gate between Sinkiang and China Proper) and then southward to T'eng-ch'ung in Yunnan (see Figure 5.1). The first area roughly comprises the ten most populous provinces—Chihli, Honan, Shantung, Shansi, Kiangsu, Chekiang, Anhwei, Kiangsi, Fukien, and Kwangtung. The second area includes Man-

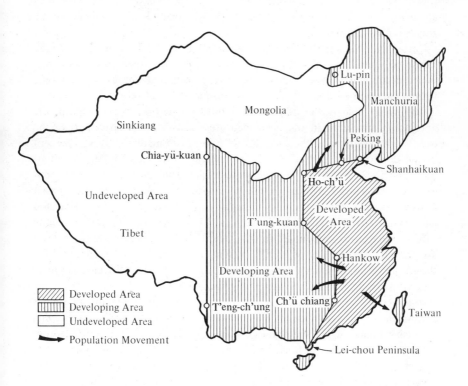

Figure 5.1. Population movement in China during the Ch'ing

churia, Shensi, Kansu, Hupei, Hunan, Kwangsi, Szechwan, Yunnan, Kweichow, and Taiwan.[2] The third covers a vast region encompassing Outer and
Inner Mongolia, Sinkiang, Tibet, and Tsinghai. Although the first area
experienced a certain degree of growth during Ch'ing times, it was the second
that enjoyed the highest degree of development. The third was only slightly
touched before the Communists came to power in the middle of the present
century. Therefore, we may ignore the last area and concentrate our attention
on the first two areas.

Throughout the period China saw her people continuously moving out of
the developed area along four directions: one was the mass migration to
Hunan, Hupei, and particularly Szechwan, prior to the Taiping Rebellion, and
further to southwestern frontier provinces—Kwangsi, Yunnan, and Kweichow—in the late Ch'ing. The second was the movement towards the Han
River drainage, which comprises northern Hupei, southwestern Honan,
southern Shensi, and the southeastern corner of Kansu. The third was the
rapid colonization of Manchuria in the last decades of the dynasty. The
fourth was the eastward migration to Taiwan.[3] All pointed to the developing
area as their destination. Consequently, population and cultivated land in the
area went up simultaneously.

Unfortunately, quantitative data on population and land are inadequate.
Those presented in Table 5.1, which cover a period rather close to the one
under discussion are probably the most reliable though the validity of some
figures are open to doubt.[4] The most conspicuous fact reflected by the data
is the much higher rate of growth in both population and acreage in the
developing area than in the developed area. Between the latter part of the
eighteenth century and the early 1930s, population increased by 155 percent
in the developing area but only 31 percent in the developed area. At about
the same time, cultivated acreage almost tripled in the developing area but
expanded a mere 7 percent in the developed area. Because of the uneven
growth between the two areas, the relative distribution of population and
land changed considerably. In the same period the share of the former area in
total population rose from 29 to 42 percent, and in total acreage from 26 to
46 percent. As a matter of fact, if reasonable data could be constructed for
the earlier years, perhaps the late seventeenth or the early eighteenth century,
one would find that a still greater change occurred in the Ch'ing.

It is very interesting that the economic relations between the two areas
resembled to a great extent that between the developed and developing
countries today. While the developed area exported capital, industrial products, and technical know-how, as well as financial aid, the developing area in
return shipped to the developed area primary products. Apparently, manpower was not the only thing being exported from the developed to the
developing area. The flow of capital and of industrial goods in the same

Table 5.1. Changes in population and cultivated acreage in China, 1766–1933

Area and province (1)	Population (in millions)			Cultivated land (in million mou)		
	1787 (2)	1933 (3)	(3) as percentage of (2) (4)	1766 (5)	1933 (6)	(6) as percentage of (5) (7)
Developed area	209.0 (71%)[a]	274.2 (55%)[a]	131	699 (74%)[a]	747.2 (40%)[a]	107
Chihli	23.0	34.6[b]	160	120	118.2[b]	99
Shantung	22.6	40.3	179	121	120.0	99
Honan	21.0	36.3	173	107	123.0	115
Shansi	13.2	12.4	114	51	55.8	109
Kiangsu	31.4	41.0[c]	131	84	92.2[c]	110
Chekiang	21.7	22.0	101	42	51.1	122
Anhwei	28.9	24.0	83	82	70.6	86
Kiangsi	19.2	16.5	86	47	43.0	92
Fukien	12.0	13.1	109	14	23.3	166
Kwangtung	16.0	34.0	213	31	50.0	161
Developing area	83.5 (29%)[a]	212.7 (42%)[a]	255	242 (26%)[a]	711.9 (46%)[a]	294
Manchuria	1.0	35.3	3,530	21	235.0	1,119
Shensi	8.4	9.7	115	59[d]	54.0	145[d]
Kansu	15.2[e](?)	6.5	43(?)	–	29.2	–
Hupei	19.0	27.3	144	51	84.0	165
Hunan	16.2	33.4	206	50	79.3	159
Kwangsi	6.4	16.6	259	9	43.0	478
Szechwan	8.6	55.4	644	41	129.0	315
Yunnan	3.5	15.9	454	8	36.0	450
Kweichow	5.2	12.6	242	3	22.4	747
Undeveloped area[f]	–	16.2 (3%)[a]	–	1	74.6 (5%)[a]	7,460
Total	292.5	503.1	172	942	1,533.7	163

Sources:
1. Ping-ti Ho, *Studies on the Population of China, 1368-1953*, p. 283.
2. Perkins, *Agricultural Development in China*, p. 234.
3. Ta-chung Liu and Kung-chia Yeh, pp. 129, 178.

Notes:
[a]The figures in parentheses are the percentage shares of the respective area in the total population or total acreage of the country.
[b]Including two special municipalities–Peking and Tientsin (provided that the share of the two municipalities in the total land and population of the four municipalities is 40 percent).
[c]Including two special municipalities–Shanghai and Nanking.
[d]Including Kansu.
[e]The fact that the reliability of official population figures of Kansu before 1851 is doubtful has been pointed out by Perkins, *Agricultural Development in China*, pp. 207–208.
[f]Including Outer and Inner Mongolia, Sinkiang, Tsinghai, and Tibet.

direction was no less important. It is easy to understand that many immigrants carried with them not just two bare hands to the new lands. Rather, they settled there with whatever capital, knowledge, and skill they possessed. Moreover, the commercial capital, especially that for interregional and international trade, was mostly supplied by merchants of the developed area. In the greater part of the Ch'ing period two groups of merchants—those of Anhwei and those of Shansi—largely monopolized interregional trade. While Anhwei merchants were engaging in trades like salt, money shops, porcelain, grain, tea, iron, and textiles throughout the country,[5] Shansi merchants were especially active in the banking business.[6]

As for the export of industrial goods, the cotton textiles of Kiangsu may serve as a good example. The market of these products extended to the interior provinces along the Yangtze River, to Manchuria by sea, and overland to the northwestern provinces.[7] In the last few decades of the dynasty when modern technology for manufacturing textiles was introduced, Kiangsu (Shanghai in particular) became the country's greatest center of the cotton industry. In 1918 the share of Kiangsu in the total spindles of the country amounted to 80 percent. Even the rest of the spindles were still mostly located in the developed area. Hupei, the only textile manufacturing center of the developing area, had a share of less than 8 percent.[8] The consumption needs for cotton textiles of the latter area, therefore, had to depend upon the more advanced area in the east.

Another aspect of the economic relations between the two areas was the transfer of financial resources from the developed area to the developing area. As discussed before, from the early part of the eighteenth century the provinces of China Proper were divided into three groups according to their financial status: the self-sufficient, the deficit, and the surplus. The last group of provinces, mostly in the developed area, was required to give financial aid to the needy provinces in the second group, all in the developing area.[9] The situation largely remained the same in the late Ch'ing though Szechwan had by then emerged as a surplus province.[10]

Without doubt what the developing area could offer in exchange for imported goods and services consisted mostly of primary products. Of these the first and foremost was grain. The Ch'ing period witnessed one-way traffic in the shipment of grain from the developing to the developed area—from Szechwan and Hukwang to Kiangsu and Chekiang, from Taiwan to Fukien, from Kwangsi to Kwangtung, from Manchuria to Chihli, Shantung, and the southeastern coast, and from Shensi to Shansi.[11] In that way, the food shortage of the developed area found its solution in the development of the midwest, Taiwan, and Manchuria. In fact, it was mainly by this development that China was able to register a recorded increase in population during the Ch'ing. The next most important item for export was copper from Yunnan.

Since copper was the primary material of coinage and no other part of the country had a rich deposit of this metal, Yunnan under the Ch'ing, especially in the eighteenth century, played an all-important role in supplying the monetary metal to the economy. In the greater part of the eighteenth century and the early nineteenth this province's annual output was almost always maintained at more than 10 million catties.[12] According to one estimate, the supply of copper from this province could match 80 to 90 percent of the country's demand for coinage at the height of the Manchu dynasty.[13] And finally, northwestern provinces and Manchuria also exported such products as wool, fur, leather, and timber to the developed area.[14]

The foregoing discussion clearly demonstrates that both of the areas played a vital role in the economy. While the developed area provided the developing area with manpower, capital, and technical know-how, the latter area in the course of development supplied the former with foodstuff and raw materials. What effects did this regional division of labor have on land tax yield? Without doubt, under normal circumstances land tax yield would increase together with the extension of cultivated acreage and the bulk of the tax increase would come from the developing area. It is worth noting that, in spite of institutional defects and administrative inefficiency, changes in the geographical distribution of land tax yield followed the same pattern, though not in the same degree, as that of population and acreage. As shown in Table 5.2, between the latter part of the eighteenth century and the early twentieth century the share of the developing area in the country's total land tax yield increased from 19.1 to 30.3 percent, a rise quite comparable to its growing share in population (from 28.5 to 42.3 percent) and acreage (from 25.6 to 46.4 percent). Nevertheless, it is also obvious that the Ch'ing government always heavily relied upon the developed area as a source of revenue; the latter still contributed about two-thirds of the country's land tax yields at the end of the dynasty.[15]

Further examination of the table gives the following findings. First, the greatest proportion of the tax was contributed by the southern provinces of the developed area. Of special importance were the two provinces (Kiangsu and Chekiang) in the Yangtze delta, for their combined share constituted about a quarter of the country's total land tax revenue. Second, over the period between 1753 and 1908 the percentage contribution of all provinces except Chihli in the developed area declined somewhat. Third, the increase in the share of the developing area resulted mainly from a substantial gain in Manchuria and Szechwan, the two most rapidly developing areas in the country.

What, then, specifically brought about the change in geographical distribution of land tax yield in this period? This can be explained by two variables: tax quota and the rate of collection. The substantial growth of the share of

Table 5.2. Changes in geographical distribution of population, cultivated land, and land tax yield in China

Area and province (1)	Percentage distribution of land tax yield		Percentage distribution of population		Percentage distribution of cultivated land	
	1753 (2)	1908 (3)	1787 (4)	1933 (5)	1766 (6)	1933 (7)
Developed area	81.0	68.8	71.5	54.5	74.2	48.6
North	32.3	27.1	27.3	24.6	42.3	27.1
Chihli	5.9	6.6	7.9	6.9	12.7	7.7
Shantung	9.8	8.4	7.7	8.0	12.8	7.8
Honan	9.0	7.4	7.2	7.2	11.4	8.0
Shansi	7.6	4.7	4.5	2.5	5.4	3.6
South	48.7	41.7	44.2	30.0	31.9	21.5
Kiangsu	15.8	14.1	10.7	8.1	8.9	6.0
Chekiang	10.4	8.7	7.4	4.4	4.5	3.3
Anhwei	7.0	4.7	9.9	4.8	8.7	4.6
Kiangsi	7.1	6.7	6.6	3.3	5.0	2.8
Fukien	3.6	3.0	4.1	2.6	1.5	1.5
Kwangtung	4.8	4.5	5.5	6.8	3.3	3.3
Developing area	19.1	30.3	28.5	42.3	25.6	46.4
Manchuria	0.3	6.2	0.3	7.0 (4.7)[a]	2.2	15.3(9.1)[a]
Interior	13.9	13.3	20.1	15.2	16.9	16.1
Shensi	4.5	3.9	2.9	1.9	6.2[b]	3.5
Kansu	1.9	1.6	5.2	1.3	-	1.9
Hupei	3.8	4.7	6.5	5.4	5.4	5.5
Hunan	3.7	3.1	5.5	6.6	5.3	5.2
Southwest	4.9	10.8	8.1	20.0	6.5	15.0
Kwangsi	1.2	1.2	2.2	3.3	1.0	2.8
Szechwan	1.6	7.7	2.9	11.0	4.4	8.4
Yunnan	1.4	1.3	1.2	3.2	0.8	2.3
Kweichow	0.7	0.6	1.8	2.5	0.3	1.5
Undeveloped area	-	1.0	-	3.2	0.1	4.9
Total	100.1	100.1	100.0	100.0	99.9	99.9

Sources: See Tables 4.1, 4.4, and 5.1.

Notes:
a Figures in parentheses dated 1913 are derived from Perkins, Agricultural Development in China, pp. 212, 236.
b Including Kansu

Manchuria from the trifling 0.3 percent to 6.2 percent was accomplished by an upward movement in both variables. In the middle of the eighteenth century Manchuria was largely an unpopulated area (except the Liaotung Peninsula) mainly because of a rigid policy banning Chinese from settling in the Manchu homeland. But the last half century of the dynasty saw a reversal of the policy from prohibition to encouragement of Chinese immigrants by the Ch'ing government with the objective of counteracting foreign encroachment. Population and land acreage therefore increased at great speed. In particular, with the appointment of Hsü Shih-ch'ang as governor-general in 1907 the provincial authorities made a vigorous effort to register land and population and to modernize the administrative and educational systems, financed by imposing a special land tax surcharge (*mou-chüan* or *hsiang-chüan*). Consequently, the area of registered land exceeded 85 million mou, the tax quota in silver went up to 1,282,000 taels, and that in grain to 131,000 shih in 1908 as compared with 2.5 million mou, 38,000 taels, and 76,000 shih respectively in 1753. Moreover, the rate of collection for the *ti-ting* tax rose three to fivefold and that for the grain tax to more than eightfold between these two dates. This phenomenal growth produced in turn a remarkable increase in the annual land tax yield, from an almost negligible sum of 141,000 taels to more than six and a quarter million taels (see Tables 4.1 and 4.4).

The enormous increase in the land tax in Szechwan, however, took the form exclusively of an increase in the rate of collection. During this period the land tax yield of this province multiplied more than ninefold, but its area of registered land and its land tax quota remained virtually the same. That the inflexibility of land tax quota was an inherent characteristic of the Ch'ing tax system has been discussed in the preceding two chapters. What is worthy of note is why there occurred no strong opposition to the multiplication of surcharges to such an extent that the rate of collection came to almost twelve times as much as the quota, far higher than the rate in any other province of the country. For this there are two good reasons. First, in the early part of the Ch'ing period the tax quota of Szechwan in terms of registered acreage, not to say in terms of cultivated acreage, was by far the lowest in the country through the land there was generally fertile and highly productive (see Table 4.1). In other words, the province was the most under-taxed in the mid-eighteenth century. Second, during the Ch'ing period Szechwan was the most rapidly growing province in China Proper (see Table 5.1). As the province obviously possessed great potential for tax increase, the provincial and local governments there were able to raise in the late Ch'ing the rate of collection without running into serious difficulties, while leaving the tax quota and registered acreage as they had been before.

Besides Manchuria and Szechwan, the share of the remaining provinces in

the developing area changed but slightly. On the whole, they held their line
over the one and a half centuries between 1753 and 1908. For instance, the
decrease in the share of Shensi and Kansu, which was due to the reduction of
tax quota following the Moslem Rebellion (1862-73), was compensated by an
increase in the share of Hupei. To be sure, the share of the developing area
would have been larger than that showed in the table if much of the increased
acreage under cultivation was taxed, because the provinces of the area had a
much greater increase of cultivated acreage than most of the developed
provinces during the period.

The relative decline in the share of most developed provinces resulted partly
from the rising importance of Szechwan and Manchuria and partly from the
reduction of the tax quota (especially the grain quota). During and immediately after the Taiping Rebellion the newly emerging scholar-generals in the
south strongly advocated a movement of land tax reduction in order to
relieve the distress of the populace and to win their support. As a result, the
grain quota in much of Kiangsu and Chekiang was reduced by a quarter or a
third.[16]

In addition, three other provinces witnessed an even more drastic reduction
in their tax quotas. Between 1753 and 1908 the grain quota decreased by
about two-thirds in Anhwei, a half in Fukien, and almost a third in Shansi
(see Tables 4.1 and 4.4). The diminution of Anhwei's quota was brought
about partly by the Taiping warfare and partly by other causes, for example,
the intermittent floods of the Huai River.[17] The change in Fukien's quota
was largely effected by the promotion in 1885 of Taiwan's status from being
a prefecture of Fukien to a separate province (which was later ceded to Japan
following the Sino-Japanese War of 1894-95). As for the decrease in the
quota of Shansi and, to a lesser extent, Honan, it was most probably the
result of a severe drought and catastrophic famine in 1877-78.[18] Moreover,
Shansi's average rate of collection in 1908 was by far the lowest in the
country (see Table 5.6). All these reasons account for the diminishing weight
of the developed area in the geographical structure of Ch'ing land tax yields.

*Shift in Relative Burden between the Developed
Area and the Developing Area*

To measure changes in the relative burden of the land tax between different
areas we must have data not only on land tax yield but also on the income of
individual areas. Let us assume a simple hypothetical case as shown in
Table 5.3. There are two areas, M and N, in a certain country. Between years
A and B the share of taxes contributed by area M dropped from 80 to 60
percent, while the share contributed by area N rose from 20 to 40 percent. In
the same period, the share of national income generated in area M declined

Table 5.3. Shift in relative burden between areas: a hypothetical case
(in percentage)

Area	Tax A	Tax B	Income A	Income B	Relative burden A	Relative burden B
(1)	(2)	(3)	(4)	(5)	$(6) = \frac{(2)}{(4)}$	$(7) = \frac{(3)}{(5)}$
M	80	60	80	50	100	120
N	20	40	20	50	100	80
Total	100	100	100	100		

from 80 to 50 percent while the share yielded in area N increased from 20 to 50 percent. As a result of all these changes, the relative burden shifted in favor of area N. In the later year (year B) both areas produced an equal amount of income, but area N bore less taxes. To put it specifically, area N had shifted 20 percent of its burden to area M because of changes in the regional structure of income and taxes (see figures in column 7 of Table 5.3).

Perhaps these changes can be better illustrated by graphs. In Figures 5.2 and 5.3, the vertical axis measures the percentage of income and taxes contributed by individual areas, and the horizontal axis stands for time (year). The solid line T indicates changes in the share of taxes; the broken line I denotes changes in the share of income. The direction of these lines indicates increase or decrease in these two variables—a downward line showing decrease in percentage and an upward line showing increase in percentage. Finally, the degree of change in either direction is measured by the slope of the line concerned—a steep slope indicating a great degree of change and a horizontal line denoting no change at all.

Figure 5.2 represents the situation of area M. At the beginning (year A) both lines coincided with each other; for this area produced 80 percent of national income and the same percentage of taxes. Yet, since line I moved downward more rapidly than line T, the area had to bear in year B 60 percent of the taxes, though its share in national income was reduced to 50 percent. The gap between T and I shows the relative amount of tax shifted to area M from area N because of the structural changes in income and taxation. The situation presented in Figure 5.3 is a portrayal of area N, it is clear without further explanation.

We may now apply this hypothetical framework to the land taxation of Ch'ing China. In the absence of income data we may employ the data of population and cultivated acreage as substitutes on the ground that more people and more cultivated land will produce more income. Moreover, as reliable data for both years of 1753 and 1908 are lacking, we have to use

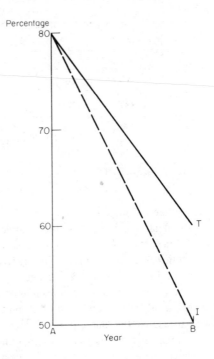

Figure 5.2. Area M. Changes in the relative distribution of income and taxes between areas

those presented in Table 5.1 as substitutes. All these data together with those on land tax yield have been rearranged in percentage form in Table 5.2. Surely, these data are by no means perfect. Some figures are probably unreliable. Nevertheless, even though derived from different sources, these three sets of data show a general consistency among themselves. We have therefore good reason to believe that they can provide a rough guide for the analysis of relative changes in land tax burden between different areas.

The changes in these three variables—land tax yields, population, and cultivated land—can best be observed by the aid of the type of graphs just illustrated. In Figures 5.4 and 5.5 T, O, and L stand for the share of land tax yields, population, and cultivated acreage respectively. Figure 5.4 depicts a lower rate of decrease in T than in O and L, whereas Figure 5.5 portrays a lower rate of increase in T than in O and L. This means that at the end of the Ch'ing the developing area enjoyed the advantage of lighter land taxation

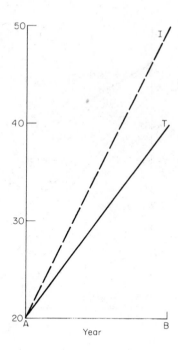

Figure 5.3. Area N. Changes in the geographical distribution of population, land, and land tax yields

vis-à-vis the developed area. In other words, by the late Ch'ing the developing area was able to shift part of its tax burden to the developed area because the regional structure of these three variables changed in favor of the former area. Comparing Figures 5.4 and 5.5 with Figures 5.2 and 5.3 the situation of the developed area is seen to be similar to that of area *M* and the situation of the developing area to that of area *N*.

It is easy to explain the shift of the land tax burden between the two areas in the late Ch'ing. Since a greater part of the land brought under cultivation in the nineteenth century was not officially registered and most of the newly cultivated land was found in the developing area, the area had a natural advantage over the developed area with regard to the redistribution of the land tax burden. Just how much land was unregistered in these two different areas during the latter part of the dynasty can be roughly measured by a comparison between the registered acreage and cultivated acreage as pre-

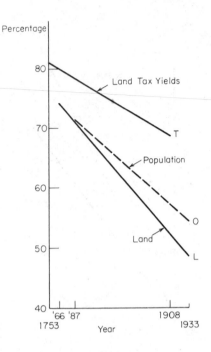

Figure 5.4. The developed area

sented in Table 5.4 below. The comparison illustrates that the proportion of cultivated land registered in the developed area had remained around the level of three-quarters from the mid-eighteenth century down to the early twentieth century but that the proportion in the developing area had declined from 88 percent to 43 percent (to be sure, the percentage for the early

Table 5.4. Comparison between registered acreage and cultivated acreage

Area (1)	Registered acreage (in million mou)		Cultivated acreage (in million mou)		Registered acreage as percentage of cultivated acreage	
					(2) as percentage of (4)	(3) as percentage of (5)
	1753 (2)	1908 (3)	1766 (4)	1933 (5)	(6)	(7)
Developed area	548.6	540.5	699	747.2	78	72
Developing area	212.9	307.1	242	711.9	88	43

Sources: See Tables 4.1, 4.4, and 5.1.

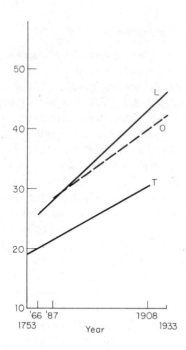

Figure 5.5. The developing area

twentieth century would be somewhat higher for both areas if reliable data on cultivated acreage for 1908 were available). By the same token, whereas about a quarter of the cultivated land was untaxed in the developed area throughout the latter part of the Ch'ing period, the land under cultivation that bore no taxes at all in the developing area swelled from a mere 12 percent to well over a half of its total acreage.

Not only population and cultivated acreage but also land productivity increased at a greater rate in the developing area than in the developed area. We may take rice yields in Kiangsu and Hunan as examples. In the Soochow area of Kiangsu, the most developed part of the country, the rice yields had reached the level of around two shih (husked rice) per mou in the early seventeenth century, if not earlier; but remained so through the late Ch'ing.[19] In Hunan, on the other hand, land productivity had been steadily on the rise. Roughly speaking, one mou of medium- or high-grade land could produce about three shih of unhusked rice in the middle of the eighteenth century, four shih a century later, and five shih in the late nineteenth and early twentieth centuries.[20] Without doubt, the uneven degree of change in land productivity between these two areas was another factor favorable to the developing area with respect to tax shifting.

Provinces with High, Medium, and Low Revenue

In Chapter 3 I touched upon a conventional classification of local offices into *fei-ch'üeh* (lucrative post), *chung-ch'üeh* (medium post), and *chi-ch'üeh* (lean post) depending on the revenue productivity of the district where the office concerned was located. A *fei-ch'üeh* suggests generally an official post in a relatively rich district—a district with a large amount of taxes, especially of land tax yield—that would yield the appointee a handsome income, whereas a *chi-ch'üeh* refers to the post that could offer him little financial reward, or even cause him a net loss. This does not mean that official salaries were much higher in the well-endowed districts than in those less affluent ones; in fact few magistrates, if any, depended upon salaries (including *yang-lien yin*) for a living in the late Ch'ing. Nor does it necessarily mean that local officials could more easily enrich themselves by extortion in the former places than in the latter. Rather, the differences in the "profitability" of local offices lay in the amount of tax surcharges that were left at the disposal of the magistrate after all kinds of public expenses and fiscal obligations had been met (that is, the surplus of revenue over expenditure).

Since surcharge was commonly assessed on the basis of tax quota and the magistrate's freedom in the increase of the surcharge rate was severely limited, the amount of surcharge and hence the amount of surplus that could be transferred to his own purse rested to a great extent upon the size of the quota. The larger the quota, the more the surplus. Therefore a post that would almost certainly assure the appointee, even if he was conscientious and incorruptible, rich material rewards and be the envy of his fellow magistrates would be in a district with a large tax quota. The marked differences in financial remuneration among various posts depending upon the revenue productivity of the locality were universal phenomena in Ch'ing China.[21] In the remaining part of this chapter, I intend to make some exploratory statistical observations, on the basis of the data gathered thus far, with regard to where the lucrative posts were concentrated, what relationships existed between the factors (the tax quota, the rate of collection, and the tax yields) that determined the financial status of different groups of districts or provinces, and to what extent changes had occurred in the geographical distribution of these districts and in the relationships between these factors.

As indicated in Tables 5.5 and 5.6, there was a wide range of difference in land tax yield per district among different provinces with Kiangsu at one extreme and Kweichow at the other. In 1753 Kiangsu yielded an average amount of the land tax for 130,000 taels per district whereas Kweichow could produce a mere 6,000 taels per district. Meanwhile the average for the entire country stood at 36,100 taels. The corresponding figures for 1908 are 209,300, 9,800, and 62,500 taels respectively. While one may definitely say that in general local posts in Kiangsu were the most sought after in the

Table 5.5. Differences in land tax yield per district among provinces, 1753

Group and province (1)	Number of districts (2)	Land tax yield (in 1,000 taels)			Land tax quota per district		Average rate of collection	
		per district (3)	Amount and percentage (in parenthesis) contributed by		Ti-ting (in 1,000 taels) (6)	Grain (in 1,000 shih) (7)	Ti-ting (taels per tael of quota) (8)	Grain (taels per shih of quota) (9)
			Ti-ting (4)	Grain (5)				
All Groups	1,501	36.1	25.0 (69)	11.1 (31)	20.3	6.0	1.2	1.9
High-revenue	303	76.9	44.9 (58)	32.0 (42)	37.7	15.8	1.2	2.0
Kiangsu	66	130.0	58.8 (45)	71.2 (45)	51.6	33.5	1.1	2.1
Chekiang	78	72.2	41.4 (57)	30.8 (43)	36.3	14.5	1.1	2.1
Anhwei	54	70.6	40.0 (57)	30.6 (43)	33.3	17.5	1.2	1.8
Shantung	105	50.5	41.4 (82)	9.1 (18)	32.4	4.8	1.3	1.9
Medium-revenue	794	34.1	27.2 (80)	6.9 (20)	21.8	3.8	1.3	1.8
Kiangsi	81	47.5	28.1 (59)	19.4 (41)	23.4	11.1	1.2	1.8
Honan	104	47.0	42.5 (90)	4.5 (10)	33.7	2.4	1.3	1.9
Shansi	95	43.5	40.2 (92)	3.3 (8)	31.9	1.8	1.3	1.9
Hupei	67	31.0	21.1 (68)	9.9 (32)	17.3	5.7	1.2	1.8
Kwangtung	88	29.9	19.2 (64)	10.7 (36)	14.3	5.0	1.3	2.1
Fukien	66	29.2	23.0 (79)	6.2 (21)	18.5	5.0	1.2	2.1
Shensi	82	28.5	24.5 (83)	4.0 (17)	18.8	4.0	1.3	1.3
Hunan	70	28.5	21.6 (76)	6.9 (24)	18.0	4.0	1.2	1.8
Chihli	141	22.5	21.2 (94)	1.3 (6)	17.1	0.7	1.2	1.9
Low-revenue	404	9.4	5.6 (60)	3.8 (40)	4.2	2.8	1.3	1.4
Kansu	60	17.1	6.5 (38)	10.6 (62)	5.0	6.5	1.3	1.3
Fengtien	14	10.1	3.3 (33)	6.8 (67)	2.7	5.4	1.2	1.3
Yunnan	73	10.0	5.1 (51)	4.9 (49)	2.9	3.2	1.8	1.5
Kwangsi	68	9.8	6.9 (71)	2.9 (29)	5.8	1.9	1.2	1.5
Szechwan	129	6.8	6.6 (98)	0.2 (2)	5.1	0.1	1.3	1.5
Kweichow	60	6.0	2.1 (35)	3.9 (65)	1.7	2.6	1.3	1.5

Sources:
1. For the number of districts, see Chao Ch'eng-ch'üan, *Ch'ing-tai ti-li yen-ke piao* (Shanghai, 1941).
2. The rest of data are derived from Table 4.1.

Table 5.6. Differences in land tax yield per district among provinces, 1908

Group and province (1)	Number of districts (2)	Land tax yield (in 1,000 taels)			Land tax quota per district		Average rate of collection	
		Land tax yield per district (3)	Amount and percentage (in parenthesis) contributed by		Ti-ting (in 1,000 taels) (6)	Grain (in 1,000 shih) (7)	Ti-ting (taels per tael of quota) (8)	Grain (taels per shih of quota) (9)
			Ti-ting (4)	Grain (5)				
All Groups	1,639	62.5	43.6 (70)	18.9 (30)	18.5	4.4	2.4	4.3
High-revenue	*437*	*109.4*	*64.0 (59)*	*45.4 (41)*	*30.2*	*10.0*	*2.1*	*4.6*
Kiangsu	69	209.3	85.2 (41)	124.1 (59)	44.0	24.3	1.9	5.1
Chekiang	78	114.6	70.2 (61)	44.4 (39)	35.5	11.5	2.0	3.9
Anhwei	55	88.2	57.9 (66)	30.3 (34)	28.9	7.0	2.0	4.3
Kiangsi	82	83.4	54.1 (65)	29.3 (35)	23.5	10.1	2.3	2.9
Fengtien	49[a]	83.2	55.5 (67)	27.7 (33)	11.1	2.7	5.0	10.4
Shantung	104	82.7	60.0 (73)	22.7 (27)	32.1	4.2	1.9	5.4
Medium-revenue	*813*	*56.4*	*47.6 (84)*	*8.8 (16)*	*18.4*	*2.0*	*2.6(2.2)[b]*	*4.4*
Honan	101	75.2	60.3 (80)	14.9 (20)	28.1	2.3	2.1	6.5
Hupei	67	71.6	50.8 (71)	20.8 (29)	17.5	4.6	2.9	4.6
Kirin	22[a]	63.6	63.6 (100)	0 (0)	22.1	0	2.9	–
Szechwan	134	59.0	59.0 (100)	0 (0)	5.0	0	11.8	–
Kwangtung	84	55.1	33.2 (60)	21.9 (40)	14.6	4.5	2.3	4.8
Heilungkiang	15[a]	53.3	53.3 (100)	0 (0)	16.9	0	3.2	–
Shansi	91	53.1	49.2 (93)	3.9 (7)	32.9	1.3	1.5	3.0
Chihli	144	46.7	43.0 (92)	3.7 (8)	17.0	0.7	2.5	5.4
Hunan	69	46.3	34.4 (74)	11.9 (26)	18.1	4.3	1.9	2.8
Shensi	86	46.1	37.8 (82)	8.3 (18)	18.9	2.3	2.0	3.6
Low-revenue	*389*	*22.6*	*12.3 (54)*	*10.3 (46)*	*5.7*	*3.2*	*2.2*	*3.3*
Fukien	78	38.7	33.4 (86)	5.3 (14)	15.7	1.2	2.1	4.3
Sinkiang	39[a]	26.6	0 (0)	26.6 (100)	0	7.7	–	3.4
Kansu	62	26.5	9.4 (36)	17.1 (64)	3.6	5.3	2.6	3.2
Yunnan	77	16.9	8.2 (48)	8.7 (52)	3.8	2.6	2.2	3.3
Kwangsi	72	16.8	10.8 (64)	6.0 (36)	5.3	2.0	2.0	3.0
Kweichow	61	9.8	3.2 (33)	6.6 (67)	1.6	2.7	2.1	2.5

Sources:
1. For the number of districts, see Chao Ch'eng-ch'üan's work cited in Table 5.5
2. The rest of data are derived from Table 4.4.

Notes:
[a]Prefectures, independent departments, and independent subprefectures are included for the reason that a substantial part of these provinces was directly administered by prefects without being divided into districts.
[b]The average rate exclusive of Szechwan.

country and those in Kweichow the least attractive to office seekers, certain arbitrary assumptions have to be made to classify those in between. Let us leave aside the differences in tax yields among districts within individual provinces and assume that any province with an average yield of over 50,000 taels per district in 1753 and of over 80,000 taels in 1908 is a high-revenue province, one with an average between 20,000+ and 50,000 taels in 1753 and between 40,000+ and 80,000 taels in 1908 a medium-revenue province, and one with an average of 20,000 taels or less in 1753 and of 40,000 taels or less in 1908 a low-revenue province. In these two tables provinces are arranged by this classification.

We shall immediately find here that in the middle of the eighteenth century the high-revenue provinces (Kiangsu, Chekiang, Anhwei, and Shantung) were concentrated in the well-developed coastal area on the east and especially the lower Yangtze valley. The lower-revenue provinces were scattered in the developing area of the southwest (Kwangsi, Szechwan, Yunnan, and Kweichow), the northwest (Kansu), and Manchuria (Fengtien). The medium-revenue group included a majority of developed provinces (Kiangsi, Honan, Shansi, Kwangtung, Fukien, and Chihli) and three developing provinces (Hupei, Hunan, and Shensi). One and a half centuries later, however, Fengtien made a spectacular jump into the top rank while Kiangsi in the middle Yangtze valley also edged into the group. Elsewhere Szechwan and two newly established Manchurian provinces (Kirin and Heilungkiang) advanced into the medium rank, but Fukien sank to the low-revenue group.

Certainly, within each province land tax yields also varied from one district to another. In Table 5.8 I have arranged the districts for each of those provinces about which district-by-district data (though by no means complete) are available into three groups according to amount of the yields in a descending order, namely: the high-revenue districts that produced the highest yields among all districts in the province and whose yields combined amounted to one-third of the provincial total; the medium-revenue districts that collectively yielded the second third of the total; and the low-revenue districts that contributed the remaining lower third. By this classification, for example, of 107 districts of collection in Honan in 1908 only fifteen could be considered the *fei-ch'üeh* for official appointment, and a majority of them (sixty-two) yielded well below the provincial average.[22]

Moreover, it was not unusual that a high-revenue district in a low-revenue province was financially more productive than a low-revenue or a medium-revenue district in a high-revenue province, or than a high-revenue district in a medium-revenue province. A case in point is that of Wu-wei hsien and Chang-yeh hsien of Kansu. In 1908 these two districts yielded to the government a land tax revenue (exclusive of surcharges for collection expenses) of 101,800 taels and 94,400 taels respectively,[23] amounts well above the average yields per district of the medium-revenue provinces and comparable to the average of the high-revenue provinces (see Table 5.6). It is interesting that the two districts were so valued by office seekers that even in the republican period there had been current in the northwest a proverb, *Chin Chang-yeh, yin Wu-wei* (lit., "golden Chang-yeh, silver Wu-wei").[24]

Having classified the districts of the country and located their geographical distribution, we may ask why certain districts or provinces yielded more than others. Obviously, in Ch'ing times the amount of land tax yields depended upon two factors: land tax quota (including the *ti-ting* and grain quotas) and the rate of collection. On the basis of the data in Tables 5.5 and 5.6, a few observations may be made regarding the relationship between the tax yields and quota on the one hand, and the relationship between the yields and the rate of collection on the other. In the first place, there is a positive correlation between the yields and the quota. The high-revenue provinces are characterized by quota high above the national average. To put it specifically, the average *ti-ting* quota per district for the entire country stood at 20,300 taels in 1753 and the average grain quota at 6,000 shih, while the corresponding figures for the high-revenue provinces were 37,700 taels and 15,800 shih respectively. When the national average of the *ti-ting* quota declined to 18,500 taels and that of the grain quota to 4,400 shih in 1908, the average for the high-revenue provinces decreased likewise to 30,200 taels and 10,000 shih respectively.[25] The medium-revenue provinces had a *ti-ting* quota (21,800 taels in 1753 and 18,400 taels in 1908) very close to the national average but their grain quota (3,800 shih in 1753 and 2,000 shih in 1908) was substantially lower. And both of the *ti-ting* and grain quotas of the low-revenue provinces were far below the national average; for they had on the average merely 4,200 taels (the *ti-ting* quota) plus 2,800 shih (the grain quota) in 1753 and 5,700 taels plus 3,200 shih in 1908. In short, the larger the tax quota, the higher the tax yields.

In the second place, there exists to a certain extent a negative correlation between the yields and the *ti-ting* rate of collection. This means that local administration in the lower- and medium-revenue provinces generally collected the *ti-ting* tax at an average rate somewhat higher than that in the high-revenue provinces. As shown in Tables 5.5 and 5.6, while the average *ti-ting* rate of collection for the high-revenue provinces was 1.2 taels for each tael of the quota in 1753, the rate for the provinces in the other two groups was 1.3 taels. In 1908 the average rate stood at 2.1, 2.6, and 2.2 taels for the high-, medium-, and low-revenue provinces respectively. It should be noted here that the highest rate (2.6 taels) for the medium-revenue provinces in the latter year resulted almost entirely from the extremely high rate of a single province, Szechwan (11.8 taels). If the province is excluded, the average rate for the group of the medium-revenue provinces would be the same as that for the lower-revenue provinces (2.2 taels).

In the third place, in contrast to the relationship between the *ti-ting* rate of collection and the tax yields, that between the grain rate of collection and the yields is positive. In other words, the average rate of collection for the grain quota was the highest in the high-revenue provinces and the lowest in the low-revenue provinces. This contrast appears paradoxical, but there is good reason for it. The grain tax had by the late Ch'ing been almost completely converted into payment in money. Local administration could collect the tax at higher rates in the high-revenue provinces than elsewhere because the level of grain prices was by and large the highest in those provinces. Roughly speaking, the level of grain prices averaged in 1908 at 3.3 taels per shih in the high-revenue provinces, 3.2 taels in the medium-revenue provinces, and 2.6 taels in the low-revenue provinces as compared with the average rate of collection for the grain quota at 4.6, 4.4, and 3.3 taels respectively.[26]

I have illustrated in a rough manner the functional relationship between land tax yields and the tax quota, and between the yields and the rate of collection for the three groups of provinces and for the country as a whole. For measuring more precisely the degree of, and changes in, correlation between these variables over the latter part of the Ch'ing period it is most appropriate to employ a statistical concept: the coefficient of correlation. The coefficient varies between +1 and −1. The plus sign indicates a positive correlation between two variables under examination, the minus sign a negative correlation. The highest degree of correlation, either positive or negative, is expressed by 1 whereas the absence of any correlation by 0. Let us now apply this concept to our tax data. Yet, for the sake of simplicity we shall confine the scope of observation to the *ti-ting* tax, which contributed seven-tenths of the country's total land tax yields in both 1753 and 1908 and a still larger proportion in the medium-revenue provinces (see columns 4 and 5 in Tables 5.5 and 5.6).

Several remarks can be made by an examination of the figures in the last three columns of Table 5.7. First, the correlation between yields and quota is positive and extremely high (only one is lower than 0.80), thus confirming our earlier observation. Second, the correlation between the rate of collection and quota is, with one exception, negative, but the degree of correlation decreases as the level of per-district revenue moves down. This finding indicates that financial needs of the local government was the primary factor accounting for differences in the rate of collection among different groups of provinces because, given a relatively small amount of quota, only a higher rate of collection could raise taxes needed for the minimal requirement of local expenditure (see Chapter 2). On the other hand, the marked difference in the coefficient between the high-revenue provinces and low-revenue provinces (−0.66 compared to −0.30 in 1753 and −0.84 compared to −0.26 in 1908) appears to suggest that the less affluent provinces of the high-revenue group probably had a more active administration and hence a greater need for

Table 5.7. Analysis of the *ti-ting* yield, 1753 and 1908

| Group[a] (1) | Year (2) | Rate of collection (tael) | | Coefficient of correlation[c] between | | |
		Average (per tael of quota) (3)	Standard deviation[b] (4)	Quota and yield (5)	Rate of collection and quota (6)	Rate of collection and yield (7)
A	1753	1.2	0.15	0.99+	−0.44	−0.40
	1908	2.4 (2.1)[d]	2.18 (0.42)[d]	0.80 (0.93+)[d]	−0.36 (−0.35)[d]	0.18 (−0.002)[d]
H	1753	1.2	0.10	0.98	−0.66	−0.52
	1908	2.1 (2.0)[d]	1.23 (0.16)[d]	0.83 (0.97)[d]	−0.84 (−0.76)[d]	−0.41 (−0.59)[d]
M	1753	1.3	0.05	0.99+	0.45	0.53
	1908	2.6 (2.2)[d]	3.03 (0.56)[d]	0.13 (0.49)[d]	−0.72 (−0.56)[d]	0.40 (0.42)[d]
L	1753	1.3	0.23	0.95	−0.30	0.002
	1908	2.2	0.24	0.99+	−0.26	−0.19

Sources: Table 5.5 and 5.6.

Notes:

[a]A stands for all groups, H for the high-revenue provinces, M for the medium-revenue provinces, and L for the low-revenue provinces.

[b]The formula of standard deviation:

$$s = \sqrt{\frac{n\Sigma x^2 - (\Sigma x)^2}{n(n-1)}}$$

[c]The formula of the coefficient of correlation:

$$\gamma = \frac{n\Sigma xy - (\Sigma x)(\Sigma y)}{\sqrt{\{n\Sigma x^2 - (\Sigma x)^2\}\{n\Sigma y^2 - (\Sigma y)^2\}}}$$

[d]Figures in parentheses indicate the computerized results when Szechwan or Fengtien or both are excluded.

raising the rate of collection than did the poorest provinces of the low-revenue group.

Third, the correlation between the rate of collection and the tax yield differs from one group to another. The coefficient is negative in the high-revenue provinces but positive in the medium-revenue provinces, while the degree of correlation in both groups is rather moderate (0.40-0.53). This means that, in spite of negative correlation between the rate and quota in the first group, most provinces with a relatively high rate still yielded less revenue (in per-district term) than did their richer neighbors; but that in the second group those with higher yields usually also had a higher rate. As to the low-revenue group, there appears to be little correlation, or at most a slight negative one, between these two variables under observation. In other words, with higher rates some provinces produced more revenue than others, but some yielded less, even with higher rates.

The first two findings are also observable from the district-by-district data for certain provinces. As shown in Table 5.8 the correlation between quota and yield is both positive and high for all groups of districts, and the correlation between the rate and quota is overwhelmingly negative for all groups, but higher in degree for the high-revenue and medium-revenue groups than for the low-revenue group. Nonetheless, the correlation between the rate and yield varies inconsistently in degree and in direction from one group of districts to another and from one province to another; hence no generalization can be made.

A final task now is to observe the changes in the financial status of different provinces and in the functioning of the factors that determined the status during the one and a half centuries between 1753 and 1908. The first part has been done (see Tables 5.5 and 5.6). On the second part we may pose, among others, two major questions which may clarify the general condition of the land tax administration in the late Ch'ing. First, were there erratic changes in relationships between the three factors mentioned above? Second, did variation in the rates of collection among different groups of provinces and districts become much greater in 1908 than in 1753? The answer to both questions is a qualified no. Comparing the coefficients in Table 5.7 we find that in most cases the degree of change between the two dates is insignificant. Although drastic shift did take place in the correlation between quota and yield (from 0.99 to 0.13) and between the rate and quota (from 0.45 to −0.72) for the medium-revenue group of provinces, and in the correlation between the rate and yield (from −0.40 to 0.18) for all groups, it resulted largely from the sharp rise in the rate of collection in two provinces—Szechwan and Fengtien. If we leave out these two provinces from computation, the extent of change in most of these latter cases, as indicated by the figures in parentheses, would also become substantially smaller. Accordingly, we might

Table 5.8. Analysis of the *ti-ting* yield in selected provinces, 1908

Province (1)	Group[a] (2)	Number of districts[b] (3)	Land tax yield[c] (in taels) Total (4)	per district (5)	*Ti-ting*[c] (in taels) Quota (6)	Yield (7)	Rate of Collection (taels) Average[c] (per tael of quota) (8)	Standard deviation (9)	Coefficient of correlation between (6) & (7) (10)	(6) & (8) (11)	(7) & (8) (12)
Honan	A	107	6,137,743	57,362	2,839,365	4,921,030	1.73	0.275	0.957	-0.134	0.120
	H	15	2,017,750	134,517	848,714	1,421,170	1.67	0.232	0.894	-0.401	0.035
	M	30	2,047,040	68,235	921,757	1,618,274	1.76	0.261	0.855	-0.429	0.083
	L	62	2,072,953	33,435	1,068,894	1,881,586	1.76	0.289	0.895	0.074	0.490
Shansi	A	111	–	–	2,987,826	4,477,573	1.50	0.136	0.993	0.446	0.527
	H	14	–	–	935,197	1,482,314	1.59	0.118	0.849	-0.443	0.096
	M	22	–	–	1,005,980	1,509,500	1.50	0.114	0.943	-0.486	-0.173
	L	75	–	–	1,046,649	1,485,759	1.42	0.118	0.990	0.179	0.293
Kansu	A	78	1,496,362	19,184	225,424	532,226	2.36	–	0.986	–	–
	H	7	480,157	68,594	26,944	67,036	2.49	–	0.999	–	–
	M	18	498,721	27,707	56,311	138,237	2.45	–	0.997	–	–
	L	53	517,484	9,764	142,168	326,953	2.30	–	0.967	–	–
Fukien	A	80	–	–	1,227,712	2,485,212	2.02	0.196	0.993	0.043	0.143
	H	11	–	–	391,150	822,488	2.10	0.117	0.918	-0.601	-0.236
	M	22	–	–	421,896	832,884	1.97	0.223	0.888	-0.608	-0.186
	L	47	–	–	414,666	829,840	2.00	0.192	0.996	-0.008	0.067
Kwangtung	A	93	–	–	1,223,258	2,532,566	2.07	0.086	0.987	0.060	0.180
	H	11	–	–	415,059	880,863	2.12	0.219	0.946	-0.177	0.144
	M	24	–	–	398,159	837,524	2.10	0.293	0.865	-0.299	0.202
	L	58	–	–	410,040	814,179	1.99	0.298	0.964	-0.189	0.032
Hunan	A	75	2,503,410	33,379	1,147,246	1,817,909	1.58	0.408	0.957	-0.541	-0.460
	H	9	803,174	89,242	279,848	407,550	1.46	0.155	0.630	-0.595	-0.028
	M	15	828,646	55,243	409,502	590,553	1.44	0.234	0.816	-0.327	-0.273

L	51	871,590	17,090	457,896	819,806	1.79	0.420	0.947	-0.366	-0.286
Kwangsi	A	71	1,079,370	15,202	378,857	692,563	1.83	0.649	0.893	-0.124	0.174
	H	6	356,629	59,438	85,798	185,221	2.16	0.707	0.941	0.875	0.977
	M	16	354,768	22,173	159,673	272,983	1.71	0.589	0.758	-0.427	0.236
	L	49	367,973	7,510	133,386	234,359	1.76	0.656	0.940	-0.247	0.012
Kweichow	A	72	559,098	7,765	95,585	188,852	1.98	0.731	0.962	-0.058	0.144
	H	11	191,898	17,445	30,488	60,500	1.98	0.883	0.975	-0.113	0.022
	M	20	182,982	9,149	27,223	49,773	1.83	0.539	0.968	-0.460	-0.261
	L	41	184,217	4,493	37,874	78,579	2.07	0.764	0.910	0.100	0.429

Sources: Tables 4, 5, 9, 13, 14, 17, 18, and 23 in my work, *An Estimate of the Land Tax* . . .

Notes:

[a] A stands for entire province, H for the high-revenue districts, M for the medium-revenue districts, and L for the low-revenue districts.

[b] Figures are the number of the districts of collection, not of administrative districts.

[c] Figures are all understated because some amounts (e.g., surcharges for tax collection) estimated on provincial basis are not included.

say that there was in general no substantial change in the functional relationships between the three essential factors in land taxation.

To measure how much the rates of collection vary among different groups of provinces and districts the formula of standard deviation is chosen for computation. The results are presented in column 4 of Table 5.7 for data on the provincial level and in column 9 of Table 5.8 for data on the district level. The figures in the first table denote a sizable increase in variation for all but the low-revenue group of provinces. These appear to indicate that the variation in the average rates of collection for all provinces was far greater in 1908 than in 1753. It should again be pointed out, however, that the extraordinary rise of the rate in the two most rapidly developing provinces—Szechwan and Fengtien—produces a distorted picture for 1908. Should these two provinces be excluded, we would find a much more moderate degree of change. After the adjustment is made, for example, the standard deviation of the average rate for all groups of provinces changes from 0.15 in 1753 to 0.42 tael instead of 2.18 taels in 1908, or from about one-eighth of the average rate to one-fifth. The degree of deviation in the figures for the latter date is still a moderate one.

More valuable are the statistics in Table 5.8. They support the observation just made, for they show a small degree of variation in the rates of collection for all groups of districts in most provinces. They also reveal a rather high degree of deviation for all groups of districts in Kwangsi and Kweichow, the two financially least productive provinces in 1908. This suggests that the rates of collection varied more within individual provinces of the low-revenue group than within those of the high- or medium-revenue group.

What significance, then, do all these findings have as far as Ch'ing land taxation and local finance are concerned? They imply that land tax administration in the late Ch'ing was far more orderly and stable than generally believed. Given the fact that the land tax quota of most provinces and districts either remained practically unchanged or even decreased somewhat, all magistrates throughout the country had to raise from time to time the rate of collection so as to carry on their public duties and to meet their private expenses. If they and their staff could increase the rate with ease, conscientious officials would exert self-restraint but less scrupulous ones would push up the rate in order to enrich themselves. Under these circumstances, there would have been great variation in the rates of collection for different groups of provinces and for different groups of districts within individual provinces. As a result, the functional relationships between the quota, rate, and yield would have been changed erratically. This was, however, hardly the case.

Rather, as our data demonstrate: the relationships between the three essential factors were stable; variations in the rates of collection were mostly small; the *ti-ting* tax was generally collected at rates between two and three taels for each tael of the quota; and in most provinces the grain was taxed at rates somewhat higher than the prevailing grain prices. All of these appear to indicate that fiscal order in local administration had been to a considerable extent maintained until the last days of the Manchu dynasty, and confirm our institutional analysis that the nonstatutory system of land tax administration worked reasonably well. Although the rates were much higher in Szechwan and Manchuria, these two areas were still undertaxed as compared with other areas. That is to say, the seemingly exorbitant rates there indicate not excessive exaction but a belated adjustment to a rapidly growing economy. On the whole, we may conclude that chaos and instability in local finance occurred probably to a considerable extent only in a few low-revenue provinces (as reflected in the high variation in the rates of collection).

6 The Price Movement and the Land Tax Burden

With regard to the land tax burden during the Ch'ing, students in this field hold two divergent views. The one which might be described as the traditional view is that the land tax became increasingly oppressive as the dynasty drew to an end; the other view is just the opposite. Those who maintain the traditional view contend that the land tax had been greatly increased by levying various surcharges though the tax quota remained almost unchanged.[1] Those who challenge the orthodox view, however, argue that since there had been a substantial decrease in the purchasing power of money during the dynastic period, the real burden of the tax was diminishing instead of increasing in the late Ch'ing.[2] Both these arguments deserve credit for having put forward the most crucial points for a critical examination of the issue, but a comprehensive study is yet to be made.

The Real Burden of the Land Tax: A Macroanalysis

The primary objective here is to examine the issue first through a macroscopic analysis by bringing into focus the major elements that affected the land tax burden in Ch'ing times and then through a minute observation of a number of specific cases of land taxation made available from diverse sources. The real burden of a tax upon the whole population or a particular segment of the population in a country depends on two variables: the tax as a proportion of the total income; and the level of per capita income. Other things being equal, the greater the proportion of income taken away through taxation by the government, the heavier the tax burden upon the people; and the reverse is true. However, if the per capita income increases, taxpayers may not feel it more burdensome to contribute to the government through taxation a greater proportion of their income than before; should the per capita income decrease, even the same proportion would constitute a heavier burden.

For the sake of simplicity we may assume an unchanged per capita income and focus our attention on land taxation. Following the same reasoning just laid out we may state that for the population of the agricultural sector as a whole the land tax burden would be unchanged if the government appropriates the same proportion of land produce over a period of time (provided that all income is derived from farming); the burden would become heavier if the proportion swells; it would be less if the proportion diminishes. This proposition may be expressed by a simple formula as follows:

$$\text{Real burden of the land tax} = \frac{\text{Land tax}}{\text{Land produce}}$$

Before the formula can be applied to practical cases, however, we have to add to it a new element, that is, the level of prices. There are two obvious reasons for the addition. First, the Ch'ing government collected most (in fact, in the last decades of the dynasty, virtually all) of the land tax in money instead of in kind. Second, measuring the tax burden is impossible if the numerator in the formula is expressed in money while the denominator is expressed in kind. In addition, it goes without saying that both the denominator and the numerator can each be differentiated into two elements—the cultivated acreage and land yield from the denominator and the tax quota and the rate of collection from the numerator. Accordingly, the above formula can be transformed into a somewhat complicated but workable one as below:

$$\text{Real land tax burden} = \frac{\text{Land tax quota} \times \text{rate of collection (in money)}}{\text{Cultivated acreage} \times \text{land yield} \times \text{price}}$$

or a slightly simpler one like this:

$$\text{Real land tax burden} = \frac{\text{Amount of land tax (in money)}}{\text{Cultivated acreage} \times \text{land yield} \times \text{price}}$$

Let us choose the second formula and observe the functional relationship between the tax burden and the elements on the other side of the equation. It is apparent that four variables determine the burden, namely, the amount of tax collected, the cultivated acreage, the land yield, and the price level. An upward movement of the first variable tends to increase the burden and a downward movement to reduce it. On the other hand, a rise in either of the last three variables tends to lessen the burden and a fall to increase it. The final outcome depends upon the degree of change in all variables combined over the period under consideration.

To illustrate the possible outcome of the changes in the four variables we may envisage a number of hypothetical cases. In Table 6.1 L stands for cultivated acreage, Y for land yield, P for the price level, I for the total income from land at current prices, T for the land tax collected, B for the real burden of the tax on the population who lived on land, and n_1, n_2, n_3, n_4 ... for different years. For the purpose of comparison, the figures in the table (except the case numbers) are all in index form. Let year n_1 be the base year and suppose no change occurs in L and Y but prices go up by 100 percent between year n_1 and year n_2. Accordingly, people's total income at current prices doubles even though their real income remains the same. If the government still collects the same amount of taxes in year n_2 as in year n_1, the real tax burden would be reduced by a half (case 1). If taxes double in line with price increase, people would find their burden unchanged (case 2). Finally, if for one reason or another taxes outrun prices, then a heavier burden would become inevitable (case 3). The remaining cases in the table are clear without explanation. Consider, for example, case 7. During the period between year n_1 and year n_4 both cultivated acreage and prices double while land yield increases by 50 percent. As a result, the total income at current

Table 6.1. Changes in income, taxes, and real tax burden: hypothetical cases

Case Number (1)	Year (2)	L (3)	Y (4)	P (5)	I^a (6)	T (7)	B $(8) = \dfrac{(7)}{(6)} \times 100$
–	n_1	100	100	100	100	100	100
1	n_2	100	100	200	200	100	50
2	n_2	100	100	200	200	200	100
3	n_2	100	100	200	200	400	200
4	n_3	100	100	50	50	100	200
5	n_3	100	100	50	50	50	100
6	n_3	100	100	50	50	25	50
7	n_4	200	150	200	600	300	50

Note:

$$a_I = \frac{Ln_x}{Ln_1} \times \frac{Yn_x}{Yn_1} \times \frac{Pn_x}{Pn_1} \times 100$$

In this equation n_1 refers to the base year and n_x to the year for which real tax burden is to be measured.

prices registers a sixfold increase. Under these circumstances, even if taxes triple, the real tax burden would actually decrease by 50 percent.

The formula developed above can be now applied to Ch'ing China. Taking 1750 as the base year, the real burden of the land tax in 1910 for the country as a whole and for a few provinces is illustrated in Table 6.2. Roughly speaking, China's cultivated acreage had increased by a half, her land yields by about 20 percent, and prices had tripled between 1750 and 1910. Therefore, her total income from land at current prices had by the latter date grown into a size that was 5.4 times as large as it had been in 1750. On the other hand, during the period the land tax actually collected less than doubled. We may thus conclude that at the end of the Ch'ing dynasty the real burden of the land tax for the agricultural sector of the country as a whole was merely a little more than a third of what it had been in the mid-eighteenth century when the dynasty was at its height.

Although the situation differed from one province to another, the fact that the land tax burden was lighter at the end than in the middle of the Ch'ing was present in all parts of the country. In most cases the increase in land tax yield could hardly keep step with price inflation. In Kiangsu the burden in 1910 was somewhat more than a half what it had been in 1750 owing not merely to the trailing of the rate of collection behind prices but in particular a sizable reduction in the grain quota after the Taiping Rebellion.[3] In Hunan, it was reduced to less than a quarter. This was because the province had achieved in the period a substantial rise in land acreage and land yield and at

Table 6.2. The real burden of the land tax in China, 1750–1910

Case (1)	Year (2)	L (3)	Y (4)	P (5)	I (6)	T (7)	B (8)
–	1750	100	100	100	100	100	100
Whole country	1910	150	120	300	540	189	35
Kiangsu	1910	100[a]	100[a]	300	300	168	56
Hunan	1910	150[a]	160[a]	300	720	160	22
Szechwan	1910	300[a]	160[b]	300	1,440	900	63

Sources: See Tables 1.1, 3.4, 4.1, 4.4, 5.1, and p. 97.

Notes:

[a]A rough estimate.

[b]Though the data on land yields in Szechwan are lacking, there is clear evidence indicating a 50–100% rise in land rent (rent deposit included) over the period. Hence we may assume roughly the same degree of rising land productivity in Szechwan as in Hunan.

For rising land rents, see, for example, *Kuan-hsien chih* (1786 preface), 4.68; *Chung-hsiu Kuan-hsien chih* (1886 preface), 6.20–21, 7.51–52.

the same time its tax quota remained practically unchanged and its rate of collection registered nearly the least increase among all provinces.[4] Even in Szechwan where the land tax multiplied ninefold during the period the real burden still decreased by more than a third.

To be sure, this analysis may not be applicable if China's population increase had far outstripped the combined gain of cultivated acreage and land productivity during the period. This was, however, hardly the case. Although China's population almost doubled in the course of one and a half centuries, her agricultural output rose by four-fifths during the same period because of the increase in land acreage and land yields.[5] In other words, her per capita output was nearly the same in 1910 as in 1750. Therefore we have good reason to maintain the conclusion drawn above.

Nevertheless, the conclusion should not be accepted uncritically. It does not mean that the tax burden was lessening all the time throughout the one and a half centuries under consideration. In fact, the tax was the most onerous in the middle of the nineteenth century and undoubtedly contributed in no small measure to the Taiping Rebellion. While it is outside the scope of this book to discuss the socio-economic background of the social uprising, a few remarks must be made with regard to the impact of the drastic fall in prices upon the land tax burden and the economy as a whole in mid-century.

The formula mentioned above has made clear the effect of price changes on the real burden of taxes. Other things being equal, the higher prices rise, the lighter the tax burden; the lower prices fall, the heavier the burden. Hence a 50 percent decline in the level of prices means a 100 percent increase in the tax burden (see case 4 in Table 6.1). Almost exactly the same situation occurred in China in the second quarter of the last century. In the three and a half decades before 1850, prices fell by a half, that is, an almost 100 percent appreciation in the value of silver.[6] In a word, China was in the depths of a deflation on the eve of the Taiping Rebellion when, as described by Pao Shih-ch'en (1775-1855), "The rice price has never been so cheap as it is now in the past several decades and the value of silver never so high in the past several centuries."[7] The severe deflation worked against the peasantry on two fronts: it compelled them to relinquish more of their crops in order to pay the same amount of taxes as before; at the same time it reduced sharply their incomes such as those from cash crops and off-season employment.

There is ample evidence indicating the hardship of an increased tax burden before the Taiping Rebellion. Tseng Kuo-fan (1811-72), the architect of victory over the Taiping rebels, submitted in 1851 a memorial on the worsening economic condition of the people because of falling prices. He said in the memorial that in the southeastern part of the country rice was sold in the earlier years at three taels per shih, but nowadays at merely one and a half taels. Hence, although the government did not raise the tax rate, the people paid in effect 100 percent more than they did before.[8] The same concern was expressed in the mid-century by Tseng's contemporaries. For example, P'eng Yün-chang (1792-1862), then the commissioner of education in Fukien, noted that although there was a continuing increase in the rate of collection of the land tax from the late years of the Ch'ien-lung period (1736-95) to the early Tao-kuang period (1821-50), the people's ability to pay had not been exhausted, as rice prices were rising at the same time. Yet, the 1840s saw a spectacular rise in the value of silver and a precipitous fall in the price of rice. As a consequence, many people were unable to pay their land tax and the government fell into grave financial straits.[9] Another official, Miu Tzu (1807-60), memorialized in 1849 that the appreciation of silver and the cheapness of rice had made land taxation in the late forties twice as heavy as in the early Tao-kuang period, and three times as heavy as in the Ch'ien-lung and Chia-ch'ing (1796-1820) periods.[10]

A more serious effect of deflation upon the populace was a conspicuous contraction of business activities and the concomitant decrease in employment and income. Take southern Kiangsu, the richest part of the country, as an example. By mid-century, it was said, "All great and wealthy merchants have gone bankrupt and business of all kinds decreased by 50 to 60 percent."[11] As peasants had to sell their surplus produce or handicraft products in order to pay taxes and in exchange for other necessities, the depression in the commercial sector thus spread to the countryside. Driven by a shrinking income and a heavier tax burden, they increasingly broke out into violence. Therefore, peasant riots against land taxation occurred in the 1840s one after another in Hunan, Hupei, Fukien, Chekiang, Kiangsi, and so on.[12] In view of this explosive situation, it is no wonder that the Taiping Rebellion should have developed into such a catastrophic social upheaval.

Tax Increase and Inflation in the Late Ch'ing: Some Specific Cases

To find out whether the real burden of a tax increased over a period of time we may also apply the formula developed in the preceding section to a number of specific cases such as the income and taxes of a family, a village, or a district. I have presented below five cases for examination. Short of data on changes in cultivated acreage and land yield, however, close observation of merely two variables—land tax yields and prices—can be made. Nonetheless, even such a partial comparison can clarify the state of land tax burden in the late Ch'ing.

Of the five cases two are geographically confined to the Soochow-Shanghai area where the tax quota per mou was the highest in the country; the rest are scattered in provinces outside Kiangsu. The most comprehensive land tax data for a series of several decades I have ever found are those of Ch'uan-sha t'ing, a small district close to Shanghai. The data dating from 1879 through the very end of the dynasty are rendered in Table 6.3, including rates of collection, amounts collected from the *ti-ting* tax and the grain tax (regular surcharges such as those for office expenses and the Boxer indemnity included), amounts collected from surcharges temporarily imposed for famine relief, construction of water control works, and so on, and total amount collected each year. However, all these are stated in cash instead of silver; for, as we shall soon see, after the Taiping Rebellion the provincial authorities fixed the rate of collection in cash. In order to compare tax increase with the movement of prices (in silver) the amounts of tax originally stated in cash will have to be converted into silver.

Fortunately, a long series of the exchange rate between silver and cash for the city of Ningpo (based on the daily transaction accounts of a store in the city) are preserved in a local gazetteer. As Ningpo has long been an important commercial port on the edge of the Yangtze delta and is separated from Ch'uan-sha merely by the Hangchow Bay, it is safe to say that the silver-cash ratios were very close between the two places. On this assumption we can solve the problem of conversion just mentioned.

A final task is to transform the converted data into index numbers and render them in a chart together with the index number of prices at hand. Figure 6.1 is the end product of this statistical process. Let us leave aside for the moment the *ti-ting* rate and grain rate series and compare the two essential ones—taxes and prices. These two lines illustrate clearly an upward trend of both variables from the mid-eighties through the end of the dynasty. This trend can be divided into two distinct phases. First, during the two decades between the mid-eighties, and the middle of the 1900s the increase in taxes was, with few exceptions, trailing further and further behind the movement of prices. Taking 1879 as the base year, by 1886 both the Nankai index number of prices and the index number of taxes collected remained around the 100 level, but thereafter the former rose to 150 in 1894 and further to 224 in 1905, while the latter merely increased to 112 and 154 respectively. In other words, in spite of a gradually rising monetary burden on the taxpayers, their real burden was actually lessening. Second, in the last half decade of the dynasty taxes swung up much faster than did prices, so that the taxpayers began to feel the pinch of the tax increase as the dynasty came to an end. However the last point deserves further consideration.

In converting the amounts of tax collected in cash into silver we have assumed all along that besides silver the traditional copper cash was the only means of tax payment. As a matter of fact, a new-style, yet debased, money, the 10-cash coin, made its appearance in 1900 and henceforth spread rapidly.

A 10-cash coin which was worth nominally ten copper cash could by no means be exchanged for that much in the market. As shown in column 2 of Table 6.3, there appeared from 1906 onwards in Ningpo two quoting systems in the exchange market: one in terms of the traditional copper cash and the other in terms of the 10-cash coin; by 1910 the copper cash had been virtually driven out of circulation by the 10-cash coin so that the exchange quotations in terms of copper cash were discontinued. People would pay their taxes in the 10-cash coin but local officials would insist on accepting only copper cash or its equivalent in silver. This chaotic situation gave rise to constant conflicts between the taxpayers and tax collectors. Consequently, the provincial authorities in Kiangsu struck a compromise by allowing people to pay 30 percent of their taxes in 10-cash coins.[13] If this ruling was adhered to, the amounts of tax in silver for the last few years of the dynasty, which are calculated on the assumption that all taxes were paid in copper cash or its equivalent in silver, have to be adjusted downward. The adjusted amounts are in parentheses in column 13 of Table 6.3 and are represented by a thin broken line in Figure 6.1. Such being the case, it might be said that because of inflation landowners in Ch'uan-sha were still better off in the late 1900s than in the early 1880s even though their gains in this regard had been greatly reduced in the last several years of the Ch'ing period.

Before we go on to examine the next case, however, a significant question must be raised and answered. That is, why did land tax yields in this small district increase more slowly than prices for the greater part of the period and then suddenly outrun the latter in the several years before the fall of the Manchu regime? An anatomy of the present case will not only make it easier for us to comprehend other cases but in particular will have an important bearing upon the whole issue of the land tax burden.

The data in Table 6.3 indicate that of the two major components of the land tax—the *ti-ting* and the grain tax—the grain tax was from the beginning quantitatively more important and became even more so in the course of rising prices. During the three decades between 1879 and 1909, for instance, the *ti-ting* tax collected in cash increased merely by 10 percent whereas the grain tax more than doubled. Accordingly, the former component which yielded about three-quarters as much as the latter in 1879 could produce only a third in 1909. In other words, it was primarily the increase in the grain tax that caused the land tax yield to rise in the district.

Then, why was the grain tax yield able to keep pace with price inflation while the *ti-ting* yield lagged far behind? The answer lies in the different measures by which the rate of collection for these two components of the tax was determined. As pointed out in Chapter 2, after the Taiping Rebellion the power of determining the rate was removed from local officials to the provincial authorities in Kiangsu. The latter then established new regulations

Table 6.3. The rise in land tax yield and prices in Ch'uan-sha t'ing, Kiangsu, 1879–1911 (index number 1879 = 100)

Year (1)	Silver-cash ratio in Ningpo[a] (number of cash per tael) (2)	Ti-ting				Grain			
		Rate of collection per tael				Rate of collection per shih			
		Cash (3)	Silver tael (4)	Index number (in silver) (5)	Amount collected cash (6)	Cash (7)	Silver tael (8)	Index number (in silver) (9)	Amount collected cash (10)
1879	1,585	2,200	1.39	100	21,729,844	3,452	2.18	100	29,043,4
1880	1,613	2,200	1.36	98	21,569,185	3,152	1.95	89	26,886,6
1881	1,604	2,200	1.33	96	21,729,844	3,252	2.03	93	27,727,1
1882	1,607	2,200	1.37	98	21,569,185	3,452	2.13	98	29,445,6
1883	1,609	2,200	1.37	98	21,569,185	3,352	2.06	95	28,592,6
1884	1,620	2,200	1.36	98	21,729,844	3,252	2.01	92	27,727,1
1885	1,602	2,200	1.37	98	21,569,185	3,452	2.15	99	29,445,6
1886	1,603	2,200	1.37	98	21,569,185	3,652	2.28	105	31,151,6
1887	1,511	2,200	1.46	105	21,729,844	3,352	2.22	103	28,580,3
1888	1,514	2,200	1.45	104	21,569,185	3,352	2.21	101	28,592,6
1889	1,520	2,200	1.45	104	21,569,185	3,352	2.20	101	28,592,6
1890	1,530	2,200	1.44	104	21,729,844	3,452	2.26	104	29,431,1
1891	1,532	2,200	1.44	104	21,569,185	3,452	2.25	103	29,445,6
1892	1,529	2,200	1.44	104	21,729,844	3,552	2.32	106	30,285,0
1893	1,536	2,200	1.43	103	21,569,185	3,552	2.31	106	30,298,6
1894	1,528	2,200	1.44	104	21,569,185	3,952	2.59	119	33,710,6
1895	1,524	2,200	1.44	104	21,729,844	3,952	2.59	119	33,695,4
1896	1,338	2,000	1.49	107	19,608,350	3,752	2.80	128	32,004,6
1897	1,271	2,000	1.57	113	19,608,350	3,952	3.11	143	33,710,6
1898	1,305	2,000	1.53	110	19,754,396	4,252	3.26	150	36,253,3
1899	1,321	2,000	1.51	109	19,608,350	4,252	3.22	148	36,269,0
1900	1,306	2,000	1.53	110	19,754,396	3,852	2.95	135	32,842,8
1901	1,288	2,000	1.55	112	19,608,350	4,352	3.38	155	37,122,6
1902	1,305	2,200	1.69	122	21,569,185	4,952	3.79	174	42,240,6
1903	1,197	2,200	1.84	132	21,729,844	4,952	4.14	190	42,221,6
1904	1,211	2,200	1.82	131	21,569,185	4,652	3.84	176	39,681,6
1905	1,245	2,200	1.77	127	21,569,185	4,452	3.58	164	37,975,6
1906	1,354 (1,512)	2,400	1.77	127	23,705,275	5,552	3.67	188	47,337,3
1907	1,366 (1,484)	2,400	1.76	127	23,530,020	6,252	4.21	210	53,329,7
1908	1,271 (1,638)	2,400	1.89	136	23,530,020	6,752	5.31	244	57,594,7
1909	1,295 (1,666)	2,400	1.85	133	23,705,275	7,552	5.83	267	64,389,7
1910	(1,792)	2,400	?	?	23,530,020	7,552	?	?	64,419,7
1911	(1,792)	2,400	?	?	11,852,638	–	–	–	42,630,9

Sources:
Ch'uan-sha-hsien chih (1937), 8.26–27.
Yin-hsien tung-chih (1935), "*Shih-huo chih*," pp. 219b–229b.
Nankai Institute of Economics, *Nankai Weekly Statistical Service*, 5.15 (April 11, 1932), 70.

Notes:
[a]The ratios are originally stated in terms of silver dollar. I have converted them into those in terms of tael according to the rate of 1.4 dollars to a tael. Figures in parenthesis are however ratios in terms of 10-cash coins to a tael.

[b]The figures in parentheses are calculated on the assumption that 30 percent of taxes was paid in 10-cash coins, 70 percent in the traditional cash.

[c]The amount in silver dollars.

| Temporary surcharges cash (11) | Total amount collected | | | Nankai index number of prices (15) |
	Cash (12)	Silver[b] tael (13)	Index number[b] (14)	
1,258,032	52,031,349	32,827	100	100
2,516,064	50,971,933	31,601	96	104
1,258,032	50,715,031	31,618	96	104
–	51,014,839	31,745	97	96
1,048,360	51,210,197	31,827	97	96
1,048,360	50,505,359	31,176	95	91
1,048,360	52,063,199	32,499	99	94
524,180	53,245,025	33,216	101	102
–	50,310,218	33,296	101	124
–	50,161,837	33,132	101	125
–	50,161,837	33,001	100	128
–	51,162,037	33,439	102	120
–	51,014,839	33,300	101	119
4,403,112	56,417,967	36,899	112	119
1,048,360	52,916,202	34,451	105	125
1,048,360	56,328,213	36,864	112	150
–	55,425,329	36,368	111	156
1,048,360	52,661,373	39,358	120	162
–	53,319,018	41,950	128	180
–	56,007,737	42,918	131	175
–	55,877,427	42,299	129	189
–	52,597,263	40,274	123	192
–	56,731,031	44,046	134	190
–	63,809,881	48,896	149	208
–	63,951,515	53,426	163	232
1,048,360	62,299,232	51,444	157	235
3,354,752	62,899,618	50,522	154	224
1,600,000	72,642,657	53,650 (51,968)	163 (158)	217
5,848,360	82,708,151	60,548 (59,103)	184 (180)	235
14,378,387	95,503,152	75,140 (70,089)	229 (214)	248
15,887,539	103,982,568	80,295 (74,931)	245 (228)	242
15,887,539	103,837,326	?	?	253
3,574,440	15,428,078 42,630.928[c]	?	?	252

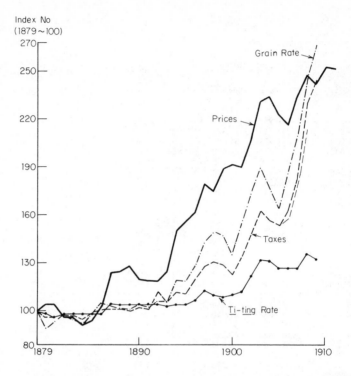

Figure 6.1. The rise in land tax yields and prices in Ch'uan-sha ting, Kiangsu, 1879–1911

for the administration of the land tax. For the area under the jurisdiction of the Soochow financial commissioner the regulation on the determination of the rate contained two essential points. First, the rate of collection for both the *ti-ting* and grain quotas was to be set in terms of cash, that is, how many cash per tael of the *ti-ting* quota or per shih of the grain quota.[14] Second, each year the rate for the *ti-ting* quota was to be decided with reference to the exchange rate between silver and cash and the rate for the grain quota to the price of unpolished rice current in the market (in both cases a fixed amount of regular surcharge was to be added).[15] Therefore, the increase of the *ti-ting* tax depended primarily upon the market exchange rate between silver and cash while the increase of grain tax depended on the market price of rice.

Over the three decades under consideration the *ti-ting* rate of collection, as shown in column 3 of Table 6.3, remained rather stable. Because of the appreciation in value of copper relative to silver, it was even reduced from 2,200 cash per tael of the quota to 2,000 cash in the last half decade of the

1890s. In the following decade the rate was raised twice: first from 2,000 to 2,200 cash in 1902 for paying the Boxer indemnity and then from 2,200 to 2,400 cash in 1906 in accordance with rising silver-cash ratio (actually silver-copper coin ratio) in the market. Still, the rate increase had been a modest one as compared with price inflation; the index number of the rate rose merely a third whereas that of prices by one and a half times over the entire period. Therefore, the gap between prices and the rate became greater as the level of prices surged upwards. It follows as a matter of course that a smaller proportion of the taxpayers' income was needed to pay off their *ti-ting* tax.

The grain tax was of a different nature. Being linked with the market prices of rice, its rate of collection had been increased first moderately and later rapidly from 3,452 cash per shih in 1879 to 7,552 cash in 1909-10, or from 100 to around 250 in terms of index number; it was therefore able to keep pace more or less with prices. This means that, as far as the grain tax is concerned, under normal circumstances inflation worked to the advantage of neither party—taxpayers or the government. The real burden upon the taxpayers would depend upon the composition of the land tax. The greater the proportion of the *ti-ting* component, the greater the decrease of the real tax burden in times of inflation; whereas the greater the proportion of the grain component, the less the decrease. Since the grain tax was the leading component in Ch'uan-sha, it was able to pull the land tax yield upwards to a substantial extent as prices rose.

How do we account, then, for the more rapid increase in taxes over that in prices in the closing days of the dynasty? This can be explained by two factors. First and foremost was a drastic increase in temporary surcharges in these years. As indicated in column 11 of Table 6.3, before 1907 the amount of temporary surcharges, if any, rarely exceeded two million cash as compared with an annual yield of 50-70 million cash from the *ti-ting* tax and the grain tax (including tax quota and regular surcharges) combined. These surcharges were therefore quantitatively insignificant. In 1907, however, they added up to 5.8 million cash. The next three years witnessed an even more dramatic increase—more than 14 million in 1908 and nearly 16 million in 1909 and 1910—because of the simultaneous imposition of several temporary surcharges: one for famine relief, one for water control works, one for the establishment of modern schools, and one for the preparation for self-govern-ment.[16] These surcharges inevitably pushed up substantially the total amount of tax collection.

The second factor was the extra collection of the grain tax caused by the depreciation of 10-cash coins. That is to say, while the provincial authorities adjusted upwards the grain rate of collection in the latter part of the 1900s apparently in accordance with the market price of rice in terms of the debased 10-cash coins, local officials accepted the traditional copper cash only for 30 percent of the tax in 10-cash coins at the most.[17] As a consequence, people were actually paying the grain tax in those few years at rates (even surcharges excluded) higher than the market prices.

The second case is taken from Professor Muramatsu Yūji's detailed study of a landlord bursary in Soochow. In the late Ch'ing the land rent in Soochow was still stated in terms of grain (for example, one shih of rice per mou) in the lease, but the bursary collected it in cash according to the rice price in the local market. Hence the price at which the rent in kind was commuted could serve as a reliable indicator of current grain prices. On the other hand, taxes paid by the bursary were also recorded in cash. It is therefore quite appropriate to compare the two sets of data—commutation prices and taxes—simply on the cash basis.

Contained in Table 6.4 are the said data about some fifty-five mou of land (later increased to fifty-eight mou) owned by Chi-hao and managed by the Wu-clan bursary in Soochow. Even though the data cover only thirteen years before 1911, they are highly revealing. When converted into index numbers, taxes and rice prices in Soochow appear to move very closely in the same direction except for the last few years. However, after a close look we shall find that taxes changed generally at a slower pace than did the rice price.[18]

Table 6.4. The rise in land tax payment and rice prices in Soochow: the case of Chi-hao's land under the management of the Wu-clan bursary, 1893–1910 (index number: 1900 = 100)

	Commutation price		Average tax paid	
Year (1)	Cash per shih (2)	Index number (3)	Cash per mou (4)	Index number (5)
1893	2,202	87	517	84
1899	2,900	115	641	105
1900	2,523	100	612	100
1901	3,051	121	620	101
1902	3,302	131	753	123
1903	3,424	136	810	132
1904	3,075	122	753	123
1905	2,869	114	732	120
1906	3,792	150	800	131
1907	4,351	172	1,028	168
1908	6,015	238	1,008	165
1909	5,922	235	1,079	176
1910	5,562	220	1,202	196

Source: See Muramatsu Yūji, "Shin-matsu Min-sho no Kōnan ni okeru hōran kankei no jittai to sono kessan-hōkoku—Soshū Go-shi Yoeki-san 'Hōshō kakugō bisa' satsu no kenkyū," Kindai Kōnan no sosan, pp. 679–747.

Hence this sample confirms our earlier observation that rising prices benefited but falling prices hurt taxpayers. As the level of prices was apparently on the rise during the last quarter of the dynasty, so their unearned benefit was growing. In this particular case, for example, ignoring the temporary aberrations, there is a growing gap between taxes and prices. Taking 1900 as the base year, the index number of the rice price was 10 percentage points above that of taxes in 1899 but nearly 24 percentage points above that in 1910.

Again, there are two questions in this case that should not be left unanswered. First, why is a favorable trend to the taxpayers not as clearly shown in Table 6.4 as in Table 6.3 or Figure 6.1? Second, why is the gap between taxes and the rice price in Table 6.4 wider instead of narrower in the last few years than before? For the inconspicuousness of the trend in Table 6.4 two reasons can be given. Obviously, the two series (taxes and price) in this case are too short to present a secular trend in perspective; for short-term aberrations are likely to obscure the long-term development. Another reason lies in the difference in the composition of land tax quota between Soochow and Ch'uan-sha. Although, these two places had the same rate of collection in the late Ch'ing,[19] the grain quota weighed more heavily on the land in the Su-chou Prefecture (in which Soochow was the capital city) than in Ch'uan-sha.[20] In fact, the grain tax quota of the prefecture was the heaviest in the country. And, as I have explained above, the greater the proportion of the grain component in the land tax structure, the more sensitively would the tax yield respond to price changes. Such being the case, the tax yield would naturally follow the course of prices more closely in Soochow than elsewhere.

As to the second question I am unable to answer it on sure ground. Several reasons may be suggested here, however. One is the extraordinary rise of the rice price in Soochow in 1908 that left taxes far behind (see Table 6.4). Another is that, being a member of the prominent gentry in the provincial capital, the owner of the bursary might ignore a number of temporary surcharges required of the taxpayers. A more probable reason could be that the bursary simply paid all the taxes in the debased 10-cash coins instead of copper cash.

So much can be said about the two cases in the Soochow-Shanghai area, the richest part of the country. We may thus conclude that, as far as this particular area is concerned, the real burden of the land tax was declining in the last two decades of the nineteenth century. Taxpayers maintained the advantage more or less unchanged or probably still gained some ground at the expense of the government exchequer in the early part of the 1900s, but their favorable position was rapidly eroded in the last few years of the dynasty. Nonetheless, they probably still felt somewhat better off on the eve of the 1911 revolution than a quarter-century before, and certainly much better off than before the Taiping Rebellion.[21]

Still, in pursuing the research on the land tax burden issue we cannot stop here because what was true in one corner of the country was not necessarily true in other areas. In other words, it is of crucial importance to find out whether the case of the Soochow-Shanghai area was typical in the country. Although the data on the following three cases are not as comprehensive as those on the preceding cases, they are just as invaluable in illustrating the state of land tax burden in the last several decades of the dynasty. The first two cases—the *ti-ting* rate of collection in T'ang-ch'i hsien, Chekiang, and the rate of collection for both *ti-ting* and grain quotas in Nan-ch'ang hsien, Kiangsi—show a 20-30 percent increase in the *ti-ting* rate of collection in the three or four decades before 1910, a magnitude quite comparable to the increase in Ch'uan-sha. Moreover, in all these three cases the rate, when surcharges for collection expenses were added, would be around two taels per tael of quota, a rate indeed typical in most part of the country (see Table 5.6). Accordingly, it can be said that, excpet in Szechwan and Manchuria, in the course of these few decades the increase of the *ti-ting* tax was, as indicated in Tables 6.5 and 6.6, lagging further and further behind that of prices almost everywhere in the country.

The case of Nan-ch'ang portrays, however, a picture of the increase in the grain rate different from that in Ch'uan-sha; for the grain rate in Nan-ch'ang, much like the *ti-ting* rate, moved up merely 37 percent against an almost 100 percent rise in prices. This was because the two provincial authorities adjusted the rates on different bases. As pointed out before, the grain rate in the Soochow-Shanghai area was adjusted roughly according to the current grain

Table 6.5. The *ti-ting* rate of collection in T'ang-ch'i hsien, Chekiang, 1862–1911 (index number: 1878 = 100)

Year (1)	The Ningpo series of silver-cash ratio number of cash per tael (2)	Rate of collection for each tael of quota			Nankai index number of prices (6)
		Cash (3)	Silver (tael) (4)	Index (5)	
1862	1,539	2,750	1.8	120	?
1864	1,399	2,550	1.8	120	?
1865	1,339	2,050	1.5	100	?
1878	1,541	2,250	1.5	100	100
1897	1,271	2,110	1.7	113	182
1902	1,305	2,410	1.8	120	210
1909	1,295	2,510–2,530	1.9	127	245
1911	?	2,610–2,630	?	?	255

Sources:
   1. *T'ang-ch'i-hsien chih* (1931), 5.11.
   2. *Yin-hsien tung-chih* (1935), "*Shih-huo chih*," pp. 219b–229b.
   3. For Nankai index number of prices, see source 3 in Table 6.3.

Table 6.6. The rate of collection for the *ti-ting* and grain quotas in Nan-ch'ang hsien, Kiangsi, 1861–1908 (index number: 1873 = 100)

Year (1)	Rate of collection for each tael of the *ti-ting* quota			Rate of collection for each shih of the grain quota			Nankai index number of prices (8)
	Cash (2)	Silver (3)	Index (4)	Cash (5)	Silver (6)	Index (7)	
1862	–	1.5	100	–	1.9	100	?
1868	–	1.5	100	3,000	1.9	100	103
1873	2,682	1.5	100	3,420	1.9	100	100
1897	2,582	1.9[a]	127	3,280	2.4[a]	126	144
1901	2,782[b]	2.0[a]	133	3,580[b]	2.5[a]	132	152
1908	–	1.8	120	–	2.6	137	198

Sources:
  1. *Nan-ch'ang-hsien chih* (1919), 10.22b–24.
  2. *Cheng-chih kuan-pao*, 3.333–339.
  3. For Nankai index number of prices, see source 3 in Table 6.3.

Notes:
  [a]Converted from the rate in cash according to current silver-cash ratio: 1,354 cash per tael (1897), and 1,419 cash (1901), see Lo Yü-tung, *Chung-kuo li-chin shih*, p. 541.
  [b]200 cash per tael and 300 cash per shih added as surcharge for the Boxer indemnity.

prices in the market. But changes in the grain rate in Kiangsi had nothing to do with market grain prices whatsoever. In 1862 the provincial authorities fixed the rate at 1.9 taels per shih and subsequently substituted it with a cash rate equivalent to the same amount of silver. They adjusted the cash rate more or less according to the silver-cash ratio in the market. For example, when silver appreciated in value in 1873, they raised the rate (in cash). When the value of cash increased in 1897, they reduced the rate. For a half-century after 1862 the only adjustments made not in connection with changes in the silver-cash ratio were the levying in 1901 of a surcharge at 300 cash per shih for the payment of the Boxer indemnity and the imposition of another surcharge for the preparation of self-government in the last year of the Manchu regime.[22] As a result, the landowners in this province gained in the course of inflation double advantage with respect to their tax payment.[23] That is to say, both the *ti-ting* tax and the grain tax became less burdensom upon them in the late Ch'ing. The same can be said of the taxpayers in other provinces where the grain rate was also unresponsive to price changes, for example, Chekiang, Anhwei, Kwangtung, Hupei, and the area of Kiangsu under the jursidiction of the Kiangning financial commissioner.[24]

At this juncture it is of significance to bring out another point already discussed. That the land tax yields in the Shanghai-Soochow area were able to keep up with prices in the last decade of the Ch'ing period resulted not simply from annual adjustment of the grain rate of collection in response to market conditions but also from a lopsided tax structure in which the grain tax occupied a predominant position. Of the total grain quota in the country,

Kiangsu's share amounted to nearly a quarter, and of the latter, four-fifths fell in the Shanghai-Soochow area (that is, the area under the jurisdiction of the Soochow financial commissioner).[25] The financial importance of the grain tax in the area was such that it yielded approximately 70 percent of the land tax in 1908.[26] Except Sinkiang where all land tax consisted of grain, in no other provinces in the country had such a high proportion of the land tax been yielded by the grain component. In fact, four out of five provinces in the country collected the bulk of their tax revenue from the *ti-ting* tax instead of the grain tax (see Table 5.6). Therefore, even in those provinces where tax officials raised the grain rate of collection in parallel to rising prices, as did their counterparts in the Soochow-Shanghai area, they could by no means completely or even substantially offset the cumulative gain the taxpayers derived from the lessening burden of the *ti-ting* tax over decades.

The last case we are going to examine is the land tax burden per mou in Ting-chou of Chihli province. The district had no grain quota and hence all land tax consisted of the *ti-ting* tax. That the tax did not increase at all for a quarter-century from 1874 to 1899 seems doubtful. But it is obvious that for three decades from 1875 to 1906 the landowners' burden decreased a great deal owing to rising prices; only in the last few years of the dynasty did the tax increase outrun prices in this particular district of the metropolitan province (see Table 6.7). All in all, in no case do we see an increasing burden

Table 6.7. The land tax burden in Ting-chou, Chihli, 1874–1911 (index number: 1875 = 100)

Year (1)	Land tax burden (silver dollar per mou) (2)	Index number of tax burden (3)	Nankai index number of prices (4)
1874	0.05339	100	111
1875	0.05339	100	100
1880	0.05339	100	105
1899	0.05339	100	191
1900	0.05768	108	194
1901	0.05725	107	192
1902	0.05775	108	210
1903	0.05762	108	234
1904	0.05766	108	237
1905	0.05785	108	226
1906	0.05750	108	219
1907	0.08202	154	237
1908	0.07935	149	250
1909	0.07793	146	245
1910	0.07833	147	256
1911	0.07814	146	255

Sources:
1. Feng Hua-te and Li Ling, "Ho-pei sheng Ting hsien chih t'ien-fu," *Cheng-chih ching-chi hsüeh-pao*, 4.3 (April 1936), pp. 443–520.
2. For Nankai index number of prices, see source 3 in Table 6.3.

Table 6.8. The land tax as percentage of land yield or land value in the late Ch'ing

Province (1)	District (2)	Approximate date (3)	Area or quality of the land (4)	Land tax[a] per mou (5)	Gross value of land yield per mou (6)	Land value per mou (7)	(5) As percentage of (6) (8)	(5) As percentage of (7) (9)
Chihli	–	1883	in general	$0.1+	$3	–	3.3	–
	Ting chou	1894–1911	whole district	$0.05–0.08	–	$17–24	–	0.25–0.37
	Wu-ch'ing hsien	1888	medium grade	Tl 0.01	Tl 1.5	Tl 5	0.7	0.20
Shantung	Lai-chou fu	1888	medium grade	Tl 0.1+	Tl 3.4	Tl 40	3.0	0.25
	I-tu hsien	1888	growing grain	$0.39	$11–12	–	3.4	–
	Lin-ch'ü hsien, Lin-tzu hsien	1888	growing tabacco	$0.39	$60	–	0.7	–
	Ar. Chefoo	1907	40 mou	Ca 150	Ca 6,150	–	2.4	–
Shansi	P'ing-yang fu	1888	in general	Ca 300	Ca 6,000	–	5.0	–
Fengtien	–	1908	34,029 mou	$0.14	$3.7	–	3.8	–
Kiangsu	Ar. Shanghai	1907	medium grade	$1.0–1.5	$12–20	$50–60	7.5–8.0	2.50
	Ar. Soochow	1893–1910	55–58 mou	Ca 816 (Av.)	Ca 8,151[b]	–	10.0 (Av.)	–
	Ar. Soochow	a.1906	medium grade	$0.9	–	$20+ (?)	–	a.4.00 (?)
Fukien	Ar. Foochow	1907	medium grade	$1.0	–	$80	–	1.25
Kwangtung	Ar. Swatow	1888	average	$0.25	$15	–	1.7	–
	Hai-yang hsien	1907	medium grade	$0.70	–	$115 (Av.)	–	0.60
Kiangsi	–	1888	high grade	$0.25	$12	–	2.1	–
Hunan	Ar. Changsha	1906	high grade	Tl 0.2	–	Tl 100	–	0.20
Hupei	Kuang-chi hsien	1888	medium grade	Ca 300	Ca 8,520[c]	–	3.5	–

Sources:

1. CKCTNYS, pp. 633–636, 639, 644–651, 667.
2. Gaimushō Tsūshōkyoku, Shinkoku jijō (Tokyo, 1907), I, 332–333, 581, 584, 667; II, 42, 321–322, 485–487, 643–644.
3. Feng-t'ien sheng nung-yeh shih-yen-ch'ang, Feng-t'ien ch'üan-sheng nung-yeh t'iao-ch'a-shu, 1.4 (February 1909).
4. Feng Hua-te and Li Ling, "Ho-pei sheng Ting hsien . . . ," p. 492; Muramatsu Yūji, "Shin-matsu Min-sho no Kōnan . . . ," pp. 43, 51,

Notes:

[a] $ stands for silver dollar, Tl for tael, and Ca for cash.

[b] Estimate based on the assumption that land rent amounted to one third of the land produce which generally amounted to three shih of rice including secondary crops in the Yangtze delta. See CSWP, 36.23, 38.3b.

[c] My estimate based on the land yield in the ordinary year and on the prevailing prices of the land products.

of the tax upon the people in the late Ch'ing, and all cases indicate a secular trend of lessening burden except in some areas in the last few years of the dynasty.

Finally, to view the issue of the land tax burden in its true light let us make an inquiry about the weight of the tax against income from land. At the present stage a comprehensive study is impossible because of the dearth of data, but some relevant evidence does exist. In 1888 a number of Westerners in China, most of them Christian missionaries, made a survey of land tenure and the peasants' economic conditions in various provinces. In 1906-07 the Japanese consulates in the treaty ports undertook a broader economic survey of China. The reports of both surveys contain some information on taxation. In addition, there are some data gathered by Chinese. Without doubt, among these data some are apparently unreliable, and some are too ambiguous to be quantified. The figures presented in Table 6.8 are derived from those data whose reliability is either self-evident or least doubtful.

Examining this table we shall find that in the last quarter-century of the Ch'ing the land tax fell within the range between 2 and 4 percent of the land produce in most districts and provinces. Only in the Soochow-Shanghai area did it amount to 8-10 percent. And it was less than 1 percent of the land value in all but the suburban areas around the few treaty ports in the south.[27] Yet, in the late 1920s of the Republican period the average burden of direct taxes upon the peasants accounted for, according to John L. Buck's survey, approximately 5 percent of their income.[28] In Meiji Japan, moreover, the land tax was estimated to be around 10 percent of the land produce.[29] By comparison, therefore, one can hardly say that the real burden of the land tax was oppressive in late Ch'ing China.

7 Towards a Reconstruction of the Land Tax Administration in the Late Ch'ing

In this book I have attempted to make an overall reconstruction of China's land taxation in the late Ch'ing. Towards this objective I proposed in the beginning five major aspects for examination: the administration of the land tax; the essential factors contributing to the increase of the tax; its fiscal importance as a source of public revenue; its geographical structure; and its real burden upon the people in the agricultural sector. Each of them has been dealt with in a separate chapter above. What remains to be done is to piece together the findings from institutional analysis into a whole structure. Moreover, on the basis of the known data, some remarks may be made on the overall tax burden (not just the land tax burden) before the downfall of the Manchu dynasty.

In the late nineteenth and the early twentieth century China's fiscal administration and especially the land tax administration on the local level were characteristically dualistic in the sense that there existed side by side two systems, or two sets of rules or procedures, for the management of public economy: one being statutory or formal and the other nonstatutory or informal. The demarcation between the statutory system and the non-statutory system was clear-cut; anything called into being by imperial statutes and regulations or done in accordance with them was statutory and vice versa. Hence the magistrate, his subordinate officers, and regular clerks and runners were the statutory staff in the district yamen, while secretaries and extra clerks and runners were the nonstatutory staff. With regard to revenue and expenditure, while tax quotas were without doubt the statutory revenues, all kinds of surcharge (except *hao-hsien* which had long been incorporated in the imperial statutes) belonged to the nonstatutory category. Accordingly, in the respect of the land tax assessment, what was required in the formal system was a decennial assessment of the tax quota on the occasion of the revision of *Fu-i ch'üan-shu*, but the assessment of the rate of collection, which constituted a vital part of the tax administration, had no place in the statutes whatsoever.

The informal system came into being because the rigid statutes simply could not meet the needs of public administration in an everchanging society. Hence it included a large body of practices and procedures tailored to financial and administrative necessities as they occurred. Viewed from the standpoint of legality, these practices and procedures may be divided into three groups: legal, conventional, and illegal. Included in the legal category were those which owed their existence to the explicit approval of the imperial or provincial authorities. They were not included in the imperial statutes primarily because the court at Peking considered them temporary arrangements to be removed as soon as conditions permitted. The surcharges for the Boxer indemnity, for the construction of railroads, and for the establishment of modern schools are the most obvious examples.

Yet, most nonstatutory activities fell within the conventional category. They were established by customs and precedents which were, in the minds of high authorities and the public alike, not inappropriate and hence were allowed to exist without objection. For instance, the collection of surcharges for defraying administrative costs and for constructing irrigation works in the locality, the determination of the rate of collection by the magistrate in consultation with local gentry, and the establishment of the country chest for facilitating tax payment of those living in the countryside are all of this kind. Even sending seasonal and birthday gifts to superiors were then treated by the magistrate as regular and routine expenses required of the local government; most magistrates would roughly follow the precedents of their predecessors as to how much was to be presented to which superior official. This custom was certainly not an ideal arrangement for maintaining a huge bureaucracy, but it was a way of life in traditional China. As long as officials did not go to excess, it was generally accepted as a matter of course. As a matter of fact, in the absence of explicit administrative regulations social conventions played a very significant role in keeping official abuses and corruption within reasonable limits.

The practices in the illegal category were those clearly against the intent of superior authorities. For example, tax farming and raising the rate of collection without consultation with local gentry or the approval of higher authorities were repeatedly prohibited by the government. However, even in this category certain activities such as tax farming were not necessarily abusive in nature and, as pointed out before, by no means always worked to the disadvantage of the taxpayers. Rather, they were often the outcome of adaptation to local conditions and to the magistrate's administrative ability. Therefore, while illegal increase of the rate of collection would likely result in heavy punishment, no higher authorities ever took any disciplinary action against local officials involved in tax farming.

On the whole, it can be said that the land tax administration was far less chaotic than it appears to be. Judging from a strictly legal point of view, many would undoubtedly deplore the situation because a great part of official activities were out of formal control. But many nonlegal practices and activities were just as vital to the maintenance of public interests as legal ones and were regulated reasonably well by social conventions. Only by seeing things in this light will we be able to understand the true nature of Ch'ing fiscal administration in general and of its land tax administration in particular (see Table 7.1).

In retrospect, the greatest defect of the Ch'ing land tax administration was rather its inability to capture increased income as the economy grew. Moreover, its decentralized nature deprived the imperial government of a controlling hand over the management of the country's largest source of public revenue. Consequently, the land tax in China played a diminishing part in government financing in the late Ch'ing just as the public expenditure was greatly expanding and thereby the need for additional revenue enormously increasing. Should the land tax, like its counterpart in Meiji Japan, have played the crucial role in the fiscal system of late Ch'ing, not only the financial condition then but also the political development of modern China might have been decisively different.[1]

Let us now turn to the tax burden issue. That the real burden of the land tax was lighter at the end than in the middle of the Ch'ing does not necessarily mean that the same can be said of the overall burden of taxes. A great deal of research should be done on the size and distribution of income and on the incidence of taxes before we can come up with a definite answer. At the present stage, nevertheless, a few remarks may be made and a tentative conclusion drawn in this regard. On the one hand, during the period between 1753 and 1908 indirect taxes rose much faster than the land tax, for the land tax yield hardly doubled whereas the yield of all other taxes combined multiplied nearly tenfold. As a result, the total tax revenue quadrupled (see Table 4.8). On the other hand, this study shows that the ability-to-pay at current prices of the agricultural sector grew more than five times during the same period (see Table 6.2). Supposing that the ability-to-pay of the non-agricultural sector increased as much as that of the agricultural sector, the overall tax burden would still be somewhat less in the 1900s than in the mid-eighteenth century. Moreover, in view of the increasing monetization of the economy in the latter part of the Ch'ing period it was quite probable that the commercial sector grew faster than the agricultural sector. Accordingly, it is likely that the people as a whole gave up a smaller proportion of their

Table 7.1. A reconstruction of local land tax administration in the late Ch'ing

Aspects of Administration	Statutory System	Non-statutory System		
		Legal	Conventional	Illegal
Administrative staff	Magistrate, subordinate officers, regular clerks and runners		Secretaries, extra clerks and runners	
Revenues[a]	Tax Quotas	Surcharges in groups III and IV, and, in some provinces, group I, too.	Generally Surcharges in Groups I and II.	Extra-collection exacted by magistrates or clerks and runners (see tax assessment and tax collection)
Expenses[a]	Funds earmarked for ts'un-liu and ch'i-yün	Assigned contributions, part of administrative expenses	Part of administrative expenses; Seasonal gifts, birthday gifts, and errand gifts to superiors; Donations for public welfare	
Tax Assessment	Assessment of tax quotas	Assessment of the rate of collection by the provincial authorities	Assessment of the rate of collection by the magistrate in consultation with local gentry	Raising the rate by the magistrate without consultation with local gentry or the approval of the superior authorities
Tax collection[b]	Direct collection ("city chests" exclusively)		Direction collection: "city chests" and clerks and runners in the countryside, "city chests" and "country chests"	Indirect collection: pao cheng, pao-shou

Notes:
[a]See the section on local finance and land tax surcharges in Chapter 3.
[b]See Chapter 2.

income for the upkeep of the Manchu regime in its closing years than at its height.

Perhaps we may also venture to make a guess by extrapolation with respect to the share of the government sector in national income. Ta-chung Liu and Kung-chia Yeh have estimated that China's net domestic product was valued at 28.86 billion yuan and her population numbered 501.1 million in 1933.[2] The per capita income would therefore be 57.3 yuan. During the quarter of a century between 1908 and 1933 the purchasing power of silver declined by nearly 40 percent, for a yuan (=0.72 tael) in 1908 was worth 1.38 yuan in 1933.[3] Assuming that the real per capita income did not change in these two and a half decades, it would be 41.5 yuan or about 30 taels in 1908. Assuming further that China's population in the same year was around 400 million, or 30 million less than Perkins' estimated population for 1913 (see Table 1.1), the net domestic product in 1908 would be about 12 billion taels. It follows that a total tax revenue of 292 million taels amounts to merely 2.4 percent of her net national product at the time, an extremely low figure by today's standard.[4] This again refutes the traditional thesis of excessive tax burden.

However, if there was a trend towards concentration of land ownership and greater inequity in the allocation of tax burden, the peasants might still find their real tax burden increasing in spite of the decrease in the overall burden of the whole population. Among all taxes in Ch'ing China the land tax was by nature the least regressive; the decline of its fiscal importance in her tax structure thus indicates a more inequitable distribution of tax burden in the late Ch'ing. So does the increasing proportion of land unregistered. On the other hand, whether land ownership was increasingly concentrated in eighteenth- and nineteenth-century China cannot be answered before extensive research is done.[5] Nevertheless, in view of the fact that on the eve of the 1911 revolution the government merely shared a few percent of national income and that there occurred no major social uprisings, I doubt strongly that the inequity of tax burden had more than minimal effect on the fall of the dynasty.

Notes
Bibliography
Glossary
Index

Abbreviations

Ad	The section on administrative expenditure in *TCSMS*
CKCTNYS	*Chung-kuo chin-tai nung-yeh-shih tzu-liao*
CSWP	*Huang-ch'ao ching-shih wen-pien*
CTCC	*Chung-kuo chin-tai ching-chi-shih yen-chiu chi-k'an*
CTLT	*Huang-ch'ao cheng-tien lei-tsuan*
CYYY	*Chung-yang yen-chiu-yüan li-shih yü-yen yen-chiu-so chi-k'an*
DR	*Decennial Reports*
E	The section on expenditure in *TCSMS*
G	The section on the grain tax in *TCSMS*
HT	*Ta-Ch'ing hui-tien*
HTTL	*Ta-Ch'ing hui-tien tse-li*
HTSL	*Ta-Ch'ing hui-tien shih-li*
HWHTK	*Ch'ing-ch'ao hsü wen-hsien t'ung-k'ao*
L	The section on the land tax in *TCSMS*
R	The section on revenue in *TCSMS*
RT	*Returns of Trade and Trade Reports*
TCSMS	*Ts'ai-cheng shuo-ming-shu*
TCTF	*Tsui-chin t'ien-fu chi-yao*
TFAT	*T'ien-fu an-tu lei-pien*
WHTK	*Ch'ing-ch'ao wen-hsien t'ung-k'ao*

Notes

INTRODUCTION

1. See, e.g., Wang Yü-ch'üan, "The Rise of Land Tax and the Fall of Dynasties in Chinese History," *Pacific Affairs*, 9.2 (June 1936), 201-220; Wang Tan-ch'en, *Chung-kuo nung-min ke-ming shih-hua* (Shanghai, 1952); Li Cheng-shui, *Chung-hua jen-min kung-ho-kuo nung-yeh-shui shih-kao* (Peking, 1959), p. 36; Kwang-ching Liu, "Nineteenth-Century China: The Disintegration of the Old Order and the Impact of the West," in Ping-ti Ho and Tang Tsou eds., *China in Crisis*, vol. 1, bk. 1 (Chicago, the University of Chicago Press, 1968), 93-178, esp. 108-120.

2. E.g., Shao-kwan Chen, *The system of Taxation in China in the Tsing Dynasty, 1644-1911* (New York, Columbia University, 1914); Han Liang Huang, *The Land Tax in China* (New York, Columbia University, 1918); H.B. Morse, *The Trade and Administration of China* (London, Longmans, Green, and Co., 1908); S.R. Wagel, *Finance in China* (Shanghai, North-China Daily News and Herald, 1914); Yen Ts'ai-chieh, *T'ien-fu ch'u-i* (Peking, 1915); Kimura Masutaro, *Shina zaiseiron* (Tokyo, 1927).

3. E.g., H.B. Morse, pp. 85-98, S.R. Wagel, pp. 363-374.

4. H.S. Brunnert and V.V. Hagelstrom, *Present Day Political Organization of China*, trans. A. Beltchenko and E.E. Moran (Shanghai, Kelly and Walsh, 1912), pp. 188-189. Note that Ch'ing-li ts'ai-cheng chü is translated in that book as "branch offices of the committee for the reorganization of the financial affairs of the empire." I prefer it as "the provincial bureau for financial reorganization" and Ch'ing-li ts'ai-cheng ch'u as "the central bureau for financial reorganization." The reasons are several. The provincial bureau was not a branch office of the central bureau, just as the office of the financial commissioner was not a branch of the ministry of finance. I see no justification in translating *chü* and *ch'u* in this case as committee because the new establishment was an administrative office composed of a head and his staff, not a consultative or advisory organ formed by a group of people with more or less equal status. Also, the authors' translation appears tedious. See also Chuan-shih Li, *Central and Local Finance in China* (New York, Columbia University, 1922), pp. 70-71.

5. *Ta-Ch'ing Hsüan-t'ung cheng-chi* (Taipei, Hua-wen shu-chü, 1964 reprint), p. 460.
6. *Ta-Ch'ing Hsüan-t'ung hsin-fa-ling* (Shanghai, The Commercial Press, 1910), 1.26-30.
7. E.g., *TFAT; TCTF*; Wei Sung-t'ang, comp., *Hu-pei ts'ai-cheng chi-lüeh* (1917); Wei Sung-t'ang, comp., *Che-chiang ts'ai-cheng chi-lüeh* (1929 preface).

1. CHINA'S ECONOMY AND FISCAL SYSTEM IN THE CH'ING PERIOD

1. Chi-ming Hou, "Economic Dualism: the Case of China, 1840-1937," *Journal of Economic History*, 13.3 (September 1963), 277-297.
2. Kazushi Ohkawa and Henry Rosovsky, "A Century of Japanese Economic Growth," in William W. Lookwood, ed., *The State and Economic Enterprise in Japan* (Princeton, Princeton University Press, 1965), pp. 47-92, esp. Table 2 on p. 90.
3. Percentage figures are derived from Ta-chung Liu and Kung-chia Yeh, *The Economy of the Chinese Mainland, 1933-1959* (Princeton, Princeton University Press, 1965), pp. 66, 69. Note that as late as 1957 77 percent of China's labor force was still employed in the agricultural sector. See *ibid.*, p. 69.
4. For the percentage contribution to increased grain output between yield and acreage, see Dwight H. Perkins, *Agricultural Development in China, 1368-1968* (Chicago, Aldine Publishing Co., 1969), p. 33.
5. E.g., see Liu Yo-yün, *Kuang-hsü k'uai-chi-piao* (1901), I, 1-2.
6. Profits from public enterprises did not appear as a source of public revenue even at the end of the nineteenth century. In the last decade of the dynasty, however, various provincial authorities started setting up stamping and printing machines and employed them with increasing frequency as a means of financing their expanding activities. Because of the decentralized nature of late Ch'ing monetary management, no comprehensive statistics on the profits from note and cash issue are available. The 1911 budget put the revenue from this source as high as 47.2 million taels against an estimated total revenue of 302 million taels. But the former figure was soon found to be unrealistically high and was therefore reduced to about 15 million in the 1912 budget, the second and last budget of the Ch'ing dynasty. See Shao-kwan Chen, p. 43; Chia Shih-i, *Min-kuo ts'ai-cheng shih* (Shanghai, the Commercial Press, 1917), pp. 26, 840.
7. T'ung-tsu Ch'ü, *Local Government in China under the Ch'ing* (Cambridge, Harvard University Press, 1962), pp. 169-173.
8. For detailed description of the system, see Hsü Ta-ling, *Ch'ing-tai chüan-na chih-tu* (Peip'ing, 1950), pp. 77-96; see also Chung-li Chang, *The Chinese Gentry* (Seattle, University of Washington Press, 1955), pp. 1-31.
9. Hsü Ta-ling, p. 110-111; Wei Yüan, *Sheng-wu chi* (1927), 11.6. The selling of public offices lasted one year or a few years on each occasion.
10. Lo Yü-tung, *Chung-kuo li-chin shih* (Shanghai, The Commercial Press, 1936), pp. 6-7.
11. See Liu Yo-yün, I, 1-2, 9-11; Hsü Ta-ling, p. 111.
12. See Ping-ti Ho, "The Salt Merchants of Yang-chou: A Study of Commercial Capitalism in 18th-century China," *Harvard Journal of Asiatic*

Studies, 17.1-2 (June 1954), pp. 130-168; Liu Chün, "T'ao-kuang ch'ao Liang-huai fei-yin kai-p'iao shih-mo," *CTCC*, 1.2 (May 1933), pp. 123-188.

13. T'ao Chu, *T'ao Wen-i-kung ch'üan-chi* (c. 1840), XI, 19b-20; Liu Chün, 135.

14. On the structural change of Ch'ing tax system after the Taiping Rebellion, it is worth noting two pioneer studies: Kato Shigeshi, "Shin chō koki no zaisei ni tsuite," in his collected works *Shina keizaishi kōshō* (Tokyo, The Tōyō Bunko, 1953), II, 478-492; James T.K. Wu, "The Impact of the Taiping Rebellion upon the Manchu Fiscal System," *Pacific Historical Review*, 19.3 (August 1950), 265-275.

15. Ping-ti Ho, *Studies on the Population of China, 1368-1953* (Cambridge, Harvard University Press, 1959), chap. 2.

16. See my article, "Ch'ing Yung-cheng shih-ch'i ti ts'ai-cheng kai-ke," *CYYY*, 32 (1961), 47-75.

17. Wu Ch'ao-tzu, *Chung-kuo shui-chih shih* (Shanghai, The Commercial Press, 1937), II, 48-60; H.B. Morse, *The Trade and Administration of China*, pp. 100-101. It should be noted here that the salt likin was collected separately from the likin levied on other commodities and thus treated as part of the salt tax, not part of likin. See also Lo Yü-tung, *Chung-kuo li-chin shih*, p. 55.

18. Lo Yü-tung, *Chung-kuo li-chin shih*, pp. 15-22; Edwin G. Beal, Jr., *The Origin of Likin (1853-1864)* (Cambridge, Harvard University Press, 1958), pp. 24-45.

19. Likin was finally abolished in 1931, see Wu Ch'ao-tzu, II, 133.

20. Lo Yü-tung, *Chung-kuo li-chin shih*, pp. 55-56.

21. Chiang Heng-yüan, comp., *Chung-kuo kuan-shui shih-liao* (Shanghai, 1931), VIII, 1-2.

22. E.g., the brokerage tax for the first-class shop was set at 0.8 tael a year in the eighteenth century; it was 15 taels in 1902. See *Feng-hua-hsien chih* (Taipei, 1957 reprint), VII, 380-381.

23. Thomas A. Metzger, "The Organizational Capabilities of the Ch'ing State in the Field of Commerce: The Liang-huai Salt Monopoly, 1740-1840," in W.E. Willmott, ed., *Economic Organization in Chinese Society* (Stanford, Stanford University Press, 1972), pp. 9-45. In this article he sees five kinds of office in Ch'ing bureaucracy: executive offices, supervisory offices, advisory offices, coordinating offices, and client offices. This conceptual framework helped me a great deal in making a preliminary examination of Ch'ing fiscal administration. However, for the sake of locating administrative responsibility I have used his framework in a slightly modified form.

24. E-tu Zen Sun, "The Board of Revenue in Nineteenth-Century China," *Harvard Journal of Asiatic Studies*, 24 (1962-1963), 175-227.

25. Fu Tsung-mao, *Ch'ing-tai chun-chi ch'u tsu-chih chi chih-chang chih yen-chiu* (Taipei, 1967), pp. 371-381.

26. See P'eng Yü-hsin, "Ch'ing-mo chung-yang yü ko-sheng ts'ai-cheng kuan-hsi," *She-hui ko-hsüeh tsa-chih*, 9.1 (June 1947), 83-110.

27. Lo Erh-kang, *Hsiang-chün hsin-chih* (Changsha, The Commercial Press, 1939), pp. 243-244; P'eng Yü-hsin, pp. 86-87.

28. E-tu Zen Sun, "The Board of Revenue . . . ," pp. 192-194; Lo Yü-tung, *Chung-kuo li-chin shih*, p. 72.

29. For the shipment of the grain tribute to Peking, see Harold C. Hinton,

The Grain Tribute System of China, 1845-1911 (Cambridge, Harvard University Press, 1970), pp. 10-12.

30. See E-tu Zen Sun, "The Board of Revenue . . . ," pp. 195-196. Note that there were two kinds of native customs station—most of them under the jurisdiction of the Board of Revenue known as Hu-kuan and a small number (which levied duties on timber and bamboos) under the jurisdiction of the Board of Works called Kung-kuan. As far as administration is concerned, the Board of Works did not play any part in it. The superintendents of Hu-kuan also took charge of collecting Kung-kuan duties and forwarded them to the Board of Works. See Wu Ch'ao-tzu, II, 75.

31. Stanley F. Wright, comp., *The Collection and Disposal of the Maritime and Native Customs Revenue since the Revolution of 1911* (Shanghai, the Inspectorate General of Customs, 1925), pp. 1-7; Stanley F. Wright, *Hart and the Chinese Customs* (Belfast, Wm. Mullan and Son, 1950), pp. 263, 266-267; H.B. Morse, *The Trade and Administration of China*, pp. 357-368.

32. See, e.g., *TCSMS* (Kwangtung), 4.48-50; *TCSMS* (Kansu), 4A.67-131.

33. *TCSMS* (Chihli), 6.5; *TCSMS* (Hunan), R−8.1-6; *TCSMS* (Kwangtung), 7.27-31.

34. See John F. Due, *Government Finance* (Homewood, Illinois, Richard D. Irwin, Inc., 1954), pp. 412-425; George F. Break, *Intergovernmental Fiscal Relations in the United States* (Washington D.C., The Brookings Institution, 1967), pp. 28-39; L.L. Ecker-Racz, *The Politics and Economics of State-Local Finance* (Englewood Cliffs, N.J., Prentice-Hall, 1970), pp. 66-67, 220.

35. *HTTL* (1764 preface), 36.1-2, 17-18.

36. P'eng Yü-hsin, p. 83.

37. P'eng Yü-hsin, pp. 83-84.

38. P'eng Yü-hsin, p. 84; *HTSL*, 1899, chüan169. Two remarks should be made here for clarification. First, the salt tax and native customs collected in the provinces were considered the central government revenue and thus not at the disposal of the provincial government. Second, according to the sources cited here, two provinces, Kiangsu and Anhwei, were not included in either of the three categories. But it is certain that Kiangsu was in the surplus category and Anhwei was in either the surplus or self-sufficient category.

39. In its broadest sense, the term *kuei-fei* could mean any of the following three kinds of fiscal transaction: a surcharge imposed for defraying administrative expenses; a fee collected for issuing a business license or for performing a service; or an intra-governmental financial aid from a lower-level yamen to a higher-level yamen. The common feature of all these three kinds of *kuei-fei* was that they were established by precedent or custom, not by law. To avoid confusion I have limited this term (unless otherwise specified) to the third kind of fiscal transaction.

40. Lo Yü-tung, "Kuang-hsü ch'ao pu-chiu ts'ai-cheng chih fang-ts'e," *CTCC*, 1.2 (May 1933), 189-270; see also P'eng Yü-hsin, pp. 86-102.

41. Lo Yü-tung, "Kuang-hsü ch'ao . . . ," pp. 242-253.

2. THE ADMINISTRATION OF THE LAND TAX

1. Haskell P. Wald, *Taxation of Agricultural Land in Under-developed Economies* (Cambridge, Harvard University Press, 1959), pp. 47-50.

2. Ping-ti Ho, *Studies on the Population of China*, pp. 3-4, 107-108.

3. According to *Ho-nan t'ung-chih* (1660 preface), 12.1, the compilation of *Fu-i ch'üan-shu* began in the Wan-li period (1573-1620).

4. For an evaluation and reconstruction of the early Ming land data (c. 1400), see Dwight H. Perkins, *Agricultural Development in China*, pp. 222-226.

5. Shimizu Taiji, "Chō Kyosei no tochi jōryō ni tsuite," *Tōyō Gakuhō* 29.2 (May 1942), 167-198.

6. In his article on the land survey of 1578-82 Shimizu noted that the governor-general of Kwangtung and Kwangsi and the governor of Kweichow also reported the survey results. After an examination of land data for these provinces I am convinced that the acreage (about 33 million mou) reported by the former was the acreage of Kwangtung, not of Kwangtung and Kwangsi combined, and that the acreage (559,000 mou) reported by the latter did not include land held on military tenure. Hence these two figures are discarded in favor of those recorded in local gazetteers.

7. *CTLT*, 4.2, 6.2; *TCSMS* (Shantung), R–L, 1; *TCSMS* (Chihli), 1.1-2; *CSWP*, 29.14b-16, 31.47.

8. According to Fujii Hiroshi, the *Fu-i ch'üan-shu* of Kiangsi province was printed in 1611, see his article. "Mindai tento tōkei ni kan suru ikkōsatsu," *Tōyō Gakuhō*, 30.4 (August 1944), 60-87, esp. p. 83.

9. Wan Kuo-ting et al., *Chiang-su Wu-chin Nan-t'ung t'ien-fu t'iao-ch'a pao-kao* (1934), pp. 4-5; *Ju-kao-hsien chih* (1804 preface), 4.12; *Ch'ao-chou chih hui-pien* (Hongkong, Lung-men shu-chü, 1965), p. 209.

10. For pre-survey land acreage in Yunnan, see Shimizu Taiji, p. 169.

11. Shimizu Taiji, pp. 167-180; Wan Kuo-ting, pp. 3, 111; *Ch'ang-chih-hsien chih* (1763 preface), 7.2b; *Chiang-hsi t'ung-chih* (1732 preface), 23.12-15. *Ch'ao-chou chih hui-pien* (1965), p. 209.

12. See Ping-ti Ho, *Studies on the Population of China*, pp. 136-138; Ku Yen-wu, *Jih-chih lü chi-shih* (Shanghai, Chung-hua shu-chü, 1927), 4.46; *Huang-Ming ching-shih wen-pien*, comp. Ch'en Tzu-lung, et al. (Taipei, Kuo-lien t'u-shu kung-ssu, 1964 reprint), 4.540, 5.243-244, 382-384, 444-446, 7.133-136; *CSWP*, 31.2.

13. *CTLT*, 6.2b.

14. Ch'en Teng-yüan, *Chung-kuo t'ien-fu shih* (Shanghai, The Commercial Press, 1936), pp. 205-206; Wang Ch'ing-yün, *Shih-ch'ü yü-chi* (1890), 4.19b; *HWHTK*, pp. 7550-7551.

15. *CSWP*, 31.44-47, 52; Ch'en Teng-yüan, pp. 205-209.

16. Ch'en Teng-yüan, pp. 229-230.

17. *Hu-pu tse-li* (1874), 7.21-22, 38-39, 9.18, 10.10b-11; *CTLT*, 6.1.

18. For official land acreage between 1661 and 1753, see *CKCTNYS*, p. 60.

19. For the early Ch'ing land policy, see Han Liang Huang, pp. 57-64.

20. *CTLT*, 4.2.

21. *WHTK*, p. 5025.

22. See Ping-ti Ho, *Studies on the Population of China*, p. 117.

23. *Hu-pu tse-li* (1874), 7.19.

24. Ho Ch'ang-ling, *Nai-an tsou-i ts'un-kao* (1881 preface), 7.3-6.

25. *Hu-pu tse-li* (1874), 8.1b.

26. T'ung-tsu Ch'ü, pp. 16, 132-133.

27. See Ping-ti Ho, *Studies on the Population of China*, pp. 104-116. Also see *CSWP*, 31.23-24.

28. For a comprehensive description of each of the tax assessment systems, see Haskell P. Wald, pp. 9-41.

29. See *WHTK*, pp. 4855-4857; Han Liang Huang, pp. 90-91; Ping-ti Ho, *Studies on the Population of China*, pp. 102-103.

30. *TCSMS* (Kiangsu), R–L, 10.

31. *TCSMS* (Fengtien), pp. 12-14.

32. Ping-ti Ho, *Studies on the Population of China*, pp. 103-116.

33. For a discussion of the decrease in land tax quota in a number of provinces after the Taiping Rebellion, see Chapter 5.

34. Wang Yü-ch'üan; Kwang-ching Liu, pp. 115-119; Kung-chuan Hsiao, *Rural China* (Seattle, University of Washington Press, 1967), pp. 113-124.

35. *Chu-p'i yü-chih* (1738 preface), I.1.81b; Wang Ch'ing-yün, 3.41b.

36. *HWHTK*, p. 7515; *Liu K'un-i i-chi* (Peking, 1959), pp. 2780-2781.

37. Chung-li Chang, *The Chinese Gentry*, pp. 32-51; T'ung-tsu Ch'ü, chap. 10.

38. *Cheng-hsien chih* (1934), 4.35.

39. *Nan-ch'uan-hsien chih* (1926 preface), 4.3b.

40. Pao Shih-ch'en, *An-wu ssu-chung* (1872 preface), 6.5b-6; *Liu K'un-i i-chi*, pp. 2780-2781; *Shan-hsi Tzu-yang-hsien chih* (1925), 2.3b; *Lo-p'ing -hsien chih* (1932), 2.26; *Chung-hsiu Chen-yüan-hsien chih* (1935), 7.10b.

41. *TCSMS* (Fengtien), L, 6; *TCSMS* (Honan), R–L, 78; *Nan-hui-hsien hsü-chih* (1928), 22.33b; *HWHTK*, pp. 7511-7512; Sasaki Masaya, "Kampō ninen Yin-ken no Kōryō bōdō" (The riot against land taxation in Yin hsien in 1852), *Kindai Chūkoku kenkyū* (Studies on modern China), Vol. 5 (1963), Tokyo, pp. 185-299.

42. *HWHTK* pp. 7511-7512.

43. See my article, "Ch'ing Yung-cheng shih-ch'i ti ts'ai-cheng kai-ke" *CYYY*, 32 (Taipei, 1961), 41-75

44. See *Hu-pu tse-li* (1874), 6.8-15.

45. Hsia Nai, "T'ai-p'ing t'ien-kuo ch'ien-hou Ch'ang-chiang ko-sheng chih t'ien-fu wen-t'i," *Tsing-hua hsüeh-pao*, 10.2 (April 1935), 409-474.

46. Hsia Nai, pp. 440-468; *TCSMS* (Kiangsu-Kiangning), 1.84; *TCSMS* (Kwangtung), R–LA, 12.

47. *TCSMS* (Shansi), I,13-14; *TCSMS* (Shantung), R–L, 1-2.

48. See, for example, *TCSMS* (Shansi), I,13-14; *TCSMS* (Hupei), p. 6; *TCSMS* (Kwangtung), R–LA, 12; *Cheng-hsien chih*, 1934, 4.41b.

49. *HWHTK*, p. 7537; *TCSMS* (Kiangsu-Soochow), R–L, 19.

50. See my work, *An Estimate of the Land Tax Collection in China, 1753 and 1908* (Cambridge, Mass., East Asian Research Center, Harvard University, 1973), chap. 1, section on southeastern provinces, 13, 14; *TCSMS* (Kiangsu-Soochow), R–L, 19.

51. *TCSMS* (Szechwan), pp. 3-4; *TFAT*, III, Szechwan, 7. All but three of the twenty-three districts in the latter group were also among those in the first group.

52. *CKCTNYS*, p. 317.

53. *TCSMS* (Anhwei), R–G, 31.

54. Ting Jih-ch'ang, *Fu Wu kung-tu* (1876 preface), 22.2, 4b-25.

55. *Hu-pei t'ung-chih* (Shanghai, The Commercial Press, 1921), pp. 46, 1284-1285; *Shao-hsing hsien-chih tzu-liao* (1939), First Collection, X, Section on the land tax, pp. 24b-32.

56. *CKCTNYS*, p. 344.

57. *CKCTNYS*, pp. 346-348.

58. Also see *TCSMS* (Kwangsi), *Ko-lun shang–kuo shui pu*, 93.

59. *TCSMS* (Honan), R–L, 44-45; *TCSMS* (Hupei), p. 2; *TCSMS* (Fukien), R–L, 9-10, R–G, 29-30; *TCSMS* (Kwangtung), R–LA, 22-23; *TCSMS* (Kwangsi), *Ko-lun shang–kuo-shui pu*, 95-98; *TCSMS* (Hunan), *Tsung-shuo*, 6; *TCSMS* (Kweichow), R–L, 136-153; *TCSMS* (Kiangsu-Soochow), R–L, 18-19; *TFAT*, II, Shansi, 9.

60. T'ung-tsu Ch'ü, pp. 133-134.

61. *Hu-pu tse-li*, 1874, 9.5b-8; T'ung-tsu Ch'ü, pp. 134-135.

62. *TCSMS* (Kweichow), R–L, 151; *TCSMS* (Kwangsi), *Ko-lun shang–kuo-shui pu*, 102.

63. *TCSMS* (Kiangsu–Soochow), R–L, 19; *TFATW*, II, Shansi, 9.

64. *TCSMS* (Honan), R–L, 78; *TCSMS* (Kweichow), R–L, 139, 143; Kung-chuan Hsia, p. 114; Ch'en Teng-yüan, p. 219.

65. *TCSMS* (Hupei), p. 2.

66. *TCSMS* (Fukien), R–L, 5-8; *TCSMS* (Kweichow), R–L, 136-162; *TCSMS* (Kwangsi), *Ko-lun shang–kuo-shui pu*, 93.

67. *TFAT*, II, Shansi, 9; *TCSMS* (Kwangsi), *Ko-lun shang–kuo-shui pu*, 96-98; *TCSMS* (Kwangtung), R–LA, 23; *TCSMS* (Fukien), R–L, 9-10, R–G, 29-30; *TCSMS* (Kweichow), R–L, 136-162.

68. T'ung-tsu Ch'ü, pp. 21, 36-37; Han Liang Huang, pp. 117-119.

69. T'ung-tsu Ch'ü, pp. 36-37, 56-57, 63-64.

70. *TCSMS* (Kwangtung), R–LA, 22-23; *TCSMS* (Hunan), *Tsung-shuo*, 6.

71. *Tz'u-ch'i-hsien chih*, (1899), 23.38b-39.

72. *Hsin-ch'ang-hsien chih*, (1918), 3.14b.

73. *TCSMS* (Kweichow), R–L, 155; *TFAT*, III, Szechwan, 6b.

74. T'ung-tsu Ch'ü, pp. 136-137; Ch'en Teng-yüan, p. 219; *TFAT*, II, Shansi, 9.

75. See Muramatsu Yuji, *Kindai Kōnan no sosan* (Tokyo, Tokyo University Press, 1970). It includes the author's eight articles on the landlord bursary in China in the late nineteenth and early twentieth centuries.

76. For example, taxes in certain part of Tu-shan chou in Kweichow were collected by tax farmers while taxes in the rest of the district were collected directly by the local administration. In another district of the same province, Ta-t'ang chou, the local government collected taxes directly within the ninth month of the year, taxes uncollected in the period were let out to tax farmers. See *TCSMS* (Kweichow), R–L, 136, 146.

77. *TCSMS* (Honan), R–L, 44-45; *TCSMS* (Kweichow), R–L, 136-153

78. *TCSMS* (Hupei), p. 2.

79. *TCSMS* (Kiangsu–Soochow), R–L, 20; *TCSMS* (Anhwei), R–L, 3-4; Muramatsu Yuji, "Shinmatsu Minsho no Kōnan ni okeru hōran kankei no jittai to sono kessan hōkoku," in *Kindai Kōnan no sosen*, pp. 391-436.

80. *TCSMS* (Kwangsi), *Ko-lun shang–kuo-shui pu*, 99; *TCSMS* (Kweichow), R–L, 137-151.

81. *TCSMS* (Kwangtung), R–LA, 23-24; Feng Hua-te and Li Ling, "Hopei sheng Ting hsien chih t'ien-fu," *Cheng-chih ching-chi hsüeh-pao* 4.3 (Tientsin, April 1936), 443-520 (see pp. 503-504); *HWHTK*, p. 7794.

82. T'ung-tsu Ch'ü, pp. 138-139.

83. *TCSMS* (Kiangsu–Soochow), R–L, 27.

84. *TCSMS* (Kiangsi), R–G, 14.

85. *TCSMS* (Kweichow), R–L, 112-119.

3. INCREASE IN LAND TAX SURCHARGE

1. For instance, in times of flood or drought, the emperor would usually grant total or partial exemption of taxes to be collected in the area affected and approve extra-"budgetary" expenditure for famine relief.

2. Properly speaking, local government refers to the lowest administrative units—those of district, department, and sub-prefecture. But in addition to the local government just defined, a number of the intermediate administrative units (between the local and provincial government)—i.e., prefecture, independent department, and independent subprefecture—were also in charge of collecting either part or whole of the land tax within their jurisdiction. On the other hand, there were cases in which the land tax of a special section of a district or department was collected independently by an assistant magistrate. For this reason I have to extend somewhat the definition of local government to include all administrative offices which had responsibility for land tax collection. Moreover, since the areas of administrative jurisdiction and land tax administration were not necessarily identical, I have used the term "district of collection" to designate the latter. For a description of administrative units from the province down in Ch'ing China, see T'ung-tsu Ch'ü, pp. 1-13.

3. See Feng Kuei-fen, *Chiao-fen-lu k'ang-i* (1884), 1.9; Pao Shih-ch'en, 4.30b-31; *TCSMS* (Kwangtung), R–LA, 26. For further discussion, see Chap. 5.

4. See my work, *An Estimate of the Land Tax . . .*, Chap. 1; *TCSMS* (Kiangsu-Soochow), R–L, 22; *TCSMS* (Kweichow), R–L, 95-112; *TCSMS* (Anhwei), R–tsa-chüan, 22-23, etc.

5. See Tables 5.5 and 5.6.

6. See Haskell P. Wald, pp. 9-41.

7. As a rule the imperial government granted tax remission in the event of agricultural disaster or crop failure to the area affected, see *WHTK*, pp. 5275-5287; *HWHTK*, pp. 8385-8394.

8. See my article, "The Secular Trend of Prices during the Ch'ing Period," *Hsiang-kang Chung-wen ta-hsüeh Chung-kuo wen-hua yen-chiu-so hsüeh-pao*, 5.2 (1973).

9. See T'ung-tsu Ch'ü, p. 26.

10. With regard to regulations on expenditure, the only practical change made during the Ch'ing was the increase of official salary known as *yang-lien* implemented in the Yung-cheng period (1723-35). See Chap. 4.

11. James T.K. Wu, "The Impact of the Taiping Rebellion upon the Manchu Fiscal System."

12. *Ibid.*

13. T'ung-tsu Ch'ü, pp. 93, 97.

14. See T'ung-tsu Ch'ü, pp. 112; *Ch'uan-sha-hsien chih* (1937), 8.51b.

15. T'ung-tsu Ch'ü, p. 23.

16. T'ung-tsu Ch'ü, pp. 45, 64.

17. *TCSMS* (Shensi), E–Ad, 17.

18. "Fu-i o-cheng ti-ts'ao feng-kung teng-k'uan ch'ien-liang ping k'ou-lien k'uan-mu-pu" (c. 1906), ms. in Harvard-Yenching Library.

19. *Ch'uan-sha-hsien chih* (1937), 8.48-51.

20. Note that a number of customary fees bore the same name as land tax surcharges. The term *chieh-fei* (delivery expenses) is a case in point. It meant different things on different occasions. As a customary fee it was a fiscal transaction between two yamen on different levels, but as a surcharge it was one between the people and the local government.

21. *Ch'uan-sha-hsien chih* (1937), 8.52b, 53b; *TCSMS* (Hunan), *Tsung-shuo*, 26-29; *TCSMS* (Kwangsi), *Ko-lun shang – sheng-shui pu*, 124.

22. *TCSMS* (Honan), *Fu-pien*, 33-37.

23. *TCSMS* (Shensi), E–Ad, 18; *TCSMS* (Honan), *Fu-pien*, 29.

24. *TCSMS* (Honan), *Fu-pien*, 38-41.

25. See Chung-li Chang, *The Income of the Chinese Gentry* (Seattle, University of Washington Press, 1962), pp. 19-29.

26. See T'ung-tsu Ch'ü, pp. 38-41.

27. *CSWP*, 24.11.

28. *Huai-yang-hsien chih* (1933), 4.12.

29. T'ung-tsu Ch'ü, p. 226: n. 15; Shang-hai t'ung-hsin-she, comp., *Shang-hai yen-chiu tzu-liao* (Shanghai, Chung-hua shu-chü, 1936), p. 533; *Kuan-hsien chih* (1932), "Kuan-chih chang-ku," 1.4-5.

30. Hsü Keng-pi, *Pu-ch'ien-chai man-ts'un* (1882), 5.123.

31. *TCSMS* (Shensi), E–Ad, 15-18.

32. *Chung-hsiu Kuan-hsien chih* (1886), 6.17.

33. For a brief description of "parallel bimetallism" (parallel standard), see Karl Helfferich, *Money* (London, Ernest Beun Ltd., 1927), II, 356, 363.

34. For a structural relationship between silver and cash, see Frank H.H. King, *Money and Monetary Policy in China, 1845-1895* (Cambridge, Harvard University Press, 1965), chap. 2.

35. Yen Chung-p'ing, *Ch'ing-tai Yün-nan t'ung-cheng k'ao* (Peking, 1957), pp. 8, 15, 22-24.

36. *Chung-kuo chin-tai huo-pi-shih tzu-liao*, comp. Chung-kuo jen-min yin-hang (Peking, 1964), First Collection, I, 102.

37. For an analysis of the political and social background of the Boxer uprising, see Chester C. Tan, *The Boxer Catastrophe* (New York, Columbia University Press, 1955), chaps. 1, 2, and 3.

38. For detail, see T'ang Hsiang-lung, "Min-kuo i-ch'ien ti p'ei-k'uan shih ju-ho ch'ang-fu ti?" *CTCC*, 3.2 (November 1935), 262-291.

39. Lo Yü-tung, "Kuang-hsü ch'ao pu-chiu ts'ai-cheng chih fang-ts'e," pp. 246-248.

40. Ch'üan Han-sheng, "Chia-wu chan-cheng i-ch'ien ti Chung-kuo kung-yeh-hua yün-tung," *CYYY*, 25 (1954), 189-270.

41. For detail, see Meribeth E. Cameron, *The Reform Movement in China, 1898-1912* (New York, Octagon Books, Inc., 1963), chaps. 4 and 6.

42. M.E. Cameron, pp. 67-75.

43. H.S. Brunnert and V.V. Hagelstrom, pp. 115-116, 167, 432; M.E. Cameron, p. 109.

44. See Chang Kia-ngau, *China's Struggle for Railroad Development* (New York, The John Day Company, 1943), pp. 26-45; E-tu Zen Sun, *Chinese Railways and British Interests* (New York, King's Crown Press, 1954), pp. 15-26.

45. Chang Kia-ngau, pp. 39-41.

46. Chang Kia-ngau, p. 45.

4. THE FISCAL IMPORTANCE OF THE LAND TAX

1. This chapter is an elaborated and slightly modified version of my article "The Fiscal Importance of the Land Tax during the Ch'ing Period," *Journal of Asian Studies*, 30.4 (August 1971), 829-842.

2. Conrad D. Totman, *Politics in the Tokugawa Bakufu, 1600-1843* (Cambridge, Harvard University Press, 1967), pp. 77-88.

3. Manilal B. Nanavati and J.J. Anjaria, *The Indian Rural Problem* (Bombay, Indian Society of Agricultural Economy, 1965), p. 419.

4. A rough indication can be found in Edwin G. Beal, Jr., pp. 3 and 5. According to the author's calculation, the percentage of total revenue supplied by the land tax decreased from 86.5 percent in 1651 to 77.2 percent in 1849, and to 36.9 percent in 1894. Nevertheless, as the author himself admits, the data from which the above figures are derived are very incomplete. For the sake of constructing a more realistic picture, it is imperative to gather all available data and to examine them closely. See also n. 14 of Chap. 1.

5. Note that another item known as *ying-yü* (surplus) usually appears in the annual returns of the salt tax and the native customs. The surplus resulted from either natural increase in tax revenue in times of economic prosperity or from converting hitherto concealed surcharges into part of the basic tax, or from both. From the mid-eighteenth century onwards the amount of *ying-yü* was also fixed by the imperial government and treated simply as an additional quota. In my classification of Ch'ing tax revenue, *ying-yü* is therefore included in the tax quota.

6. See the classification of surcharges in Chap. 3.

7. Customary fees here refer to surcharges levied for defraying administrative expenses and for issuing a license or rendering a service. See n. 39 of Chap. 1.

8. For financial reforms in the second quarter of the eighteenth century, see my article, "Ch'ing Yung-cheng shih-ch'i ti ts'ai-cheng kai-ke"; Abe Takeo, "Kōsen teikai no kenkyū," *Tōyōshi kenkyū*, 16.4 (March 1958), 108-261.

9. *CSWP*, 49.23-25, or 31-33.

10. *Hu-pei t'ung-chih*, Chia-ch'ing ed., 24A.9b; *Tung-hua lu*, comp. Wang Hsien-ch'ien (1884), "Yung-cheng," 5.16b.

11. *CTLT*, 83.1 and 6; *HT* (1764), 16.1-2; *HTTL* (1764), 48.34b; *Chu-p'i yü-chih*, I.4.72.

12. *HT* (1764), 17.11b; *Chu-p'i yü-chih*, IV.4.92b-93. Note that there was no customs station in Kansu; the tea tax was therefore included in the category of the miscellaneous taxes.

13. *HTTL* (1764), 50.3.

14. *CSWP*, 46.19.

15. Liu Hsün-kao et al., comps., *Chiang-su sheng chien-fu ch'üan-an* (1866), 2.13.

16. E.g., for every hundred dollars of taxes collected in 1962 the costs of collection are $0.45 in the United States and $1.15 in England. See Lillian Doris, ed., *The American Way in Taxation: Internal Revenue, 1862-1963* (Englewood Cliffs, N.J., Prentice-Hall Inc., 1963), pp. 134-135.

17. John B. Wolf, *The Emergence of the Great Powers, 1685-1715* (New York, Harper, 1951), p. 185; Stanford J. Shaw, *The Financial Administrative Organization and Development of Ottoman Egypt, 1517-1789* (Princeton, Princeton University Press, 1962), p. 75

18. See my work, *An Estimate of the Land Tax . . .* , chap. 1, section on the northern provinces, 3.

19. See my work, *An Estimate of the Land Tax . . .*

20. Yang Tuan-liu et al., comps., *Statistics of China's Foreign Trade during the Last Sixty-five Years* (Institute of Social Sciences, Academia Sinica, 1931), p. 123.

21. *Tung-hua hsü-lu*, comp. Chu Shou-p'eng (Shanghai, 1909), "Kuang-hsü," 206.12; *Yen-cheng ts'ung-k'an* (Peking, 1921), p. 129.

22. See A.P. Winston, "Chinese Finance under the Republic," *Quarterly Journal of Economics*, 30.4 (August 1916), 738-779.

23. Note also that in his study on China's salt administration in the early twentieth century S.A.M. Adshead estimates the total salt revenue being within the range of 40-50 million taels in the last decade of the Ch'ing period. See his book *The Modernization of the Chinese Salt Administration, 1900-1920* (Cambridge, Harvard University Press, 1970), p. 43.

24. Based on a single piece of evidence, H.B. Morse put the unreported amount at as much as 162 percent of the reported revenue. Also, a Japanese source gave without explanation an estimate of the unreported revenue as high as 100-200 percent of the reported revenue. See H.B. Morse, *The Trade and Administration of China*, pp. 108-110; *Shina keizai zensho*, I, 509.

25. Inspectorate General of Customs, *Working of Likin Collectorates: Kiukiang, Soochow, and Hangchow* (Shanghai, 1907), p. 166.

26. Lo Yü-tung, *Chung-kuo li-chin shih*, p. 464; *TCSMS* (Fukien), R—Likin, 29-30, 50.

27. *TCSMS* (Shensi), R—Likin, 75-110.

28. Lo Yü-tung, *Chung-kuo li-chin shih*, p. 469.

29. *Cheng-chih kuan-pao* (reprinted by Wen-hai ch'u-pan she, Taipei, 1965), XV, 203.

30. Liu Yo-yün, 1.1-2; Table 4.5.

31. Stanley F. Wright, comp., *The Collection and Disposal of the Maritime and Native Customs Revenue since the Revolution of 1911*, p. 41.

32. Nung Yeh, "Chung-kuo shih-chiu shih-chi hou-pan nung-yeh sheng-ch'an ti shang-p'in-hua," *Ching-chi yen-chiu* (Peking, 1956), no. 3, pp. 120-140, no. 4, 129-137.

5. GEOGRAPHICAL DIFFERENTIALS IN LAND TAXATION

1. For an excellent account of the chain development, see Chao-ting Chi, *Key Economic Areas in Chinese History* (New York, Paragon Book Reprint Corp., 1963). See also Perkins, *Agricultural Development in China*, chaps. 3 and 4. For a case study, see my unpublished paper, "Agricultural Development and Peasant Economy in Hunan during the Ch'ing Period."

2. It should be noted that some provinces in the developing area, such as Shensi, Szechwan, Hupei and Hunan, experienced considerable economic development long before the Manchu conquest of China, but a greater part of these provinces, especially Szechwan, suffered mass depopulation during the transition period between the Ming and the Ch'ing. Consequently, the subsequent development in large part took the form of repopulation and rehabilitation.

3. Ping-ti Ho, *Studies on the Population of China*, chap. 7 and app. 2.

4. See Ping-ti Ho, *Studies on the Population of China*, pp. 283-288; Dwight H. Perkins, *Agricultural Development in China*, pp. 207-208.

5. Fujii Hiroshi, "Shinan shōnin no kenkyū (2)," Tōyō gakuho, 36.2 (September 1953), 32-60.

6. Lien-sheng Yang, *Money and Credit in China* (Cambridge, Harvard University Press, 1952), pp. 82-83.

7. Ch'üan Han-sheng, "Ya-p'ien chan-cheng ch'ien Chiang-su ti mien-fang-chih-yeh," *Tsing-hua hsüeh-pao*, new series, 1.3 (September 1958),

25-51. Yen Chung-p'ing, *Chung-kuo mien-fang-chih shih-kao* (Peking, 1955), pp. 16-17.

8. Fang Hsien-t'ing, *Chung-kuo chih mien-fang-chih-yeh* (Shanghai, The Commercial Press, 1934), pp. 15-16.

9. See chap. 1.

10. See Chuan-shih Li, *Central and Local Finance in China* (New York, Columbia University, 1922), n. 4 on p. 54.

11. Ch'üan Han-sheng and Wang Yeh-chien, "Ch'ing Yung-cheng nien-chien ti mi-chia," *CYYY*, XXX (1959), 157-189; Abe Takeo, "Beikoku jukyū no kenkyū," *Tōyōshi kenkyū*, 15.4 (March 1954), 120-213; *Ta-Ch'ing li-ch'ao shih-lu*, "Sheng-tsu," 128.13, "Kao-tsung," 440.10b; *DR* (1901-11), II, 312; *TCSMS* (Kirin), p. 59; *Hei-lung-chiang chih-kao* (1932 comp., reprinted in Taipei, 1965), p. 1788; *P'an-yü-hsien hsü-chih* (1931 preface), 12.2.

12. Yen Chung-p'ing, *Ch'ing-tai Yün-nan t'ung-cheng k'ao*, pp. 22-23, 81-84.

13. *Ibid.*, p. 23.

14. *TCSMS* (Kansu), 1A.111; *TCSMS* (Fengtien), *Cheng-tsa ko-shui*, pp. 24-25; Ch'ou Chi-heng, *Shan-ching Han-chiang liu-yü mou-i piao*, chüan-hsia 5, in Sung Lien-k'uei, *Kuan-chung ts'ung-shu* (Shensi, 1934-35); *Tung-san-sheng cheng-lüeh*, comp. Hsü Shih-ch'ang (1911, reprinted in Taipei, Wen-hai ch'u-pan she, 1965), pp. 6309, 6619.

15. The percentage contribution from the developed area was even higher in the case of indirect taxes. For instance, the developed area yielded 90 percent of the country's total native customs in 1753 and 80 percent of total maritime customs in 1908. See *HT* (1764 preface), 16.1-2; Yang Tuan-liu, et al., pp. 124-131.

16. See Hsia Nai, "Tai-p'ing t'ien-kuo . . . ," pp. 457-458, 463-465; see my paper "The Impact of the Taiping Rebellion on Population in southern Kiangsu," *Papers on China* (Cambridge, East Asian Research Center, Harvard University), XIX (1965), 120-158.

17. *TCSMS* (Anhwei), R–G, 25-30.

18. See *HWHTK*, pp. 8409-8410.

19. See Ch'en Chen-han, "Ming-mo Ch'ing-ch'u Chung-kuo ti nung-yeh lao-tung sheng-ch'an-li, ti-tsu, ho t'u-ti chi-chung," *Ching-chi yen-chiu* (Peking, 1955), no. 3, pp. 124-139; see my paper "The Impact of the Taiping Rebellion . . . ," pp. 136-137.

20. See my unpublished paper "Agricultural Development and Peasant Economy in Hunan during the Ch'ing."

21. See Ko Shih-chün, comp., *Huang-ch'ao ching-shih wen hsü-pien* (Shanghai, 1888), 16.1, 24.7; Pao Shih-ch'en, 4.30b-31.

22. There are a few points that should be clarified. First, the number of districts in Table 5.8 is not the number of administrative districts, but that of the districts of collection. For the difference between the two, see n. 2 of chap. 3. Second, the average yields per districts computed in Table 5.8 are lower than those in Table 5.6 because certain parts of the tax yields estimated on provincial basis are not included in the totals of the former table. Third, the district (Chi hsien) that tops the lower-revenue group yields 51,561 taels, an amount well below the provincial average of 57,362 taels (see Table 5.8).

23. See Table 9 in my work *An Estimate of the Land Tax . . . .*

24. Hsü Yüan-fan, *I Lan-chou* (Hong Kong, 1941), p. 19.

25. The decrease in both of the *ti-ting* and grain quotas per district was the

result of an increase in the number of districts and a reduction in the grain quota between 1753 and 1908.

26. The grain prices for the three groups of provinces is the arithmetic mean of prices of the provinces included in each group. See Tables 1 and 26 in my work *An Estimate of the Land Tax* . . . . Note that in a number of provinces the grain rate of collection was lower than the market price of grain. This was because the provincial authorities in those provinces fixed and adjusted the rate without reference to grain prices in the market.

6. THE PRICE MOVEMENT AND THE LAND TAX BURDEN

1. See n. 1 in the Introduction; *CKCTNYS*, pp. 297-284.
2. Yen Ts'ai-chieh, 4.16-17, 26-28, 92-93.
3. See Tables 4.1, 4.4, and 5.6. For the reduction of the grain quota, see Hsia Nai, "T'ai-p'ing t'ien-kuo ch'ien-hou Ch'ang-chiang ko-sheng chih t'ien-fu wen-t'i," and my article "The Impact of the Taiping Rebellion on Population in Southern Kiangsu."
4. See Tables 4.1, 4.4, and 5.6.
5. For population increase, see Table 1.1.
   Agricultural output = cultivated acreage × land yields.
Thus the index of the output in 1910 would be 180, given 1750 as the base year. For the rising agricultural output in the period, see esp. Dwight H. Perkins, *Agricultural Development in China*, pp. 16-29.
6. See my article, "The Secular Trend of Prices during the Ch'ing Period." See also Table 3.4.
7. *CTLT*, 50.17b. For Pao Shih-ch'en, see Arthur W. Hummel, ed., *Eminent Chinese of the Ch'ing Period* (Washington, D.C., Government Printing Office, 1944), pp. 610-611.
8. *Huang-ch'ao Tao Hsien T'ung Kuang tsou-i*, comp. Wang Yen-hsi (Shanghai, 1902), 30.3.
9. P'eng Yün-chang, *Kuei-p'u-an ts'ung-kao* (1848 preface), 4.24b.
10. Miu Tzu, *Miu Wu-lieh-kung i-chi* (1881), 1.12.
11. Feng Kuei-fen, *Hsien-chih-t'ang chi* (1876), 11.30-35.
12. See *Chung-Kuo chin-tai huo-pi-shih tzu-liao*, I, 105-106; Hsia Nai, "T'ai-p'ing t'ien-kuo ch'ien-hou . . . ," pp. 427-428; Sasaki Masaya, p. 187.
13. *Ch'uan-sha-hsien chih* (1937), 8.22b.
14. Although in the case of the grain tax people may pay it either in kind or in cash, 90 percent of the tax was actually paid in cash. See *TCSMS* (Kiangsu-Soochow), R–L, 28.
15. *TCSMS* (Kiangsu-Soochow), R–L, 19, 27, and 28; *Nan-hui-hsien hsü-chih* (1928), 4.12b.
16. *Ch'uan-sha-hsien chih* (1937), 8.27.
17. According to the provincial regulation the grain rate of collection (surcharges not included) in the area under the jurisdiction of the Soochow financial commissioner was to be fixed in the early winter each year at a rate 100-200 cash less than the market price of the unpolished rice in Wu-hsi where grain was usually cheaper than in Shanghai. If the rates in these few years (1906-10) were determined on the basis of the market price in copper cash, these rates (surcharges excluded) would have been higher than the average price of rice in Shanghai. For the regulation, see *TCSMS* (Kiangsu-

Soochow), R–L, 28. For the average price of rice in Shanghai, see *DR* (1902-11), app. p. 340.

18. The only exception occurred in 1902-03 when taxes rose faster than did prices because of levying additional surcharges: one for the Boxer indemnity (1902) and one for the construction of irrigation works. See Muramatsu Yuji, *Kindai Kōnan no sosen*, p. 717.

19. After the Taiping Rebellion the rates of collection (including the tax quota and regular surcharges) were the same in all but a few districts within the area under the jurisdiction of the Soochow financial commissioner. See *TCSMS* (Kiangsu-Soochow), R–L, 19, 28.

20. The composition of the land tax quota in Su-chou Prefecture and Ch'uan-sha t'ing in the late Ch'ing is as follows:

	Ti-ting quota	Grain quota
Su-chou prefecture	558,198 taels	550,850 shih
Ch'uan-sha t'ing	9,804 taels	8,530 shih

Assuming one tael and one shih of quota each as a unit, the proportion between the *ti-ting* quota and the grain quota in Su-chou prefecture was approximately 1:1 while the proportion in Ch'uan-sha 1.2:1. For sources, see *Su-chou-fu chih* (1881), 12.60b-63; *Ch'uan-sha-hsien chih* (1937), 8.45.

21. After the Taiping Rebellion the grain quota in the Soochow-Shanghai area was reduced by about a third; therefore there is no question that the real burden of the tax upon the landowners had been substantially lessened in the late Ch'ing. There is, moreover, solid evidence indicating the same. On the eve of the rebellion Tseng-Kuo-fan observed that landlords in the area paid the government three-quarters of the rent they collected from the tenants. About the same time Pao Shih-ch'en put the proportion at 60 percent. In the last decade of the dynasty, according to the records of the Wu-clan bursary, the proportion was about 30 percent. In another article Muramatsu observed in the case of the Feng Lin-i bursary in Soochow that the land tax amounted to about 13 percent of the land rent in the post-Taiping period. The last figure is however much too low because of the unrealistic nature of the data on which his observation is based. On the one hand, his data on land rent in this case are but those on the nominal rent, not the real rent (the latter was usually 20 percent less than the former). On the other hand, his data on the land tax are those of the tax quota, not the amount actually paid to the government. See Hsia Nai, "T'ai-p'ing t'ien-kuo chien-hou . . . ," pp. 464-465; *Huang-ch'ao Tao Hsien T'ung Kuang tsou-i*, 30.3; Pao Shih-ch'en, 7B.7; Muamatsu Yuji, "Shin-matsu Min-sho no Kōnan . . . ," and "Shin-matsu Sochū fukin no ichi sosen ni okeru chishu shoyūchi no seizei kosaku kankei," in *Kindai Kōnan no sosen*, pp. 391-636, 679-747.

22. See my work, *An Estimate of the Land Tax . . .* , section on the middle Yangtze provinces, 16.

23. The rate of collection in Kiangsi in the post-Taiping period was uniformly set for all districts. Hence the case of Nan-ch'ang could serve as a good indicator of the state of land taxation for the whole province. See *ibid.*

24. The province of Kiangsu was divided into two areas: one under the jurisdiction of the Soochow financial commissioner and the other under the jurisdiction of the Kiangning financial commissioner. For the unresponsiveness of the grain rate of collection to the market grain prices, see *TCSMS* (Hupei), R–L, 6; *TCSMS* (Kwangtung), R–LA, 2; *TCSMS* (Kiangsu-Kiangning), I.84-85; *Lo-ting chih* (1934 preface), 3.3b; *Hsin-teng-hsien chih* (1922), 11.14-18.

25. See Table 4.4 and my work, *An Estimate of the Land Tax* . . . , Table 10. The heaviness of the land tax burden in the Soochow area can be traced at least to the sixteenth century. See my article "The Impact of the Taiping Rebellion . . . ."

26. See Table 10 in my work, *An Estimate of the Land Tax* . . . .

27. The reported land value of the Soochow suburb was much too low because the Japanese consulate reported at the same time the province-wide land prices per mou as follows:

> High-grade land: 40-50 taels
> Medium-grade land: 20-30 taels
> Low-grade land: 15-20 taels

Since the land in the Soochow area was the most productive in the province, it is hardly possible that the land price in the area would be much lower than the province-wide price of the same grade land. See Gaimushō Tsūshōkyoku, *Shinkoku jijō*, I, 580-581.

28. John L. Buck, *Chinese Farm Economy* (Chicago, University of Chicago Press, 1930), p. 75.

29. The new land tax of 1873 in Japan, which was fixed at 3 percent of the land value, was said to have appropriated 33 percent of the total crop at the outset—nearly as much as the share appropriated by the feudal lord in the Tokugawa period. Later, the percentage declined substantially because land values increased whereas the assessment of land tax remained unchanged. According to an estimate, in years from 1879 to 1911 the land tax in Japan comprised about 10 percent of income originating in agriculture. See William W. Lockwood, *The Economic Development of Japan: Growth and Structural Change, 1868-1938* (Princeton, Princeton University Press, 1954), p. 98; Harry T. Oshima, "Meiji Fiscal Policy and Agricultural Progress," in William W. Lockwood, ed., *The State and Economic Enterprise in Japan*, pp. 353-389.

7. RECONSTRUCTION OF THE LAND TAX ADMINISTRATION

1. For the role of the land tax in Meiji Japan, see Gustav Ranis, "The Financing of Japanese Economic Development," *Economic History Review*, 11.3 (April 1959), 440-454.

2. Ta-chung Liu and Kung-chia Yeh, pp. 66, 178.

3. *Silver and Prices in China*, comp. Ministry of Industries (Shanghai, The Commercial Press, 1935), pp. 6-7.

4. As suggested by some economists, the share of the government sector in the gross national product at 12 percent may be taken as fairly typical of low-income countries. See Wald and Froomkin, p. 67; John F. Due, *Taxation and Economic Development in Tropical Africa* (Cambridge, M.I.T. Press, 1963), pp. 25-26.

5. While there are many who assert that there had been a trend toward land concentration in the Ch'ing and the Republican periods, Ramon H. Myers finds in his detailed study of a few villages in North China little evidence of increased tenancy between 1880 and 1937. See Ramon H. Myers, *The Chinese Peasant Economy: Agricultural Development in Hopei and Shantung, 1890-1949* (Cambridge, Harvard University Press, 1970), pp. 15-16, 234-240.

Bibliography

Abe Takeo 安部健夫. "Beikoku jukyū no kenkyū" 米穀需給の研究 (The supply and demand of the staple food in the reign of the Yung-cheng Emperor), *Tōyōshi kenkyū* 東洋史研究 (The journal of Oriental research), 15.4: 120–213 (March 1954).

—— "Kōsen teikai no kenkyū" 耗羨提解の研究 (On *hao-hsien*), *Tōyōshi kenkyū*, 16.4: 108–261 (March 1958).

Adshead, S. A. M. *The Modernization of the Chinese Salt Administration, 1900–1920.* Cambridge, Mass., Harvard University Press, 1970.

An-hui t'ung-chih kao 安徽通志稿 (A draft of the general gazetteer of Anhwei). 1934.

Beal, Edwin G., Jr. *The Origin of Likin, 1853–1864.* Cambridge, Mass., East Asian Research Center, Harvard University, 1958.

Break, George F. *Intergovernmental Fiscal Relations in the United States.* Washington, D. C., The Brookings Institution, 1967.

Brunnert, H. S., and V. V. Hagelstrom. *Present Day Political Organization of China.* tr. A. Beltchenko and E. E. Moran. Shanghai, Kelly and Walsh, 1912.

Buck, John L. *Chinese Farm Economy.* Chicago, University of Chicago Press, 1930.

Cameron, Meribeth E. *The Reform Movement in China, 1898–1912.* New York, Octagon Books, Inc., 1963.

Chang Chung-li. *The Chinese Gentry.* Seattle, University of Washington Press, 1955.

—— *The Income of the Chinese Gentry.* Seattle, University of Washington Press, 1962.

Chang Jen-chia 張人价, comp. *Hunan no kokubei* 湖南の穀米 (The rice of Hunan). Tokyo, Seikatsu sha 生活社, 1940.

Chang Kia-ngau. *China's Struggle for Railroad Development.* New York, The John Day Company, 1943.

Ch'ang-chih-hsien chih 長治縣志 (The gazetteer of Ch'ang-chih-hsien). 1763 preface.

Chao Ch'eng-ch'üan 趙澄泉. *Ch'ing-tai ti-li yen-ke-piao* 清代地理沿革表 (A table of historical geography of the Ch'ing dynasty). Shanghai, 1941.

Ch'ao-chou chih hui-pien 潮州志滙編 (The comprehensive gazetteer of Ch'ao-chou). Hong Kong, Lung-men shu-chü 龍門書局, 1965.

Che-chiang t'ung-chih 浙江通志 (General gazetteer of Chekiang). Shanghai, The Commercial Press, 1934.

Chen Shao-kwan. *The System of Taxation in China in the Tsing Dynasty, 1644–1911*. New York, Columbia University, 1914.

Ch'en Chao-nan 陳昭南. *Yung-cheng Ch'ien-lung nien-chien ti yin-ch'ien pi-chia pien-tung* 雍正乾隆年間的銀錢比價變動 (Changes in the silver-cash ratios during the Yung-cheng and Ch'ien-lung periods). Taipei, 1966.

Ch'en Chen-han 陳振漢. "Ming-mo Ch'ing-ch'u Chung-kuo ti nung-yeh lao-tung sheng-ch'an li, ti-tsu, ho t'u-ti chi-chung" 明末清初中國的農業勞動生產力, 地租, 和土地集中 (Labor productivity, land rent, and land concentration in China during the late Ming and early Ch'ing, 1620–1720), *Ching-chi yen-chiu* 經濟研究 (*Economic research*), no. 3: 124–139 (Peking, 1955).

Ch'en Teng-yüan 陳登原. *Chung-kuo t'ien-fu shih* 中國田賦史 (The history of land taxation in China). Shanghai, The Commercial Press, 1936.

Cheng-chih kuan-pao 政治官報 (Political gazette). Taipei, Wen-hai ch'u-pan she 文海出版社, 1965 reprint.

Cheng-hsien chih 嵊縣志 (The gazetteer of Cheng hsien). 1934.

Chi Chao-ting. *Key Economic Areas in Chinese History*. New York, Paragon Book Reprint Corp., 1963.

Chia Shih-i 賈士毅. *Min-kuo ts'ai-cheng shih* 民國財政史 (The financial history of Republican China). Shanghai, The Commercial Press, 1917.

Chia-ting-hsien hsü-chih 嘉定縣續志 (The gazetteer of Chia-ting hsien, continued). 1930.

Chiang Heng-yüan 江恒源, comp. *Chung-kuo kuan-shui shih-liao* 中國關稅史料 (Historical materials on the maritime and native customs of China). Shanghai, 1931.

Chiang-hsi t'ung-chih 江西通志 (General gazetteer of Kiangsi). 1732 preface and 1880.

Chiang-nan t'ung-chih 江南通志 (General gazetteer of Chiangnan). 1684 preface.

Ch'ing-ch'ao hsü wen-hsien t'ung-k'ao 清朝續文獻通考 (Encyclopedia of the historical records of the Ch'ing dynasty, continued). Shanghai, the Commercial Press, 1936.

Ch'ing-ch'ao wen-hsien t'ung-k'ao 清朝文獻通考 (Encyclopedia of the historical records of the Ch'ing dynasty). Shanghai, The Commercial Press, 1936.

Ch'ou Chi-heng 仇繼恒. *Shan-ching Han-chiang liu-yü mou-i piao* 陝境漢江流域貿易表 (Table of trade in the valley of Han River in Shensi), in Sung Lien-k'uei 宋聯奎, comp. *Kuan-chung ts'ung-shu* 關中叢書 (Collected works on Shensi). Shensi, 1934–1935.

Chu-p'i yü-chih 硃批御旨 (Vermillion-endorsed edicts). 1738 preface.

Ch'uan-sha-hsien chih 川沙縣志 (The gazetteer of Ch'uan-sha hsien). 1937.

Ch'uan-sha-t'ing chih 川沙廳志 (The gazetteer of Ch'uan-sha t'ing). 1879.

Chung-hsiu Chen-yüan-hsien chih 重修鎮原縣志 (The gazetteer of Chen-yüan hsien, rev. ed.). 1935.

Chung-hsiu Kuan-hsien chih 重修灌縣志 (The gazetteer of Kuan hsien, rev. ed.). 1886.

Chung-kuo chin-tai ching-chi-shih yen-chiu chi-k'an 中國近代經濟史研究集刊

(Journal of modern Chinese economic history).

Chung-kuo chin-tai huo-pi-shih tzu-liao 中國近代貨幣史資料 (Materials on the monetary history of modern China), comp. Chung-kuo jen-min yin-hang 中國人民銀行 (The People's Bank of China). Peking, Chung-hua shu-chü, 1964, first collection.

Chung-kuo chin-tai nung-yeh-shih tzu-liao 中國近代農業史資料 (Materials on the agricultural history of modern China). First collection, 1840–1911, comp. Li Wen-chih 李文治. Peking, San-lien shu-tien 三聯書店, 1957.

Chung-kuo ching-chi, 1948 中國經濟, 1948 (The economy of China, 1948). Canton (?), Hua-nan hsin-wen-she 華南新聞社, 1948.

Chung-yang yen-chiu yüan li-shih yü-yen yen-chiu-so chi-k'an 中央研究院歷史語言研究所集刊 (Bulletin of the Institute of History and Philology, Academia Sinica).

Ch'ü T'ung-tsu. *Local Government in China under the Ch'ing.* Cambridge, Mass., Harvard University Press, 1962.

Ch'üan Han-sheng 全漢昇. "Chia-wu chan-cheng i-ch'ien ti Chung kuo kung-yeh-hua yün-tung" 甲午戰爭以前的中國工業化運動 (China's industrialization movement before the Sino-Japanese War of 1894–1895), *CYYY,* 25: 180–270 (1954).

——— "Ya-p'ien chan-cheng ch'ien Chiang-su ti mien-fang-chih-yeh" 鴉片戰爭前江蘇的棉紡織業 (The cotton textile industry of Kiangsu before the Opium War), *Tsing-hua hsüeh-pao* 清華學報 (The Tsing Hua journal), new series, 1.3: 25–51 (September 1958).

——— and Wang Yeh-chien 王業鍵. "Ch'ing Yung-cheng nien-chien ti mi-chia" 清雍正年間的米價 (Rice prices during the Yung-cheng period of the Ch'ing dynasty), *CYYY,* 30: 157–189 (1959).

Decennial Reports. Shanghai, Inspectorate General of Customs, various dates.

Doris, Lillian, ed. *The American Way in Taxation: Internal Revenue, 1862–1963.* Englewood Cliffs, N. J., Prentice-Hall, 1963.

Due, John F. *Government Finance.* Homewood, Ill., Richard D. Irwin, Inc., 1954.

——— *Taxation and Economic Development in Tropical Africa.* Cambridge, M. I. T. Press, 1963.

Ecker-Racz, L. L. *The Politics and Economics of State-Local Finance.* Englewood Cliffs, N. J., Prentice-Hall, 1970.

Edkins, J. *The Revenue and Taxation of the Chinese Empire.* Shanghai, 1903.

Fang Hsien-t'ing 方顯廷. *Chung-kuo chih mien-fang-chih yeh* 中國之棉紡織業 (The cotton textile industry of China). Shanghai, The Commercial Press, 1934.

Feng-hua-hsien chih 奉化縣志 (The gazetteer of Feng-hua hsien). Taipei, 1957 reprint.

Feng Hua-te 馮華德 and Li Ling 李陵. "Ho-pei sheng Ting hsien chih t'ien-fu" 河北省定縣之田賦 (The land tax in Ting hsien of Hopei Province), *Cheng-chih ching-chi hsüeh-pao* 政治經濟學報 (The journal of political economy), 4.3: 443–520 (Tientsin, April 1936).

Feng Kuei-fen 馮桂芬. *Hsien-chih-t'ang chi* 顯志堂集 (Collected essays of Feng Kuei-fen). 1876.

——— *Chiao-fen-lu k'ang-i* 校邠廬抗議 (Protests of Feng Kuei-fen). 1884.

Feng-t'ien-sheng nung-yeh shih-yen-ch'ang 奉天省農業試驗場 (The Agricultural Experimental Station of Feng-t'ien Province). *Feng-t'ien ch'üan-sheng nung-yeh t'iao-ch'a-shu* 奉天全省農業調查書 (Agricultural survey of the whole province of Feng-t'ien), 1.4 (February 1909).

Fu-chien t'ung-chih 福建通志 (General gazetteer of Fukien). 1737 preface.

"Fu-i o-cheng ti-ts'ao feng-kung teng-k'uan ch'ien-liang ping k'ou-lien k'uan-mu-pu" 阜邑額征地漕俸ユ等款錢糧並扣廉款目簿 (An account book of land-tax quota, salaries, wages, and deductions from *yang-lien yin*, Fu-ning hsien). c. 1906, ms. in Harvard-Yenching Library.

Fu Tsung-mo 傅宗懋. *Ch'ing-tai chün-chi ch'u tsu-chih chi chih-chang chih yen-chiu* 清代軍機處組織及職掌之研究 (A study of the organization and functions of the Grand Council in the Ch'ing dynasty). Taipei, 1967.

Fujii Hiroshi 藤井宏. "Mindai tento tōkei ni kan suru ikkosatsu" 明代田土統計に關する一考察, II (A critical examination of the statistics of the cultivated fields in the Ming dynasty), *Tōyō gakuhō* 東洋學報 (Reports of the Oriental Society), 30.4: 60–87(August 1944).

——— "Shinan shōnin no kenkyū (2)" 新安商人の研究, II (A study of the Hsin-an merchants, II), *Tōyō gakuhō*, 36.2: 32–60 (September 1953).

Gaimushō Tsūshōkyoku 外務所通商局 (The Bureau of Trade of the Foreign Office). *Shinkoku jijō* 清國事情 (General conditions of the Ch'ing empire). 2 vols. Tokyo, 1907.

Hei-lung-chiang chih-kao 黑龍江志稿 (A draft of the gazetteer of Hei-lung-chiang). comp. in 1932. Taipei, 1965 reprint.

Helfferich, Karl. *Money*. London, Ernest Beun Ltd., 1927.

Hinton, Harold C. *The Grain Tribute System of China, 1845–1911*. Cambridge, Mass., East Asian Research Center, Harvard University, 1970.

Ho Ch'ang-ling 賀長齡. *Nan-an tsou-i ts'un-kao* 耐菴奏議存稿 (The memorials of Ho Ch'ang-ling). 1881 preface.

Ho-nan t'ung-chih 河南通志 (General gazetteer of Honan). 1660 preface.

Ho Ping-ti. "The Salt Merchants of Yang-chou: A Study of Commercial Capitalism in 18th-century China," *Harvard Journal of Asiatic Studies*, 17.1–2: 130–168 (June 1954).

——— *Studies on the Population of China, 1368–1953*. Cambridge, Mass., Harvard University Press, 1959.

Hou Chi-ming. "Economic Dualism: The Case of China, 1840–1937," *Journal of Economic History*, 13.3: 277–297 (September 1965).

Hsia Nai 夏鼐. "T'ai-p'ing t'ien-kuo ch'ien-hou Chang-chiang ko-sheng chih t'ien-fu wen-t'i" 太平天國前後長江各省之田賦問題 (The land-tax problem of the Yangtze provinces before and after the Taiping Rebellion), *Tsing-hua hsüeh-pao*, 10.2: 409–474 (April 1935).

Hsiang-t'an-hsien chih 湘潭縣志 (The gazetteer of Hsiang-t'an hsien). 1889.

Hsiao Kung-chuan. *Rural China*. Seattle, University of Washington Press, 1967.

Hsin-ch'ang-hsien chih 新昌縣志 (The gazetteer of Hsin-ch'ang hsien). 1918.

Hsin-teng-hsien chih 新登縣志 (The gazetteer of Hsin-teng hsien). 1922.

Hsü Keng-pi 徐賡陛. *Pu-ch'ien-chai man-ts'un* 不慊齋漫存 (Miscellaneous notes of Hsü Keng-pi). 1882.

Hsü Ta-ling 許大齡. *Ch'ing-tai chüan-na chih-tu* 清代捐納制度 (The system of purchasing degrees and offices by contributions during the Ch'ing dynasty). Peking, Yenching University, 1950.

Hsü Yüan-fan 許元方. *I Lan-chou* 憶蘭州 (Reminiscences about Lan-chou). Hong Kong, 1941.

Hu-pei t'ung-chih 湖北通志 (General gazetteer of Hupei). Chia-ch'ing ed. Shanghai, The Commercial Press, 1921.

Hu-pu tse-li 戶部則例 (Regulations of the Board of Revenue). 1874.

Huang-ch'ao cheng-tien lei-tsuan 皇朝政典類纂 (A classified compendium of the administrative statutes of the Ch'ing dynasty), comp. Hsi Yü-fu 席裕福 et al. 1903 preface.

Huang-ch'ao ching-shih wen-pien 皇朝經世文編 (Collected essays on statecraft in the Ch'ing dynasty), comp. Ho Ch'ang-ling 賀長齡. 1886.

Huang-ch'ao Tao Hsien T'ung Kuang tsou-i 皇朝道咸同光奏議 (Memorials of the Tao-kuang, Hsien-feng, T'ung-chih, and Kuang-hsü periods of the Ch'ing dynasty), comp. Wang Yen-hsi 王延熙. Shanghai, 1902.

Huang Han Liang. *The Land Tax in China*. New York, Columbia University, 1918.

Huang-Ming ching-shih wen-pien 皇明經世文編 (Collected essays on statecraft in the Ming dynasty), comp. Ch'en Tzu-lung 陳子龍 et al. Taipei, Kuo-lien t'u-shu kung-ssu, 1964 reprint.

Hummel, Arthur W., ed. *Eminent Chinese of the Ch'ing Period*. Washington, D. C., Government Printing Office, 1944.

Inspectorate General of Customs. *Native Customs Trade Returns, No. 3—Quinquennial Reports and Returns, 1902–1906*. Shanghai, 1907.

——— *Working of Likin Collectorates: Kiukiang, Soochow, and Hangchow*. Shanghai, 1907.

Ju-kao-hsien chih 如皋縣志 (The gazetteer of Ju-kao hsien). 1804 preface.

K'ai-yüan-hsien chih 開原縣志 (The gazetteer of K'ai-yuan hsien). 1917.

Kan-su sheng-cheng-fu 甘肅省政府 (The provincial government of Kansu), comp. *Kan-su-sheng chü-pan t'u-ti ch'en-pao chi-shih* 甘肅省舉辦土地陳報紀實 (A general description of the undertaking of land reporting in Kansu province). 1942.

Katō Shigeshi 加藤繁. "Shin chō koki no zaisei ni tsuite" 清朝後期の財政につ いて (On the public finance during the latter part of the Ch'ing dynasty), in his collected works, *Shina keizaishi kōshō* 支那經濟史考証 (Studies on Chinese economic history). Tokyo, Tōyō Bunko 東洋文庫, 1953.

Kimura Masutarō 木村増太郎. *Shina zaiseiron* 支那財政論 (Treatise on the finance of China). Tokyo, 1927.

King, Frank H. H. *Money and Monetary Policy in China, 1845–1895*. Cambridge, Mass., Harvard University Press, 1965.

Ko Shih-chün 葛士濬, comp. *Huang-ch'ao ching-shih wen hsü-pien* 皇朝經世文 續編 (Collected essays on statecraft in the Ch'ing dynasty, continued). Shanghai, 1888.

Ku Yen-wu 顧炎武. *Jih-chih lü chi-shih* 日知錄集釋 (Daily notes with comments). Shanghai, Chung-hua shu-chü, 1927.

Kuan-hsien chih 灌縣志 (The gazetteer of Kuan hsien). 1932.

Kuang-tung t'ung-chih 廣東通志 (General gazetteer of Kwangtung). 1852 preface, Taipei, 1959 reprint.

Kuei-chou t'ung-chih 貴州通志 (General gazetteer of Kweichow). 1692 preface.

Li Cheng-shui 李成瑞. *Chung-hua jen-min kung-ho-kuo nung-yeh-shui shih-kao* 中華人民共和國農業稅史稿 (A draft of the agricultural history of the People's Republic of China). Peking, 1959.

Li Chuan-shih. *Central and Local Finance in China*. New York, Columbia University, 1922.

Liu Chün 劉崙. "Tao-kuang ch'ao Liang-huai fei-yin kai-p'iao shih-mo" 道光朝 兩淮廢引改票始末 (The reform of the salt gabelle system in the Lianghuai region during the Tao-kuang period), *CTCC*, 1.2: 123–188 (May 1933).

Liu Hsün-kao 劉郇膏 et al. *Chiang-su sheng chien-fu ch'üan-an* 江蘇省減賦全案

(The complete documents on tax reductions in Kiangsu Province). 1866.

Liu K'un-i i-chi 劉坤一遺集 (Posthumous works of Liu K'un-i). Peking, 1959.

Liu Kwang-Ching. "Nineteenth-Century China: The Disintegration of the Old Order and the Impact of the West," in Ping-ti Ho and Tang Tsou, eds. *China in Crisis*, vol. I, book 1. Chicago, University of Chicago Press, 1968, pp. 93–178.

Liu Ta-chung and Kung-chia Yeh. *The Economy of the Chinese Mainland, 1933–1959*. Princeton, Princeton University Press, 1965.

Liu Yo-yün 劉嶽雲. *Kuang-hsü k'uai-chi-piao* 光緒會計表 (Tables of revenue and expenditure in the Kuang-hsü period). 1901.

Lo Erh-kang 羅爾綱. *Hsiang-chün hsin-chih* 湘軍新志 (A new history of the Hunan army). Changsha, The Commercial Press, 1939.

Lo-p'ing hsien chih 羅平縣志 (The gazetteer of Lo-p'ing hsien). 1932.

Lo-ting chih 羅定志 (The gazetteer of Lo-ting). 1934 preface.

Lo Yü-tung 羅玉東. "Kuang-hsü ch'ao pu-chiu ts'ai-cheng chih fang-ts'e" 光緒朝補救財政之方策 (The government policies of meeting the financial crisis during the Kuang-hsü period), *CTCC*, 1.2: 189–270 (May 1933).

——— *Chung-kuo li-chin-shih* 中國釐金史 (The history of likin in China). Shanghai, The Commercial Press, 1936.

Lockwood, William W. *The Economic Development of Japan: Growth and Structural Change, 1868–1938*. Princeton, Princeton University Press, 1954.

———, ed. *The State and Economic Enterprise in Japan*. Princeton, Princeton University Press, 1965.

Metzger, Thomas A. "The Organizational Capabilities of the Ch'ing State in the Field of Commerce: The Liang-huai Salt Monopoly, 1740–1840," in W. E. Willmott, ed. *Economic Organization in Chinese Society*. Stanford, Stanford University Press, 1972, pp. 9–45.

Miu Tzu 繆梓. *Miu Wu-lieh-kung i-chi* 繆武烈公遺集 (Posthumous works of Miu Tzu). 1881.

Morse, Hosea B. *The Trade and Administration of China*. London, Longmans, Green, and Co., 1908.

Muramatsu Yūji 村松祐次. "Shinmatsu Minsho no Kōnan ni okeru hōran kankei no jittai to sono kessan hōkoku" 清末民初の江南における包攬關係の實態とその決算報告 (The actual condition of the operation on contract for tax payment and its balance sheet in southern Kiangsu during the late Ch'ing and early Republican period), in *Kindai Kōnan no sosen* 近代江南の租棧 (The landlord bursary in Kiangnan in modern times). Tokyo, Tokyo University Press, 1970, pp. 391–636.

——— "Shin-matsu Sochū fukin no ichi sosen ni okeru chishu shoyūchi no seizei kosaku kankei" 清末蘇州附近の一租棧における地主所有地の征稅小作關係 (The relationship between taxes and rent of certain landlords' property managed by a bursary near Soochow in the late Ch'ing), in *Kindai Kōnan no sosen*, pp. 679–747.

Myers, Ramon H. *The Chinese Peasant Economy: Agricultural Development in Hopei and Shantung, 1890–1949*. Cambridge, Mass., Harvard University Press, 1970.

Nan-ch'ang hsien chih 南昌縣志 (The gazetteer of Nan-ch'ang hsien). 1919.

Nan-ch'uan-hsien chih 南川縣志 (The gazetteer of Nan-ch'uan hsien). 1926 preface.

Nan-hui-hsien hsü-chih 南滙縣續志 (The gazetteer of Nan-hui hsien, continued). 1928.

Nanavati, Manilal B. and J. J. Anjaria. *The Indian Rural Problem.* Bombay, Indian Society of Agricultural Economy, 1965.

Nankai Institute of Economics. *Nankai Weekly Statistical Service,* 5.15 (April 11, 1932).

Nung Yeh 農也. "Chung-kuo shih-chiu shih-chi hou-pan nung-yeh sheng-ch'an ti shang-p'in-hua" 中國十九世紀後半農業生產的商品化 (The commercialization of agricultural production in China during the last half of the nineteenth century), *Ching-chi yen-chiu,* no. 3: 120–140 (Peking, 1956); no. 4: 129–137 (1956).

Ohkawa, Kazushi, and Henry Rosovsky. "A Century of Japanese Economic Growth," in William W. Lockwood, ed., *The State and Economic Enterprise in Japan,* pp. 47–92.

Oshima, Harry T. "Meiji Fiscal Policy and Agricultural Progress," in William W. Lockwood, ed., *The State and Economic Enterprise in Japan,* pp. 353–389.

P'an-yü-hsien hsü-chih 番禺縣續志 (The gazetteer of P'an-yü hsien, continued). 1931 preface.

Pao Shih-ch'en 包世臣. *An-wu ssu-chung* 安吳四種 (Four works of Pao Shih-ch'en). 1872 preface.

P'eng Yü-hsin 彭雨新. "Ch'ing-mo chung-yang yü ko-sheng ts'ai cheng kuan-hsi" 清末中央與各省財政關係 (The financial relations between the central and provincial governments in the late Ch'ing), *She-hui ko-hsüeh tsa-chih* 社會科學雜誌 (Quarterly review of social sciences), 9.1: 83–110 (June 1947).

P'eng Yün-chang 彭蘊章. *Kuei-p'u-an ts'ung-kao* 歸樸盦叢稿 (Collected works of P'eng Yün-chang). 1848 preface.

Perkins, Dwight H. *Agricultural Development in China, 1368–1968.* Chicago, Aldine Publishing Co., 1969.

Ranis, Gustav. "The Financing of Japanese Economic Development," *Economic History Review,* 11.3: 440–454 (April 1959).

Returns of Trade and Trade Reports. Shanghai, Inspectorate General of Customs, various dates.

Sasaki Masaya 佐佐木正哉. "Kampō ninen Yin-ken no kōryō bōdō 咸豐二年鄞縣の抗糧暴動 (The riot against land taxation in Yin hsien in 1852), *Kindai Chūgoku kenkyū* 近代中國研究 (Studies on modern China), 5: 185–299 (Tokyo, 1963).

Shan-hsi t'ung-chih 山西通志 (General gazetteer of Shansi). 1892.

Shan-hsi Tzu-yang-hsien chih 陝西紫陽縣志 (The gazetteer of Tsu-yang hsien in Shensi). 1925.

Shang-hai t'ung-hsin-she 上海通訊社, comp. *Shang-hai yen-chiu tzu-liao* 上海研究資料 (Research materials on Shanghai). Shanghai, Chung-hua shu-chü, 1936.

Shao-hsing hsien-chih tzu-liao 紹興縣志資料 (Materials on the local history of Shao-hsing hsien). 1939, first collection.

Shaw, Stanford J. *The Financial Administrative Organization and Development of Ottoman Egypt, 1517–1789.* Princeton, Princeton University Press, 1962.

Shimizu Taiji 清水泰次. "Chō kyosei no tochi jōryō ni tsuite" 張居正の土地丈量について (A study of land survey by Chang Chü-cheng in the latter part of the sixteenth century), *Tōyō gakuhō,* 29.2: 167–198 (May 1942).

Shina keizai zensho 支那經濟全書 (The encyclopedia of the Chinese economy), comp. Tōa Dōbunkai 東亞同文會. Tokyo, 1908.

Silver and Prices in China, comp. Committee for the Study of Silver Values and Commodity Prices, Ministry of Industries. Shanghai, The Commercial Press, 1935.

Su-chou-fu chih 蘇州府志 (The gazetteer of Su-chou fu). 1881.

Sun E-tu Zen. *Chinese Railways and British Interests*. New York, King's Crown Press, 1954.

——— "The Board of Revenue in 19th-century China," *Harvard Journal of Asiatic Studies*, 24: 175–227 (1962–63).

Ta-Ch'ing Hsüan-t'ung cheng-chi 大清宣統政紀 (Political chronicles of the Hsüan-t'ung period of the Ch'ing dynasty). Taipei, Hua-wen shu-chü 華文書局, 1964 reprint.

Ta-Ch'ing Hsüan-t'ung hsin-fa-ling 大清宣統新法令 (New laws and ordinances in the Hsüan-t'ung period of the Ch'ing dynasty). Shanghai, The Commercial Press, 1910.

Ta-Ch'ing hui-tien 大清會典 (Collected statutes of the Ch'ing dynasty).

Ta-Ch'ing hui-tien shih-li 大清會典事例 (Precedents of the collected statutes of the Ch'ing dynasty).

Ta-Ch'ing hui-tien tse-li 大清會典則例 (Precedents of the collected statutes of the Ch'ing dynasty). 1764 preface.

Ta-Ch'ing li-ch'ao shih-lu 大清歷朝實錄 (Veritable records of the successive reigns of the Ch'ing dynasty). Tokyo, 1937–1938.

Tan, Chester C. *The Boxer Catastrophe*. New York, Columbia University Press, 1955.

T'an-yen ts'ung-pao 談鹽叢報 (The salt journal). Shanghai.

T'ang-ch'i-hsien chih 湯溪縣志 (The gazetteer of T'ang-ch'i hsien). 1931.

T'ang Hsiang-lung 湯象龍. "Min-kuo i-ch'ien ti p'ei-k'uan shih ju-ho ch'ang-fu ti" 民國以前的賠款是如何償付的 (A study of the indemnity payments before 1911), *CTCC*, 3.2: 262–291 (November 1935).

T'ao Chu 陶澍. *T'ao Wen-i-kung ch'üan-chi* 陶文毅公全集 (The complete works of T'ao Chu). c. 1840.

T'ieh-ling-hsien chih 鐵嶺縣志 (The gazetteer of T'ieh-ling hsien). 1931 preface.

T'ien-fu an-tu hui-pien 田賦案牘彙編 (Collected documents on the land tax). Ts'ai-cheng pu 財政部 (The Ministry of Finance), n.d.

Ting En 丁恩. *Kai-ke Chung-kuo yen-wu pao-kao-shu* 改革中國塩務報告書 (A report on the reform of the Chinese salt administration). 1922.

Ting Jih-ch'ang 丁日昌. *Fu Wu kung-tu* 撫吳公牘 (Public documents in the governorship of Kiangsu). 1876 preface.

Totman, Conrad D. *Politics in the Tokugawa Bakufu, 1600–1843*. Cambridge, Mass., Harvard University Press, 1967.

Ts'ai-cheng shuo-ming-shu 財政說明書 (Financial reports). This collection includes the following twenty-three reports, published in twenty volumes in 1915 by Ching-chi hsüeh-hui 經濟學會 (Association of economic studies). The province in parentheses indicates the area covered by the report.
(Anhwei): *An-hui ch'üan-sheng ts'ai-cheng shuo-ming shu*
　　　　安徽全省財政說明書
(Chekiang): *Che-chiang ch'üan-sheng ts'ai-cheng shuo-ming shu*
　　　　浙江全省說明書
(Chihli): *Chih-li ch'üan-sheng ts'ai-cheng shuo-ming-shu*
　　　　直隸全省財政說明書

(Fengtien): *Feng-t'ien ch'üan-sheng ts'ai-cheng shuo-ming shu*
奉天全省財政說明書
(Fukien): *Fu-chien ch'üan-sheng ts'ai-cheng shou-ming-shu*
福建全省財政說明書
(Heilungkiang): *Hei-lung-chiang ch'üan-sheng ts'ai-cheng shuo-ming-shu*
黑龍江全省財政說明書
(Honan): *Ho-nan ch'üan-sheng ts'ai-cheng shuo-ming-shu*
河南全省財政說明書
(Hunan): *Hu-nan ch'üan-sheng ts'ai-cheng shuo-ming-shu*
湖南全省財政說明書
(Hupeh): *Hu-pei ch'üan-sheng ts'ai-cheng shuo-ming-shu*
湖北全省財政說明書
(Kansu): *Kan-su ch'üan-sheng ts'ai-cheng shuo-ming-shu*
甘肅全省財政說明書
(Kiangsi): *Chiang-hsi ch'üan-sheng ts'ai-cheng shuo-ming-shu*
江西全省財政說明書
(Kiangsu-Kiangning): *Chiang-su Ning-shu ts'ai-cheng shuo-ming-shu*
江蘇寗屬財政說明書
(Kiangsu-Soochow): *Chiang-su Su-chu ts'ai-cheng shuo-ming-shu*
江蘇蘇屬財政說明書
(Kirin): *Chi-lin ch'üan-sheng ts'ai-cheng shuo-ming-shu*
吉林全省財政說明書
(Kwangsi): *Kuang-hsi ch'üan-sheng ts'ai-cheng shuo-ming-shu*
廣西全省財政說明書
(Kweichow): *Kuei-chou ch'üan-sheng ts'ai-cheng shuo-ming-shu*
貴州全省財政說明書
(Shansi): *Shan-hsi ch'üan-sheng ts'ai-cheng shuo-ming-shu*
山西全省財政說明書
(Shantung): *Shan-tung ch'üan-sheng ts'ai-cheng shuo-ming-shu*
山東全省財政說明書
(Shensi): *Shan-hsi ch'üan-sheng ts'ai-cheng shuo-ming-shu*
陝西全省財政說明書
(Sinkiang): *Hsin-chiang ch'üan-sheng ts'ai-cheng shuo-ming shu*
新疆全省財政說明書
(Szechwan): *Ssu-ch'uan ch'üan-sheng ts'ai-cheng shuo-ming-shu*
四川全省財政說明書
(Yunnan): *Yün-nan ch'üan-sheng ts'ai-cheng shuo-ming-shu*
雲南全省財政說明書
Tsui-chin t'ien-fu chi-yao 最近田賦紀要 (Essential land-tax records of recent years), comp. Chung-kuo ts'ai-cheng (-pu) fu-shui-ssu 中國財政(部)賦稅司 (The division of taxes of the Ministry of Finance, Republic of China), c. late 1910s.
Tung-hua hsü-lu 東華續錄 (The Tung-hua records, continued), comp. Chu Shou-p'eng 朱壽朋. Shanghai, 1909.
Tung-hua lu 東華錄 (The Tung-hua records), comp. Wang Hsien-ch'ien 王先謙. 1884.
Tung-san-sheng cheng-lüeh 東三省政略 (Essential information on the three northeastern provinces), comp. Hsü Shih-ch'ang 徐世昌. 1911; Taipei, Wen-hai ch'u-pan she 文海出版社, 1965 reprint.
Tz'u-ch'i-hsien chih 慈谿縣志 (The gazetteer of Tz'u-ch'i hsien). 1899.
Wagel, S.R. *Finance in China.* Shanghai, North China Daily News and Herald, 1914.

Wald, Haskell P. *Taxation of Agricultural Land in Underdeveloped Economies.* Cambridge, Mass., Harvard University Press, 1959.

Wan Kuo-ting 萬國鼎 et al. *Chiang-su Wu-chin Nan-t'ung t'ien-fu t'iao-ch'a pao-kao* 江蘇武進南通田賦調查報告 (A report on the land-tax survey in Wu-chin and Nan-t'ung districts of Kiangsu). 1934.

Wang Ch'ing-yün 王慶雲. *Shih-ch'ü yü-chi* 石渠餘紀 (Residual notes of Wang Ch'ing-yün). 1890.

Wang Hui-tsu 汪輝祖. *Meng-hen yü-lu* 夢痕餘錄 (lit., "Reminiscences of my dreams"). 1872.

Wang Tan-ch'en 王丹岑. *Chung-kuo nung-min ke-ming shih-hua* 中國農民革命史話 (A historical account of the peasant revolution in China). Shanghai, 1952.

Wang Yeh-chien 王業鍵. "Ch'ing Yung-cheng shih-ch'i ti ts'ai-cheng kai-ke" 清雍正時期的財政改革 (Financial reforms during the Yung-cheng period of the Ch'ing dynasty), *CYYY*, 32: 47–75 (1961).

——— "The Impact of the Taiping Rebellion on Population in Southern Kiangsu," *Papers on China*, 19: 120–158 (December 1965). Cambridge, Mass., East Asian Research Center, Harvard University.

——— "The Fiscal Importance of the Land Tax during the Ch'ing Period," *Journal of Asian Studies*, 30.4: 829–842 (August 1971).

——— "The Secular Trend of Prices during the Ch'ing Period," *Hsiang-kang Chung-wen ta-hsüeh Chung-kuo wen-hua yen-chiu-so hsüeh-pao* 香港中文大學中國文化研究所學報 (Journal of the Institute of Chinese Studies of the Chinese University of Hong Kong), 5.2 (1973).

——— *An Estimate of the Land Tax Collection in China, 1753 and 1908.* Cambridge, Mass., East Asian Research Center, Harvard University, 1973.

——— "Agricultural Development and Peasant Economy in Hunan during the Ch'ing Period," unpublished paper.

Wang Yü-ch'üan. "The Rise of Land Tax and the Fall of Dynasties in Chinese History," *Pacific Affairs*, 9.2: 201–220 (June 1936).

Wei Sung-t'ang 魏頌唐, comp. *Hu-pei ts'ai-cheng chi-lüeh* 湖北財政紀略 (A brief account of public finance in Hupeh). Hu-pei li-chih yen-chiu-so 湖北吏治研究所, 1917.

——— *Che-chiang ts'ai-cheng chi-lüeh* 浙江財政紀略 (A brief account of public finance in Chekiang). 1929 preface.

Wei Yüan 魏源. *Shen-wu chi* 聖武記 (Notes on imperial military exploits). 1927.

Williams, E. T. "Taxation in China," *Quarterly Journal of Economics*, 26.3: 482–510 (May 1912).

Winston, A. P. "Chinese Finance under the Republic," *Quarterly Journal of Economics*, 30.4: 738–779 (August 1916).

Wolf, John B. *The Emergence of the Great Powers, 1685–1715.* New York, Harper, 1951.

Wright, Stanley F., comp. *The Collection and Disposal of the Maritime and Native Customs Revenue Since the Revolution of 1911.* Shanghai, Inspectorate General of Customs, 1925.

——— *Hart and the Chinese Customs.* Belfast, Wm. Mullan and Son, 1950.

Wu Ch'ao-tzu 吳兆梓. *Chung-kuo shui-chih shih* 中國稅制史 (The history of the tax system in China). Shanghai, The Commercial Press, 1937.

Wu, James T. K. "The Impact of the Taiping Rebellion upon the Manchu Fiscal System," *Pacific Historical Review*, 19.3: 265–275 (August 1959).

Yang Lien-sheng. *Money and Credit in China.* Cambridge, Mass., Harvard University Press, 1952.

Yang Tuan-liu et al., comps. *Statistics of China's Foreign Trade During the Last Sixty-five Years.* Institute of Social Sciences, Academia Sinica, 1931.

Yen-cheng ts'ung-k'an 塩政叢刊 (The journal of salt administration). Peking, 1921.

Yen Chung-p'ing 嚴中平. *Chung-kuo mien-fang-chih shih-kao* 中國棉紡織史稿 (A draft history of China's cotton textile industry). Peking, 1955.

―――― *Ch'ing-tai Yün-nan t'ung-cheng k'ao* 清代雲南銅政考 (A study on the administration of copper mining in Yunnan during the Ch'ing dynasty). Peking, Chung-hua shu-chü, 1957.

Yen Ts'ai-chieh 晏才傑. *T'ien-fu ch'u-i* 田賦芻議 (Discourse on the land tax). Peking, 1915.

Yin-hsien t'ung-chih 鄞縣通志 (General gazetteer of Yin hsien). 1935.

Glossary

ch'ai-ching 差敬
ch'ai-yao 差徭
Chang-yeh 張掖
Changsha (Ch'ang-sha) 長沙
Ch'ao-chou 潮州
ch'e-p'i fei 掣批費
Chefoo (Chih-fou) 芝罘
Chen-yüan 鎮原
Cheng 嵊
cheng(-shou) fei 征(收)費
cheng-tsa ko-shui 正雜各稅
ch'eng-kuei 城櫃
chi-ch'üeh 瘠缺
Chi-hao 祭號
chi-ku chüan 積穀捐
ch'i-yün 起運
chia 甲
Chia-ch'ing 嘉慶
Chia-ting 嘉定
Chia-ying 嘉應
Chia-yü-kuan 嘉峪關
Chiang I-li 蔣益澧
Chiao Sung-nien 喬松年
chieh-fei 觧費
chieh-hsiang 觧餉
Ch'ien-lung 乾隆
chih-pi fan-shih 紙筆飯食
chin Chang-yeh yin Wu-wei 金張掖銀武威
chin-t'ieh 津貼
Ching-ch'ien 京錢
Ching-hsiang 京餉
Ch'ing-li ts'ai-cheng-ch'u 清理財政處
Ch'ing-li ts'ai-cheng-chü 清理財政局

ch'ing-yao po-fu 輕徭簿賦
chou (department) 州
ch'uan-p'iao fei 串票費
Ch'uan-sha 川沙
chung-ch'üeh 中缺
Ch'ü-chiang 曲江
chüan-chin 捐津
chüan-hsia 卷下
chüan-na 捐納
chüan-shu 捐輸

fan-shih yin 飯食銀
fang-fei 房費
fei-ch'üeh 肥缺
Foochow (Fu-chou) 福州
fou-shou 浮收
fu (prefecture) 府
Fu-i ch'üan-shu 賦役全書
fu-ma (fei) 夫馬(費)
Fu Min 福敏
Fu-ning 阜寧
fu-pien 附編

Hai-yang 海陽
Hangchow (Hang-chou) 杭州
Hankow (Han-k'ou) 漢口
hao-hsien 耗羨
Ho-ch'ü 河曲
ho-kung chüan 河工捐
hsiang-cheng 鄉征
hsiang-chüan 晌捐
hsiang-kuei 鄉櫃
Hsiang-t'an 湘潭

Hsiao-shan 蕭山
hsieh-hsiang 協餉
hsien (district) 縣
Hsien-feng 咸豐
Hsin-ch'ang 新昌
hsin-cheng chüan 新政捐
Hsü Shih-ch'ang 徐世昌
hsüeh(-t'ang) chüan 學(堂)捐
hsün-ching chüan 巡警捐
Hu-kuan 戶關
Hu Lin-i 胡林翼
Hua-nan hsin-wen-she 華南新聞社
Huai (River) 淮
Huai-ning 淮寧
Huang-ts'e 黃冊

I-tu 益都

Ju-kao 如皋

Kao-tsung 高宗
k'ao-ch'eng 考成
Ko Feng-shih 柯逢時
ko-lun shang 各論上
kua-hao fei 掛號費
Kuan 灌
"Kuan-chih chang-ku" 灌志掌故
kuan min liang-pien 官民兩便
Kuang-chi 廣濟
Kuang-hsin 廣信
Kuang-hsü 光緒
kuei-fei 規費
kuei-fei 櫃費
kung-fei 公費
Kung-kuan 工關
kuo-shui pu 國稅部

Lai-chou 萊州
Lei-chou 雷州
Lei I-hsien 雷以誠
li 里
Li Hung-chang 李鴻章
liang-chüan 糧捐
liang-hsi 糧席
Liangkiang (Liang-Chiang) 兩江
likin (li-chin) 釐金
Lin-ch'ü 臨朐
Lin-tzu 臨淄
Lo Ping-chang 駱秉章
Lo-p'ing 羅平
lo-ti-shui 落地稅
Lu-pin 瀘濱

mei-ch'üeh 美缺
min-t'ien 民田
Miu Tzu 繆梓

mou-chüan 畝捐

Nan-ch'ang 南昌
Nan-ch'uan 南川
Ningpo (Ning-po) 寧波

pao-cheng 包征
pao-hsiao 報効
pao-lan 包攬
Pao Shih-ch'en 包世臣
pao-shou 包收
Peking 北京
P'eng Yün-chang 彭蘊章
p'iao-fei 票費
P'ing-yang 平陽

shan 山
shang-shui 商稅
Shanghai (Shang-hai) 上海
Shanhaikwan 山海關
Shen Pao-chen 沈葆楨
sheng-shui pu 省稅部
Sheng-tsu 聖祖
"Shih-huo chih" 食貨志
shou-hsien 首縣
shui-hsiang 稅項
Soochow (Su-chou) 蘇州
sui-liang chüan 隨糧捐
Swatow (Shan-t'ou) 汕頭

Ta-t'ang 大塘
Taiwan 臺灣
t'an-chüan 攤捐
tang 蕩
t'ang-kung chüan 塘工捐
Tao-kuang 道光
T'eng-ch'ung 騰衝
ti 地
ti-ting 地丁
t'iao-ch'a 調查
t'ieh-lu chüan 鐵路捐
tien-liang 墊糧
t'ien 田
ting 丁
Ting 定
Ting Jih-ch'ang 丁日昌
ting-ts'ao chia-chüan 丁漕加捐
t'ing (subprefecture) 廳
t'ou-wen fei 投文費
tsa-chüan 雜捐
ts'e-fei 冊費
Tseng Kuo-fan 曾國藩
Tso Tsung-t'ang 左宗棠
tsou-hsiao 奏銷
tsou-hsiao ts'e 奏銷冊
tsu-ku 租股

ts'ui-ch'ai 催差
ts'ui-liang fei 催糧費
ts'un-liu 存留
Tsung-li Yamen 總理衙門
tsung-shuo 總說
Tu-pan yen-cheng ch'u 督辦塩政處
Tu-shan 獨山
t'u 圖
t'uan(-lien) fei 團(練)費
t'un-t'ien 屯田
tung-ch'ien 東錢
T'ung-chih 同治
T'ung-kuan 潼關
tzu-chih chüan 自治捐
Tzu-yang 紫陽
Tz'u-ch'i 慈谿

wai-hsiao k'uan 外銷款
Wan-li 萬曆
Wu-chin 武進
Wu-ch'ing 武清
Wu-hsi 無錫
Wu-wei 武威

yang-lien (yin) 養廉(銀)
Yao Wen-t'ien 姚文田
yen-li 塩釐
ying-yü 盈餘
Yung-cheng 雍正
yung-pu chia-fu 永不加賦
yü-liang 餘糧
Yü-lin t'u-ts'e 魚鱗圖冊
yüan-o 原額

Index

Harvard East Asia Series

17. *The Origins of Entrepreneurship in Meiji Japan.* By Johannes Hirschmeier, S.V.D.
18. *Commissioner Lin and the Opium War,* By Hsin-pao Chang.
19. *Money and Monetary Policy in China, 1845-1895.* By Frank H.H. King.
20. *China's Wartime Finance and Inflation, 1937-1945.* By Arthur N. Young.
21. *Foreign Investment and Economic Development in China, 1840-1937.* By Chi-ming Hou.
22. *After Imperialism: The Search for a New Order in the Far East, 1921-1931.* By Akira Iriye.
23. *Foundations of Constitutional Government in Modern Japan, 1868-1900.* By George Akita.
24. *Political Thought in Early Meiji Japan, 1868-1889.* By Joseph Pittau, S.J.
25. *China's Struggle for Naval Development, 1839-1895.* By John L. Rawlinson.
26. *The Practice of Buddhism in China, 1900-1950.* By Holmes Welch.
27 *Li Ta-chao and the Origins of Chinese Marxism.* By Maurice Meisner.
28. *Pa Chin and His Writings: Chinese Youth Between the Two Revolutions.* By Olga Lang.
29. *Literary Dissent in Communist China.* By Merle Goldman.
30. *Politics in the Tokugawa Bakufu, 1600-1843.* By Conrad Totman.
31. *Hara Kei in the Politics of Compromise, 1905-1915.* By Tetsuo Najita.
32. *The Chinese World Order: Traditional China's Foreign Relations.* Edited by John K. Fairbank.
33. *The Buddhist Revival in China.* By Holmes Welch.
34. *Traditional Medicine in Modern China: Science, Nationalism, and the Tensions of Cultural Change.* By Ralph C. Croizier.
35. *Party Rivalry and Political Change in Taishō Japan.* By Peter Duus.
36. *The Rhetoric of Empire: American China Policy, 1895-1901.* By Marilyn B. Young.
37. *Radical Nationalist in Japan: Kita Ikki, 1883-1937.* By George M. Wilson.
38. *While China Faced West: American Reformers in Nationalist China, 1928-1937.* By James C. Thomson Jr.
39. *The Failure of Freedom: A Portrait of Modern Japanese Intellectuals.* By Tatsuo Arima.
40. *Asian Ideas of East and West: Tagore and His Critics in Japan, China, and India.* By Stephen N. Hay.
41. *Canton under Communism: Programs and Politics in a Provincial Capital, 1949-1968.* By Ezra F. Vogel.
42. *Ting Wen-chiang: Science and China's New Culture.* By Charlotte Furth.
43. *The Manchurian Frontier in Ch'ing History.* By Robert H.G. Lee.
44. *Motoori Norinaga, 1730-1801.* By Shigeru Matsumoto.
45. *The Comprador in Nineteenth Century China: Bridge between East and West.* By Yen-p'ing Hao.
46. *Hu Shih and the Chinese Renaissance: Liberalism in the Chinese Revolution, 1917-1937.* By Jerome B. Grieder.
47. *The Chinese Peasant Economy: Agricultural Development in Hopei and Shantung, 1890-1949.* By Ramon H. Myers.
48. *Japanese Tradition and Western Law: Emperor, State, and Law in the Thought of Hozumi Yatsuka.* By Richard H. Minear.
49. *Rebellion and Its Enemies in Late Imperial China: Militarization and Social Structure, 1796-1864.* By Philip A. Kuhn.
50. *Early Chinese Revolutionaries: Radical Intellectuals in Shanghai and Chekiang, 1902-1911.* By Mary Backus Rankin.
51. *Communication and Imperial Control in China: Evolution of the Palace Memorial System, 1693-1735.* By Silas H.L. Wu.